EDWARD JARVIS

God, Land & Freedom

THE TRUE STORY OF I.C.A.B.

The Brazilian Catholic Apostolic Church:
Its History, Theology, Branches,
and Worldwide Offshoots

APOCRYPHILE
PRESS

Apocryphile Press
1700 Shattuck Ave #81
Berkeley, CA 94709
www.apocryphilepress.com

Copyright © 2018 by Edward Jarvis
Printed in the United States of America
ISBN 978-1-947826-90-8 | paperback
ISBN 978-1-947826-91-5 | epub

Please join our mailing list at
www.apocryphilepress.com/free
We'll keep you up-to-date on all our new releases,
and we'll also send you a FREE BOOK.
Visit us today!

Contents

PREFACE   5

I   "A LIBERAL CATHOLICISM,
INIMICAL TO THE PAPACY"   13

II   "THE COURAGEOUS AND DEMOCRATIC
ROMAN CATHOLIC BISHOP OF MAURA"
— Genesis of a dissident bishop —   39

III   A "REBEL IN RIO" AND
A SCHISM IN BRAZIL
— ICAB in its early years —   63

IV   "PRIESTHOOD-MANIA"
AND "BISHOPS GALORE"
— ICAB in an age of revolution —   93

V   "THE CHURCH'S DOORS
WILL ALWAYS BE OPEN"
BUT "WHAT DOES 'CANONICAL' MEAN?"
— ICAB in a conciliar age —   123

VI   "FROM TRADITIONAL TO ESOTERIC
AND ULTRACONSERVATIVE TO RADICAL"
— the ICAB phenomenon, its
branches and offshoots —   151

VII   "WHERE AND WHAT IS THE CHURCH?"
— Theological critique of the
ICAB phenomenon —   187

VIII   "A FREE DECISION OF FAITH"
— Theological defense of the
ICAB phenomenon —   219

IX   GOD, LAND AND FREEDOM?
— Conclusions —   249

     ACKNOWLEDGEMENTS   279

     ABOUT THE AUTHOR   280

     SOURCES   281

PREFACE

This is the strange story of the *Igreja Católica Apostólica Brasileira* (ICAB) or Brazilian Catholic Apostolic Church – not to be confused with the *Roman* Catholic Church *in* Brazil. It is the story of a schism. ICAB broke away from the Roman Catholic Church in the immediate aftermath of World War Two and was intended to be "a national movement for a return to a pure Christianity"[1] founded "for the religious liberation of our land and our people."[2] Its aim was "to liberate Brazil from the baneful yoke"[3] of "the most odious of all the political powers, the Empire of the Vatican."[4] ICAB arose out of social, political, and ecclesiastical disciplinary grievances that had built up before World War Two and intensified during it. ICAB remains by far the biggest and most enduring schism in the world's largest Catholic population. It is also the most enduring and possibly the largest schism at world level in modern times. Calling it a schism may sound dramatic, medieval, or harsh, but that is not merely the cold assessment of some unforgiving and intolerant Vatican officials – it is how ICAB's founder Carlos Duarte Costa described it.[5] It will be worthwhile to examine the term 'schism' in Chapter I.

ICAB is without a shadow of a doubt the largest of what are referred to as 'Independent Catholic' churches even though it is much less well-known than other, smaller breakaway Catholic communities. To put ICAB's 560,781[6] adherents – in Brazil alone – into context, the faithful of the Old Catholic Churches in Europe (Union of Utrecht), a much more famous split from the Catholic Church, today only number about 74,000, while the Polish National Catholic Church in the USA only has around 26,000 members. For a UK-based comparison, ICAB membership outstrips the *combined* memberships of all the Methodists, Baptists,

United Reformed, and Congregationalists. The Episcopal Church in the USA has a communicant membership only three times ICAB's. Within Brazil itself, ICAB is much bigger than better-known minority denominations such as the Orthodox Churches (131,571) and the Anglican Episcopal Church, founded there in 1890 (approximately 120,000 members). The more recent Catholic 'schism', Archbishop Lefebvre's SSPX, does not enroll lay members as such, but estimates tend to range between 600,000 and 1 to 2 million lay adherents worldwide. Interestingly, this mirrors both the documented lower (560,781) and estimated higher (2 million) figures for ICAB.

It is much harder to establish the facts about the many independent branches, offshoots, and micro-churches that make up ICAB's worldwide network. A recent study of 'Independent Catholic' groups in the USA suggested a conservative "underestimate" of one million adherents there,[7] though this includes communities not originating from ICAB, such as offshoots and branches of the Old Catholic Churches. Though covering a very wide spectrum, ICAB branch and offshoot adherents will typically claim to be essentially orthodox Catholics, just not under the constraints of the Vatican. These days there is rarely any trace of the Communism or Socialism espoused by ICAB's founder. It is widely assumed that their sacraments and Holy Orders are theologically correct and valid, because of their roots in the official Catholic Church. While they generally recognize that their status is irregular and contrary to Canon Law, they tend to defend their priesthood as both demonstrably valid according to sacramental theology, and at least tacitly recognizable as such even by the official Catholic Church. Indeed, for one of these small 'Catholic Churches' separated from *the* Catholic Church, a large part of their claim to be a Church at all hangs on their claim to have valid Holy Orders and sacraments. But the reality of the validity issue is more complex and less certain than these communities would like. A number of historical and theological factors impair their claims, and the picture that emerges from this research may be displeasing to some.

Wherever Catholics are found in any significant number, stories regularly unfold wherein a 'Catholic Church' – be it 'independent catholic', 'ecumenical catholic', 'national catholic', 'Celtic catholic', 'holy catholic', or however they choose to style themselves – claims to have a real bishop and therefore to be a real Church. They hold that they are really Catholic because they descend from ICAB. It would be a truly gargantuan and lifelong labor of shadow-chasing to attempt to catalog every branch and offshoot of ICAB since 1945. Dozens upon dozens of them have been short-lived; they have often changed name, re-formed, or have had multiple names to begin with; leaders have often taken 'religious' names and other pseudonyms; and many offshoots, especially in pre-internet days, have left no available written trace.[8] The present study aims to discuss a number of representative cases from several countries – including the USA, UK, Italy, Portugal, Germany, Venezuela, and Argentina – and outline their often bitter conflicts with the Roman Catholic Church. I will explain why these groups' passionate affirmations of being 'real' churches and having 'real' bishops are often castles built on damp sand.[9] I will aim to offer clarity on the often upsetting clashes experienced by all the churches and communities involved. So far no serious, unbiased, full-length study of ICAB, its branches and its offshoots has ever been produced. The mere absence of such a work may not in itself be enough to justify writing one, but the fact remains that the ICAB phenomenon continues to resurface across the world under various names and forms, without their common origins being understood or identified, and without their claims being properly and fairly evaluated.

It may be surprising that no full-length book about ICAB has ever appeared until now, and in fact the available sources are somewhat sparse. There are several predictable reasons for this, including a tendency towards secrecy within the movement itself and a wider tendency towards misunderstanding and misinformation. It appears that no-one directly involved in ICAB over the years has ever felt called to produce truly scholarly writing about ICAB. The barriers of distance and language have also played their part in limiting sources – the best short writings about ICAB that do exist are in Portuguese or Spanish. Good sources include newspaper articles from 1945 onwards, contemporary reports of the founding of ICAB, and some background details about Bishop Carlos Duarte Costa, especially those written by Father Florencio Maria Dubois. Ukrainian-born Orthodox Bishop Aleksei Pelypenko published a frank and rather hostile report in 1961 as a chapter of his book on Communist infiltration in Christian Churches. Pelypenko focused on ICAB's possible links to the USSR and Freemasonry, and hunted around as well for evidence of degeneracy and scandal among its clergy. The writings of ICAB's founder, Bishop Carlos Duarte Costa, and other contributors, survive in the form of his journal *'Luta!'* – meaning *'Fight!'* or *'Struggle!'* – published at irregular intervals from the founding of ICAB until his death.[10] This was a continuation of his earlier newsletter 'Messenger of Our Lady the Child Mary' – *Mensageiro de Nossa Senhora Menina*. The archivists at the National (Roman) Catholic Bishops' Conference of Brazil (CNBB) and the Conference of Religious of Brazil showed great courtesy and patience as I hunted down their documents relating to ICAB, as well as those of the Congregation for the Doctrine of the Faith. The Internet facilitates the locating of various now-accessible Brazilian government documents and public archive collections, especially the foundation documents both of ICAB and the related Christian Socialist Party. My requests for documents and rare books at the Andrés Bello Catholic University in Caracas, the Archdiocese of Caracas, and the National University of Mexico were also received with great kindness.

There is another small body of material, produced over the years and published or self-published by members of ICAB. These include works by Bishop Gerardo Albano de Freitas and a similar self-published book by Bishop Antonio Duarte Santos Rodrigues. There is also a small series of books by ICAB's Father Marcos Martini, aimed at catechizing those new to ICAB or studying for its Holy Orders, offered through a print-on-demand company.

Unfortunately, on the whole these books offer an 'official' ICAB version of events with the warts airbrushed out; a sanitized portrait of ICAB as the beleaguered voice of liberation in the wilderness. We tend to find an uncritical defense of Duarte Costa as the persecuted prophet, usually drawing heavily but selectively on Duarte Costa's own 1945 ICAB *Manifesto*[11] – regarded as "the most important confessional document of ICAB"[12] – for assessment of his positions. It is of course the prerogative of ICAB authors to defend their founder and their organization, especially in the context of in-house manuals. They may be quite right to document Duarte Costa's merits for posterity – so much of this story seems to be extant only in the oral tradition. But I am not a member of ICAB and I owe Duarte Costa no hagiography. Besides which, the objective mistake made by these in-house authors is this: they attribute the origin of ICAB to the perceived genius and sanctity of the founder, rather than seeing the schism within the bigger picture of Catholicism in Brazil and in the context of previous schisms. In fact, ICAB was not the first significant modern deviation from official Catholicism, even within Brazil, and it sits within a clear train of historical events.[13]

ICAB often receives mention as an aside in books on world religions, new religious movements, or specific 'offshoot' issues such as women's ordination and married priests. As a generalization, these passing mentions of independent catholic groups either acknowledge them uncritically or dismiss them as irrelevant. Either way these books' scope does not usually warrant going beyond the most readily available sources, which are the ones most likely to repeat perfunctory face-value reports and hearsay. Among the best secondary sources about ICAB are chapters and articles published in journals in Brazil, Venezuela, Chile and Argentina, usually focusing on a specific aspect or personality of the ICAB story. The English texts of all these sources used here are my own translations. I have used other acclaimed secondary, reference, and some secondary-tertiary sources in order to confront the issues arising from the ICAB story with recognized Catholic theology and other relevant disciplines. The main criteria in selecting these sources have been quality, recognition, and accessibility in every sense. These sources also correspond broadly to the relevant period in the development of ICAB.

The first chapter gives the background to our story – from the arrival of Catholicism in Brazil and the factors that would make it unique, to the dawning of the twentieth century and the process of Romanization in Brazilian Catholicism. Chapter Two deals with the early life of ICAB's founder and the seeds of the schism. Chapter Three explains the unfolding of the ICAB schism itself, and Chapter Four corresponds to the hectic decade of the 1950's, the growth of ICAB, and the stories of the people involved. Chapter Five describes the development of ICAB during the 1960's and 1970's, while Chapter Six looks at more recent decades and the advent of international branches and offshoots. Chapters Seven and Eight focus on the theological issues arising from the ICAB phenomenon – presenting cases both for the prosecution and for the defense of ICAB. The concluding chapter offers an appraisal and evaluation of the story and also aims to clarify or dispel any remaining doubts, myths, and misunderstandings.

Readers with an active interest, concern, or curiosity about the state of the Catholic Church will be most likely to find this book useful, engaging, and informative, especially with regard to the Independent Catholic phenomenon. The issues raised by the story of ICAB, its branches and its offshoots pose important questions both at the practical and theoretical levels: Who says what 'Catholic' means anyway? Where does Church authority come from? Is true religious freedom compatible with or within a true faith? And what about ordination – does becoming a 'real' priest or bishop really just amount to having one's Apostolic Succession – or priestly pedigree – in order? I hope to contribute constructively to these broader debates. For the mainstream Churches, living harmoniously alongside irregular communities has rarely seemed achievable or sustainable, and misunderstandings and conflicts can be distressing for all concerned. I hope that this study may reach those many corners of the Church where ICAB's branches and offshoots are present, whether named 'Ecumenical', 'Orthodox', 'Holy', 'Celtic', 'Gnostic', or 'Luciferian', all with their apparent Apostolic Succession from Brazil. It is my intention to offer theological and historical clarity with regard to these claims of valid Holy Orders and sacraments. Naturally, any reader, individual, or group is also free to completely reject the idea itself of a 'dynastic' or 'pedigree' priesthood – sometimes derogatorily referred to as 'grace by pipeline' – transmitted sacramentally via the rite of ordination. But in the case of ICAB and its offshoots their claim to be validly ordained should be tested according to the Catholic theology that they themselves uphold.

For those readers less interested in the theological and sacramental issues arising from *God, Land and Freedom: the true story of I.C.A.B.,* I trust that they will find as many varied topics here to interest them as I certainly have: Latin American history and politics, religion and politics, Church and State, and some extraordinary individuals' stories. This unusual tale is not without truly entertaining elements – it might even be called weird. The history of the twentieth century is itself endlessly entertaining and fascinating, with its intertwining of huge national and international events, its extremes of politics and clashing ideologies, and the intrigues and interplay of religions and governments in fast-developing new moral realities – I am pleased to say that all these elements and more are to be found in the up-to-now untold true story of ICAB, its branches and its offshoots.

Edward Jarvis
25th May 2018
Feast of the Venerable Bede

Notes

1   *Luta!* issue 1, January 1947, p 2 – *Luta! [Fight!* or: *Struggle!]* was the occasional journal of the Brazilian Catholic Apostolic Church (ICAB) from 1947 to 1958.

2   *Luta!* issue 1, January 1947, p 7

3   *Luta!* issue 1, January 1947, p 31

4   *Luta!* issue 4, January-February 1948, p 31

5   Carlos Duarte Costa, 'Manifesto á Nação' [Declaration to the Nation], published in various newspapers including *O Diário de São Paulo,* 19th August 1945, and later in Duarte Costa's own journal *Luta!* issue 12, September 1950, [pp 7-15] – see p 9 – http://diocesedecabofrio. blogspot.com/p/revista-luta.html [accessed 23rd May 2018]

6   IBGE – Instituto Brasileiro de Geografia e Estatística [Brazilian Institute of Geography and Statistics], *Censo Demografico 2010: Características Gerais da População, Religião, e Pessoas com Deficiência,* [Demographic Census 2010: General Characteristics of the Population, Religion, and People with Disabilities], IGBE, Rio de Janeiro, 2010, Table 1.4.1.

7   Julie Byrne, 'Catholic But Not Roman Catholic', *American Catholic Studies* Volume 125, Number 3, Fall 2014, pp 16-19, p 18 – See also Julie Byrne, *The Other Catholics: Remaking America's Largest Religion,* Columbia University Press, New York, 2016, p 3

8   There have been several attempts to catalog groups within the phenomenon in various ways and with varying approaches – Cf. Peter F. Anson, Alan M. Bain, Karl Prüter, Gary L. Ward (see Bibliography)

9   Cf. Matthew 7: 26-27

10 ICAB's Diocese of Cabo Frio RJ has generously gone to the trouble of adding these to their website: http://diocesedecabofrio.blogspot.com/p/ revista-luta.html [accessed 23rd May 2018]

11 Duarte Costa's 'Manifesto' is found in *Luta!* issue 12, September 1950, [pp 7-15] http://diocesedecabofrio.blogspot.com/p/revista-luta.html [accessed 23rd May 2018]

12 Dom Gerardo Albano de Freitas, *Igreja Brasileira – Abençoada Rebeldía [Brazilian Church – Blessed Rebeliousness],* Centro de Estudos Teológicos ICAB, São Paulo, 1987, p 10

13 Thomas C. Bruneau's classic *The Political Transformation of the Brazilian Catholic Church* (1974) provides a thorough overview of the political history of the Church in Brazil.

I

"A LIBERAL CATHOLICISM, INIMICAL TO THE PAPACY"[1]

The founder of ICAB, Carlos Duarte Costa, described it as a schism.[2] Schism is a word that has escaped the confines of theology to be almost as frequently applied in other contexts such as politics and sociology. Many Catholics would have difficulty explaining what schism in the theological context actually is. The word is of Greek origin and means a split, cleft, or division. Theologically speaking schism indicates an organized and deliberate act of disobedience that damages the unity or wholeness of the Church. Schism also refers to the group or part that thus obstinately cuts itself off from the main body of the Church. Legally speaking, schism is a grave offense in Roman Catholic Canon Law (Canon 751). The Church considers the crime of schism serious enough to sit alongside heresy, which is the denial of a truth of the Catholic faith, and apostasy, which is the total repudiation of the faith. It is given a fairly broad definition in Canon Law as "the refusal of submission to the Supreme Pontiff or of communion with the members of the Church subject to him."[3] In practice, the *fact* of schism has long been understood as an individual or group "setting up a rival altar"[4] and in more recent times Yves Congar described it as

> "to think, pray, act – in a word, live – not in harmony with the whole Church, as a part in conformity with the whole and with the authority which presides over the whole, but according to [one's] own rules and like an autonomous being."[5]

13

It is no accident that the Catholic Church, its Canon Law, and its theologians try to offer clarity on the issue of schisms; they are a big deal for the Church. The 'Great Schism' of 1054, also known as the 'East-West Schism', irreversibly divided Christianity in two. The Great Schism achieved no less than the break between what are now commonly known as the Orthodox Church (or Churches) and the Roman Catholic Church. Just over three hundred years later, the 'Western Schism' divided the Roman (Western) Church in a confusing stand-off lasting forty years, during which there were no fewer than three simultaneous claimants to the Papacy. A few centuries later still came Protestantism, which is often understandably interpreted by Catholics in terms of another 'great schism.'

In recent centuries schisms have not stopped happening, though they may take place on a smaller scale and over different issues. The great schisms of the distant past unfolded when the Church's role was immensely different from today. Society was "an organic whole, governed by two parallel and universal powers – the Pope and the Prince."[6] The great schisms involved power and thrones, influence and empire; as all aspects of life were seen as impinging on Salvation, all aspects of life were seen as the business of the Church. But the modern Church no longer concerns itself with these things in the same way – over time it has been elbowed out of the arena of governance and power into "the apolitical realm of values and ideals."[7] It no longer (literally at least) crowns emperors and does not (or at least does not openly) forge pacts with and give its blessing to conquerors and despots. As the Church now finds itself located squarely in the field of day-to-day morality and the ethics of human living, it is on such issues – sexuality, family, class, human rights, ethnicity, and tradition versus progress – that modern-day schisms are more likely to arise. Such is the case with our subject, the Brazilian Catholic Apostolic Church – *Igreja Católica Apostólica Brasileira* in Portuguese, often shortened to *'igreja brasileira'* and also known as ICAB.

In spite of all the apparent theological and legal clarity on the nature of schism, accusations of schism are usually hotly contested and the disputes can go on for decades. Pope St. John Paul II famously coined the slightly gentler term 'a schismatic act', rather than outright schism, to describe Archbishop Marcel Lefebvre's consecrations of four new bishops – without the required papal permission – in 1988. This event was the culmination of a two-decade-long stand-off between the Vatican and Lefebvre's Society of St. Pius X (SSPX). Supporters and sympathizers of the SSPX absolutely reject the idea that this was schism *or* schismatic, and even many non-sympathizers would admit that the SSPX is still essentially Catholic. For some, the SSPX's lack of concern for unity and their disobedience to the Pope vaporize their claim to be Catholic. At the other extreme, a few *very* hard-liners would consider the SSPX to be too lukewarm in their opposition to the reforms of Vatican II, and on that basis no longer truly Catholic. The SSPX was founded in 1970 as a traditionalist bulwark against the sweeping reforms of the Second Vatican Council (1962-1965). ICAB, by contrast, was founded nearly two decades *before* Vatican II and arguably preempted some of its sweeping reforms. Readers may nevertheless notice similarities between the SSPX case and the ICAB case, but these similarities will tend to be largely superficial. The fact that ICAB split from the Church before Vatican II meant that it was not subject to – or even particularly interested in – the great reforms of that Council. ICAB's liturgy, governance, polity, and theology did not change as a consequence of Vatican II – the changes it *had* made dated back to the 1940's. This eventually helped to give ICAB a dated and 'traditional' feel; cassocks and birettas, for example, are still 'in' and are actually a key part of ICAB's identity. The ICAB Mass, furthermore, is inspired by the pre-Vatican II Mass of St. Pius V – the Tridentine Mass. These features would allow some in the ICAB movement to attempt to reposition or rebrand ICAB as a force for traditionalism rather than rebellion, moves which were mirrored by a corresponding shift in political orientation. But it would be a huge stretch to call ICAB

'Brazil's SSPX' or to label ICAB's founder 'the Brazilian Lefebvre.' Both the groups and their founders came from opposite ends of the political and theological spectra. ICAB aimed to achieve no less than "true Christian communism"[8] in opposition to "Roman Church Fascism."[9]

The SSPX and ICAB may be called the two major breakaway groups or schisms in the Catholic Church of the twentieth century, certainly among those that to this day still claim to be Catholic. There were other significant mass defections in the early years of the century, such as the Philippine Independent Church – also known as the 'Aglipayan' Church – which gradually moved a considerable distance away from its Catholic roots. There were also the Mariavite Catholic Church and the Polish National Catholic Church. These schisms owed a lot to the influence of yet another, earlier European schism, the Old Catholic movement. All these twentieth-century schisms, to varying degrees, have rigorously defended their Catholic identity and usually preserved the word Catholic in their names. How can it be that these rebels – including the SSPX and ICAB – break off from the Catholic Church and yet still call themselves Catholic? Unity – or 'oneness' – is a core element of Catholicism, one of the classic 'marks' by which the true Church is supposed to be identified, but being in a state of either schism or unity can be surprisingly nebulous. While it is in many ways highly centralized, the Catholic Church is also very diverse, as any truly worldwide organization is bound to be. It is truly universal and present in every sphere, from ecology to education, from archeology to agriculture, from medicine to the military, from sport to the stock market. With the Catholic Church's tentacles having such an all-embracing reach, it is perhaps surprising that what really constitutes 'being Catholic' is still up for debate. There is no 'card' as such for being a card-carrying Catholic. The Catholic Creeds – 'we believe in one, holy, catholic and apostolic Church', 'I believe in the Holy Spirit, the holy catholic Church, the communion of saints' etc. – do not necessarily help to define 'Catholic.' The creeds are part of the shared inheritance of all Christians, even if some non-Catholic Christians do not necessarily appreciate the word Catholic.

Flexibility as to what Catholic precisely means may be a necessary correlation of the flexibility of the institution. Could the Catholic Church adapt and operate in such diverse fields and societies if all the concepts and language had to be nailed down and copyrighted? Since Vatican II the Catholic Church has relinquished its claim to an absolute monopoly on Salvation, expressly in order to better relate to the world and move more fluently within it. But the phrase 'Catholic Church' still leaves no-one in any doubt as to what it refers to – one visible organization, a robust institution with a clear hierarchy, and a widely-spread faith. Its identity is also intricately interwoven with the history and culture of wherever it is found. It would be an awesome task to try to usurp that identity, but the perennial and reassuring qualities of 'Holy Mother Church' do attract determined competitors. Some of these rivals keep a very low profile while others do a good job of publicly imitating the Catholic Church. There are in fact rival or renegade communities all around us who would argue that 'Catholic Church' is a far more fluid and flexible concept than the Vatican would have us believe. Some would say that the Vatican *cannot* dictate what is and is not Catholic. For strict Catholics the question of being a member of the true Church is not trivial or hypothetical, it is actually necessary for the literal salvation of their souls.

Schisms have sometimes arisen with the intention of saving the 'true Church' or restoring it to its true origins. Returning for a moment to the SSPX; even before 1988 when Archbishop Lefebvre consecrated four new bishops without papal permission, the SSPX was already widely regarded as a breakaway or separatist group operating under its own steam. In other words it was a 'rival altar' and, speaking both plainly and theologically, it was an 'autonomous entity' or schism. The four bishops' consecrations were no mere protest, nor were they an end in themselves; Lefebvre was 82 at the time and since only bishops can ordain future priests, consecrating new bishops provided continuity for the SSPX and gave it a further degree of autonomy from the Vatican. In condemning the consecrations, however, even John Paul II stopped short of calling it a schism, preferring that phrase 'a schismatic act.' Much less did he declare the SSPXers – or 'Lefebvrists' – non-Catholic. So it is clear that, when pushed, the Catholic Church, even up to its highest authorities, can and does admit some ambiguity; it is possible to commit a 'schismatic act', fulfill most of the criteria for having broken with the Church, but not cease to be Catholic. So what does being Catholic mean to ICAB?

ICAB allows priests to marry and earn money however they wish; it allows divorce; it does not demand that its members shun Freemasonry, politics, other religions, Spiritualism, Umbanda, or the occult. ICAB values its own national identity high above any internationalist conception of Catholicism; it regards the Pope in Rome as just one of many admittedly influential foreign bishops. Viewed from outside this looks like a revolutionary take on Catholicism, but within the context of Brazilian history it is less of an anomaly – this is more or less Brazilian Catholicism as it has always been. Throughout most of Brazil's history, the presence there of something called Catholicism would be unrecognizable in comparison with the Catholic Church of today. For 400 years the Church in Brazil lacked cohesion, structure and even shared values in so many areas that it could barely be called a Church at all.[10] Today's worldwide Catholic Church is more diverse and more universal than ever before, and yet there is highly visible uniformity of structure, activity, training, iconography, law, language, terminology, self-understanding and role. It is clearly so much more than an international network of local churches with an HQ in Rome. Through diplomatic representation, participation in global organizations, and key presences in the fields of health and education, the Catholic Church relates to the world in complex and varied ways. Crucially, it does this in perpetual dialogue and orchestration between its many constituent parts around the world, and with constant reference back to its centre, the Holy See. This unity that the Church exerts may be a flawed unity, but the religious practices of 1.2 billion people across the world overwhelmingly have more similarities than differences. We could make the mistake of assuming that this was always the case – it is after all the same old religion with the same old set of rules and beliefs, so how much disparity could there be? But in fact no semblance of this worldwide uniformity and unity, flawed or not, existed five hundred years ago.[11]

More than 41% of Pope Francis's subjects in the whole world are currently to be found in the continent he calls home. At their foundation, however, the Catholic Churches in Latin America had a much closer and far more dependent relationship with the colonizing States of origin than with the Papacy. The Brazilian Church's connection to the Vatican was at best a formality and at worst illusory, right up until the turn of the twentieth century. When Brazil itself was founded in 1500 the Portuguese established the Church there as a simple extension of the one at home. The Portuguese Crown enjoyed an exceptionally good relationship with the Papacy. Portuguese Kings had received extraordinary concessions from the Popes in recognition of Portugal's role in defeating the Moors, and for subsequent colonial expeditions into Africa and Asia – professedly for the defence and expansion of Christian civilization. These campaigns were always imbued with strong religious overtones, and for successfully propagating the 'true faith' the Portuguese King received official recognition of his 'divine right' to rule. The papal bulls *Romanus Pontifex* (1455) and *Inter Caetera* (1456) granted the King the right to found new churches in conquered lands as he saw fit and staff the churches with whomsoever he chose. Furthermore, these bulls granted to the Portuguese Order of Christ the privilege of filling all episcopal posts in Portugal's new colonies – and since the Grand Master of the Order of Christ was the King himself, all the bases were covered. When it came to the conquest of Brazil, therefore, the Portuguese Crown was already equipped to exercise wide-ranging powers in the new colony. These included power over all Church affairs, the freedom to appoint bishops, and the entitlement to collect tithes – the *dízimo real* or 'royal tenth', so called because it was adjudged due to the Crown first and foremost with the Church receiving some of the excess at the Crown's discretion. The system of Royal domination over the Church in Brazil, therefore – known as *padroado real* or 'royal patronage' – was enforced on the basis of rights and privileges already in place before the colonization of Brazil.

This kind of arrangement and understanding of the Church's role in symbiosis with the secular authorities is usually referred to as Christendom. It was the dominant system in Europe from about the fourth century until the Reformation. For most of this period, the State as we now understand it did not exist, and the Church was the principal social institution as far as most facets of society were concerned. The idea of Church and State as distinct social entities is a thoroughly modern concept.[12]

> "Christendom consisted of a single social body, in which the ecclesial and the civil marked not spatial jurisdictions or even modalities of rule, but ends. Ecclesial authorities were concerned with the supernatural end of human community, while civil authorities concerned themselves with the temporal ends of that same community."[13]

Though the Protestant Reformation signalled the end of Christendom as the prevalent European model, it continued unabated in the Counter-Reformation countries of Spain and Portugal. The Iberian States exported the unreformed Christendom model to the New World, which they were in the process of energetically colonizing. The characteristics of the Church in Christendom are as follows: it is all-embracing, relating to all aspects of life and society; it has a monopoly on faith and salvation; and, since every human activity could be construed as having to do with one's ultimate destiny, all sectors of society are expected to support the Church – hence the *dízimo real*, the tithes system. As the message of Christ and the mission of the Church are universal, went the worldview, Christian rulers must be put in place to ensure the conversion of all peoples. If necessary, conversion was to be imposed through force – baptisms *en masse* were unfortunately a reality, with slaves being baptized prior to arrival in Brazil while still crammed on board ship. All of this is in great contrast to the Church model eventually established in the United States, for example, where Catholicism was a minority religion from the outset. Any ambitions of widespread saturation or forceful imposition would have been pointless, and the Church there focused almost exclusively on ethnic minorities. Thus, from their earliest foundations the Latin American Churches were profoundly different from the Catholic Church in other areas, even on the continent directly to the north. At that time, only by the most tenuous of links and through the most generous of interpretations could they all be considered organically (rather than spiritually or ethereally) part of the same, one, Roman Catholic Church.

In Brazil then, Christianity was intended to permeate everything, but it should not be thought that the power of the Church was total or that its leaders enjoyed great autonomy. The colonization of Brazil was a joint venture; along with the sword went the cross – Brazil was originally named Vera Cruz, the land of the True Cross. The colonizers' priority was to command materially and militarily, safe in the knowledge that spiritual domination was being taken care of by the Church. In practice the local Church came to function as an appendage of the secular civil powers. The Papacy, incidentally, was in no position to object. The European Church at that time was dogged by internal problems, with the Papacy itself threatened by the Conciliar Movement,[14] and external problems such as the threat of Turkish imperial ambitions. While the extent of the concessions given to Christian rulers may appear to have been very great, this strategy provided the Catholic Church with a safety net. If Christian Europe were to be overrun or defeated from within, the Patronage system guaranteed Catholicism an overseas base for future survival and expansion, even at the high cost of blurring the distinctions between temporal and spiritual powers, and Church powers being wielded by and in the interests of the State.

In spite of Royal endorsement, what passed for the Brazilian Church remained weak and underdeveloped due to tight civil controls, little organizational structure of its own, and a range of abuses. It was starved of tithes, which went primarily to the Crown, meaning that priests were underpaid and left susceptible to corruption. Communication with Rome was poor, as it all had to go through the secular authorities. The Church itself, Thomas C. Bruneau wrote, "was regarded by everyone as a sector of the civil bureaucracy. ... In fact, during the whole colonial period (1500-1822) it is probably misleading to talk about a Church."[15] In terms of organizational reality the Church was a random series of rural and semi-rural mission stations. This contrasted with other parts of Latin America where the Spanish soon began to establish cities; the Church there was by consequence primarily an urban reality, establishing chapels, religious houses, parishes, dioceses, and cathedrals. The colonization of Brazil was chiefly rural in character, through the development of vast country estates. The cities that did spring up were actually annexes of the estates, and priests tended to be employed by these great landowning families as chaplains. The local church building, such as it was,

> "was really the domestic chapel; the priest received his wages from the family and he often received his values from them as well. The one characteristic which seems to have most fascinated foreign observers of colonial Brazil was the immorality of the clergy. The clergy lived with the family, accepted its values, and these values did not deny the priest some form of female companionship."[16]

But it would be a mistake to imagine that these priests were the main or only point of day-to-day contact that people had with Catholicism. Just as the priests enjoyed a degree of freedom, so did the *irmandades* – lay religious fraternities – which along with the country estates were the main foci of religious activity. Though not officially part of the Church, the *irmandades* were important centres for social interaction and allowed people of the same social status to mix. Many *irmandades* would become increasingly associated with Freemasonry by the nineteenth century, often to the point of breaking from the Church completely. Where the Church did function more effectively and more *like* a Church was in the religious orders such as the Jesuits. They were more independent, more disciplined, and less corruptible. They lived in ordered, self-managing communities and failed to be wooed by country landowning society with its vast ranches. They had a robust esprit de corps which made them less likely to become vulnerable to temptations, and less likely to spend long periods isolated or with access to sympathetic female company. While these distinctions set the religious orders apart they also made them unpopular. The Jesuits, especially, made powerful enemies, and they would eventually face expulsion from Brazil and Portugal and even worldwide suppression. Brazil's already weak Church would be enfeebled by the departure of the Jesuits, and they would deliberately not be replaced. The man responsible was the Marquis of Pombal.

In 1755 a devastating earthquake flattened Lisbon. The King's chief minister, the Marquis of Pombal, was instrumental in rebuilding the city, and as a reward he was given extraordinary far-reaching powers – he became the de facto ruler of Portugal and its colonies. Pombal was a statesman of his time; he was an absolutist, favoring absolute monarchy as in Spain and France, and he was a regalist and a Jansenist, opposing submission to the Holy See in religious affairs. He took away powers from the nobility, the Church, the Papacy, and especially the Jesuits. He severely attacked the Jesuits with violent persecutions and eventually expelled them from both Portugal and Brazil. Pombal then severed relations with the Vatican itself and evicted the Nuncio. For ten years (1760-1770) the Church in Portugal and Brazil was effectively an independent national church, its bishops being completely cut off from Rome. This temporary break with Rome and the freezing of powers devastated the feeble Brazilian Church. Posts remained vacant, decisions hung in limbo, and the dynamic Jesuit missionaries who had kept things going were ousted. Even at the best of times communication with Rome had been shaky, so there was no chance of Rome intervening – and that is exactly how Pombal liked it. His effect was far-reaching and long-lasting. The clergy were by now completely integrated into colonial society and culture with little that was churchman-like about them. In 1772 Pombal took control of the University of Coimbra in Portugal and abolished the Jesuitical scholastic curriculum. He promoted the study of theories that affirmed that the civil state had the prerogative in Church control, not the Papacy, along with other teachings opposed to or condemned by the Church. Jansenism, Regalism-Gallicanism, libertine ideas (and Liberalism itself, after the French Revolution), opposition to Ultramontanism – all found their way onto the curriculum at the University of Coimbra. This was intentional and strategic on Pombal's part – Coimbra was where the more able Brazilian clergy were sent to study, with the intention of sending them back to Brazil to become bishops and then to open seminaries of their own. Pombal's aim was effectively to recraft the clergy in his own image. This 'Pombalization' of the clergy consisted of

> "a systematic indoctrination of clerical students with libertine ideas and false doctrines which made some priests ready accomplices in the Pombaline scheme of establishing in Portugal and her colonies a Liberal Catholicism, inimical to the Papacy."[17]

Underdevelopment from the start had made the Church in Brazil perfectly susceptible to this kind of indoctrination; it was neither autonomous intellectually nor self-determining in governance. The Pombal administration secured enormous concessions from Rome in return for agreeing to re-establish ties. The Vatican had to acknowledge Pombal's control over the Church and, it is presumed, agree to order the worldwide suppression of the Jesuits. The isolation and ineffectiveness of the Brazilian Church now seemed permanent. By the year 1800, after three hundred years in the vast colony, the Church was about to open only its third seminary for the training of clergy. These pitifully few seminaries were highly controlled – clergy were more an educational product of the civil administration than of the Church. They studied doctrines that discouraged any ideas of seeking greater powers for the Church itself. The Church's influence in society was practically non-existent, and its political power, especially after Pombal, was nil.

This does not mean that individual priests themselves were not politically active. Since priests boasted a better education than most of the population, infused with large elements of Liberalism, many priests were in fact leading revolutionaries in the struggle for independence from Portugal. The unsuccessful republican revolt of 1817 in Pernambuco has been called 'The Revolution of the Padres', reflecting the extent of participation by the clergy. These priests functioned individually, however, and not with any particular thought for the Church's institutional interests.[18] The Church's approval or otherwise of their actions was considered irrelevant. A considerable number of these priests recognized the compatibility of national independence with religious independence from the Vatican, opening the door to the idea of a National Church. Their schooling in Liberalism left them with serious doubts about the idea of a centralized Church ruled from overseas. A large number of priests – and a few bishops – became Freemasons, partly because the Masonic lodges were effective centres of republican opposition to Portugal. After the declaration of independence[19] in 1822 the new National Constituent Assembly was actually presided over by the Bishop of Rio de Janeiro and included fifteen members of the clergy. Even so, the mechanics of the Church-State relationship did not change. The 1824 Constitution confirmed *Roman* Catholicism as the official religion, with the addition of a somewhat paradoxical aim that Brazil's Church must be an expression of the unique national character. Thus, the Church would have to conform to Brazilian customs, the Emperor would still be the highest voice in the Church, and appointments, formation, and implementation – or not – of papal and conciliar decrees would still be the State's decision. Rome did succeed in negotiating a *modus vivendi* giving it some greater power, but this remained effectively a courtesy agreement, not a formal pact. In any case, the new State had little interest in the Church. Pedro II nominated bishops and did as he wished, and the Church was still simply one more agency of the government. Anything that might forge better links with Rome was vetoed – notably this included the proposed arrival of foreign clergy, especially from religious orders (the suppression of the Jesuits had been lifted by this time). The Church still relied mainly on the few Brazilian-born secular clergy, who were fully integrated socially and considerably politicized, and who rarely followed priestly discipline.

Religion itself in the newly-independent Brazil was not discouraged by those in power – it was still regarded as a useful tool for maintaining national unity and a way to placate the populace. The elites were uninterested in the Church but strongly opposed to any attempt by Rome to increase its control. Church development was still astonishingly slow. Even by the end of the independent monarchy period in 1889 there would be only twelve dioceses, thirteen bishops and about seven hundred priests in the whole of Brazil. Compare this to the United States at that time – smaller than Brazil, with a much smaller Catholic population – where there were eighty-four bishops and eight *thousand* priests. On the whole, Brazil was extremely successful in smothering the Church's growth. But the stand-off between Church and State would reach a head, catalysed by three things: a) increasing Ultramontanism in Rome; b) Ultramontanism's positive reception among sections of the Brazilian hierarchy, especially some Europe-educated bishops; and c) the subsequent panic-reaction to all this by sections of the State.

The lengthy pontificate of Pius IX (1846–1878) was marked by the spread of the idea of Ultramontanism – promoting the worldwide exercise of papal authority from the far-off central power base in Rome – and by the Pope's personal efforts to increase this universal centralization of Church power. Pius IX tried more earnestly than anyone previously to bring the whole worldwide Catholic Church under central control, focusing primarily on Catholic-majority countries. Not surprisingly, Pius IX's agenda was particularly cutting and relevant in Brazil. Liberals everywhere were aghast at the publication of his 'Syllabus of Errors' in 1864, which set out the Pope's vision for the Church. Among the Errors placed squarely on the chopping block, the royal 'placet' – the Crown's right to veto or ratify papal decrees – was now declared illegal. 'National' churches were also condemned. Another Error was to presume that civil law takes precedence over canon law when the two clash. Furthermore, the Syllabus of Errors lambasted Freemasonry, while the Emperor and many of the leading figures in Brazil were indeed linked to Masonic lodges. Regardless of the condemnation of the royal placet, Pedro II did not *give* his placet to the Syllabus of Errors, so it effectively did not exist in Brazil. The papal encyclical *Quanta Cura*, of which the Syllabus was an addendum, was rejected in its entirety. With the First Vatican Council Pius IX would consolidate all his efforts for defining and safeguarding the future of the Church – papal infallibility, centralization of power, and universal jurisdiction.

The Pope's campaign had several medium-term effects in Brazil. The State became wary of any glimmer of independence or autonomy among the clergy as a potential warning sign of Ultramontanism. Conversely, the bishops who saw things Pius IX's way were given a morale boost, especially those who went on to attend the First Vatican Council. The State would then be extremely wary of them on their return. The Emperor still made all the senior appointments in the Church, of course, but Pedro II had committed something of a blunder. To him the Church was just another bureau of government – he saw himself as a modern man of the Enlightenment. As a supporter of rationalism, scholarship and efficiency, by about 1850 he had staffed the Church with the most intellectually and morally stable clerics available. He was indifferent to religious fervor, passion and spirituality, so he simply appointed the men with the best academic backgrounds and reputations: principled, incorruptible men, with no pesky party political leanings and no clandestine immorality. Thus he unwittingly created a Church hierarchy much more amenable to the reactionary conservatism of Pius IX and the Ultramontanists. For some bishops it would become a sort of crusade – it seemed to be time to settle once and for all whether the Church would be forever in the pocket of the State. In 1874 a dispute erupted which would eventually settle that question.

By the middle of the nineteenth century, the lay religious fraternities – the *irmandades* – were functioning as Masonic lodges. When one 'crusading' bishop placed an interdict on one fraternity that refused to cut its ties to Freemasonry, the fraternity appealed to the State – which took their side. In solidarity, a second bishop (Europe-trained, like the first) placed a similar ban on the activities of another Masonic chapel. The State retaliated harshly by sentencing both bishops to four years' hard labor, which was soon commuted to simple imprisonment. Their 'crime' was to have shown excessive zeal in obeying the Roman Curia, and a lack of due concern for the interests of the State. The bishops were granted an amnesty the following year (1875) but the effect of the case was dramatic. It was an open acknowledgement that the State controlled the Church completely. Only two members of the National Assembly spoke out in defence of the imprisoned bishops, and these did not even include any of the five Assembly members who were priests themselves. These events accelerated the process of Church and State separation, causing Rome's campaign to intensify and adding to the government's fears of Ultramontanism.

For the State, events like the banning of the Masonic *irmandades* demonstrated the spread of Ultramontanism. A vague agreement therefore arose that the Church and State relationship should change, and the opportunity came with the establishment of the First Republic in 1889. The Church was galvanized by the *irmandades* conflict, but it did not have enough influence alone to overthrow the Empire. The abolition of slavery in 1888, without compensation for slave-owners, made plantation proprietors unhappy. Increased militarism at the time of the Paraguayan War meant that senior military men had risen to prominence and began to assume public roles, thus preparing the ground for a possible military coup. Republican ideas and movements grew across the continent, as a monarchy in the New World looked increasingly like an archaic anomaly. The 1889 provisional government duly decreed the separation of Church and State and the 1891 Constitution almost went so far as to show a complete disregard for religious issues. Freedom of worship and property-owning rights were granted to all religions, and State support was withdrawn from any one religion, thus placing the majority Catholic religion on a juridical par with all the others. Only civil marriages would be recognized, cemeteries were to be secularized, and religion was to be taken out of schools. After 400 years of establishment the Catholic Church was suddenly excluded from the public realm and stripped of its privileges, its government funding, and its schools. In spite of this effective suppression of Catholicism, the Church largely saw the new state of affairs as the lesser evil. In 1890 the bishops would retrospectively sum up the Royal Patronage period as

"a protection that smothered us … . Among us, the oppression exercised by the State in the name of a pretended patronage was a main cause of weakness in our Church and almost led to its destruction."[20]

In summarizing this period we may ask: What were the characteristics of the Catholic Church in Brazil during its first four hundred years? It was distant from Rome in every sense, and at every practical level was answerable to, and dependent on, the State. The clergy were deeply integrated into society, especially the landowning class, and lived as that class did – they earned a wage, adopted the landowning class's values, and rejected the Church's values. Inevitably it must be said that celibacy was not observed even in a token fashion – it was absolutely normal for the local priest to be a common-law husband, a father, and a grandfather. The Church had spent a considerable period of time as an independent national church, completely cut off from Rome. Political independence and church independence were seen as complementary. Consequently the Church was insular, defensive, and did not welcome outside clergy with foreign values. Its priests and bishops were politically active, independently and in spite of Church interests, and many saw no contradiction in allying themselves to Freemasonry. All of these characteristics could be seen as violating and conflicting with fundamental tenets of the Catholic Church, but they made up the unique identity of Brazilian Catholicism; this identity, even when quashed, was to become a spectre that would never go away.

Even at the beginning of the twentieth century this was still the real nature of the Church in Brazil – it was inward-looking, State-oriented, national, secular, political, sceptical of Rome, and worldly (to put it gently) in its morality. Only an immense, decades-long international effort and the mobilization of all the Church's might could begin to change this situation, driven by a succession of exceptionally determined and visionary Popes. After 400 years the beast was finally brought to heel, but the church vision that would later take the form of the ICAB schism was clearly anything but unprecedented. ICAB constituted a clarion call for the Church in Brazil to return to its four-hundred-year-old ways – to cut links with Rome, abolish celibacy, eject foreign clergy, incorporate Brazilian culture, intervene in politics, and to accept Freemasonry, Positivism, Theosophy, Umbanda, Candomblé, and Spiritualism. Nor is it remotely surprising that today's calls for the relaxation of Church discipline, including the most vociferous calls in favor of married priests, always originate in Brazil – it now seems inevitable that married priests will finally become a Roman-rite reality there.[21] The ICAB schism was arguably no great innovation and merely challenged the Brazilian Church to be true to itself. The old 1824 Constitution had perhaps presented the most realistic vision of a Brazilian Church as one that is Catholic and yet communicates the uniqueness of the national character and spirituality. Edicts emanating from the increasingly-centralized

30

Vatican were perceived as novelties, as Rome sought to reinvent itself as the international power hub of Catholicism. The start of the 'Romanization' process of the Church in Brazil was both a cause and effect of the split between Church and State. Pope Pius IX intensified this process, enforcing a vision of the Church which was unknown in Brazil – centralized rule from Rome, high moral standards for the clergy, strict doctrinal adherence, the exclusion of other beliefs (whether indigenous religions or new spiritual and philosophical ideas), and a discreet and diplomatic approach to politics. Whether incongruous with the reality of Brazil or not, Romanization was the Church model which would be enforced during the period of Brazil's First Republic and beyond. Brazilian bishops resolved to focus on what they saw as a higher priority – addressing the weak Church's chronic lack of influence, impact, and effect in society. It would lead to the most enduring schism in the Catholic Church in modern times.

In spite of its intentionally equivocal name, the Brazilian Catholic Apostolic Church of today is not connected to the Roman Catholic Apostolic Church in Brazil – the official, Vatican-authorized, or 'real' Catholic Church – and it does not want to be. Having split from Rome in 1945, ICAB is a separate, and in some senses parallel organization. ICAB has successfully defended – in court – its designation as a Catholic Church. In some lights it is also a Church of the Bizarre. In these pages the reader will meet such characters as the world's youngest bishop, aged 25, and the only married bishop (and father of seven) to sit as an actual Council Father (rather than an observer) at Vatican II. There is also, for good measure, a Jewish bishop and several Freemason bishops. But it would be a mistake to presume that ICAB is just an eccentric, glorified house-church or protest group, or a case of a few odd people playing church in their backyard. The last government census revealed a membership of well over half a million[22] and some sources venture a much higher number of around 2 to 3 million,[23] or as high as 4 million[24] if ICAB's worldwide branches and offshoots are included. In the world's biggest Catholic nation, where the official Catholic Church nurses open wounds caused by the onslaught of Pentecostalism and Evangelicalism, this 'rogue' Catholic Church shows serious signs of gaining ground. In the densely-populated industrial conurbation known as Grande ABC[25] in São Paulo State, ICAB showed astonishing growth of 95.8% between the 2000 and 2010 censuses.[26] This far surpassed even the Evangelicals' impressive growth of 35.6%. Furthermore, compare this to an actual *drop* in Roman Catholic allegiance of 9.4%. With ICAB growing by a healthy 12% at a national level as well, it would appear that something about this alternative Catholic Church is increasingly finding appeal among Brazilian Catholics.

Mainstream Catholics may be surprised, skeptical, or dismayed to learn about the size – and success – of rival, parallel Catholic Churches like ICAB in their midst. Independent Catholic Churches are easy to ignore until a scandal erupts. Members of such Churches are themselves often accused of failing to clearly differentiate themselves from the official Catholic Church. Their intentions are often the subject of speculation and suspicion. An extraordinary range of motives and a bizarre array of characters seem to lie behind the rise of ICAB. At its foundation, ICAB claimed to be reviving the third century Church, but actually started to preempt the liberal reforms of the future.[27] ICAB's founder was a man called Dom[28] Carlos Duarte Costa, once a rising star in the Catholic Church, who had studied in Rome and was a bishop by age 35. Then Duarte Costa changed tack completely. He made international news campaigning for disciplinary reforms; he was disobedient; he criticized the Pope; he accused the Church of complicity with the Nazis and Fascists. He was at least equally vocal and passionate – and uncritical – in his support of Stalin and the USSR. As a bishop he was so ecumenical that his 'Catholic' reform movement embraced Protestants, Theosophists, Spiritualists, Umbandists,[29] Freemasons and Communists. He ordained a former Presbyterian minister, ironically, as a bishop.[30] It might sound like it would never catch on, but today the movement that started as ICAB is present in fifteen countries – there may be a branch

32

or an offshoot not far from you. Although ICAB initially made international news, it became chameleon-like, growing in size but blending into the scenery and becoming "semi-secret."[31] There are several reasons for this – as time passed, some of ICAB's more sensational features became mainstream and new leaders found new things to focus on. They may have also lost the desire to grab headlines, and they became more conservative.[32] The imperative to publicize and expand was felt strongly in the early days of ICAB. New bishops were often hurriedly consecrated in order to carry the ICAB message beyond Rio de Janeiro and also overseas. This eventually gave rise to many, many ICAB offshoots – at times at least one offshoot-church per bishop, and then one more offshoot-church for each bishop consecrated by them, and so on. This was neither the first time nor the last time that a Catholic bishop, fallen out of favor with his superiors, had proceeded to ordain a multitude of hastily-chosen candidates, resulting in a vast progeny of present-day 'independent' bishops. It happened in the early years of the twentieth century in England when a former Catholic priest, Arnold Harris Mathew, managed to persuade the Utrecht Old Catholics to consecrate him bishop for the (non-existent, as it turned out) British Old Catholic Church. Having no Church to actually lead, Mathew dedicated himself to consecrating 'freelance' bishops – mainly theosophists, occultists, and various disgruntled clergy. Mathew's episcopal descendants today are impossible to count. Then, in the 1970's and 1980's a profoundly disenchanted retired Vietnamese Archbishop, Pierre Martin Ngô-dinh-Thuc, set out on a volatile second career consecrating bishops for a very strange selection of individuals and sects – the current 'Pope Peter III', the Palmarian anti-pope, owes his episcopal credentials to Thuc. This promptly earned Thuc an excommunication of course, which did not deter him much. Like Arnold Harris Mathew, Thuc spawned a large and varied ecclesiastical dynasty. In more recent years, Archbishop Emmanuel Milingo of Zambia revived this mania for consecrating bishops without papal permission. Following his marriage in Reverend Moon's Reunification Church and subsequent reconciliation with John Paul II, Milingo ordained four married priests as bishops in 2006. He then ordained and consecrated several more candidates in the USA, Brazil, Europe, and Africa. Mathew, Thuc, and Milingo were all, once upon a time, flawed but legitimate bishops. Cynics would later warn people to watch out – if you stand still too long they will probably ordain you.

As with the Mathew, Thuc, and Milingo cases, impatient candidates for Holy Orders grew wings and flocked to be ordained in ICAB. In this way, the Brazilian schism is to be found at the root of thousands of claims to 'apostolic succession' and 'real' Catholic sacraments. Today these multifarious ICAB offshoots include self-designated Orthodox Churches, traditionalists, progressives, Gnostics, charismatics, Anglicans, a 'Luciferian' Church, Women-priests (including the famous Danube Seven with their 'riverboat ordinations') and at least one contender for the Papacy from his 'Vatican in Exile' in Kansas. It surely goes without saying that some of them are sincere Christian communities with excellent intentions. ICAB's offshoots – and offshoots of the offshoots – may be referred to as Independent Catholics or sometimes Old Catholics (because of similarities with, not links to, the Union of Utrecht Old Catholic Churches). Independent Catholic bishops are sometimes described as *episcopi vagantes* – a term originally meaning bishops who were 'wandering' or not linked to a diocese. In modern usage, rightly or wrongly, *episcopus vagans* is generally used to indicate a crank or fantasist, a lover of robes and ecclesiastical paraphernalia, who, nevertheless, boasts a theoretically sound claim to having been consecrated bishop – usually by a fellow crank. Reflections on the rather sad subculture – or "ecclesiastical underworld"[33] – of *episcopi vagantes* date back to works by Henry R. T. Brandreth and Peter F. Anson in the 1960's. To designations like 'independent catholic' these individuals may add the words 'church', 'diocese', 'confederation', and even 'communion' or 'patriarchate', according to the level of grandeur they aspire to, even though membership often does not exceed a handful of people. While the story of ICAB is the story of a schism, it is also the story of an ecclesiastical subculture which ICAB energized and perpetuated.

"God, Land and Freedom" is the translation of ICAB's official motto *"Deus, Terra e Liberdade"* chosen by Carlos Duarte Costa in 1945. It is an interesting choice of slogan for a number of reasons. In the first place, 'God, Land and Freedom' encapsulates the main points about ICAB – it worships God, it is national or nationalist, and it is independent or 'free' of the Vatican. The motto is also clearly reminiscent of an older motto, 'Land and Freedom', an anarchist and revolutionary slogan which has been adopted by various political groups. It was first used as the name of a Russian revolutionary organization – *Zemlya i Volya* – and then first made its way to Latin America as a slogan of the Mexican Revolution, which had its origins in disputes over land rights. Land rights in Brazil, however, were never an issue seriously taken up by ICAB or Carlos Duarte Costa. It is more likely that the phrase appealed to him because of its wider adoption by the revolutionary left, as well as its suggestions of national character and freedom from papal subservience. This is especially likely considering the phrase's links to the Spanish Revolution, which was also anti-clerical in flavor. Even today 'Land and Freedom' is probably best known as a slogan of the Anarchist forces of the Spanish Civil War. (It is also the title of Ken Loach's film about that war.) The forces opposing the Anarchists were those most closely tied to the Church, including Italian Fascist troops as well as Franco's conservative, monarchist, Catholic army. The Catholic Church, for its part, has recognized nearly 1900 Catholic martyrs at the hands of the Republican forces, with around 2000 more cases currently under consideration. By the end of World War Two, Duarte Costa's assessment of the Church was that it had been entirely hand-in-glove with the forces of the extreme right. He believed that, as one of the major Fascist organizations to survive the war, the Church would now orchestrate a stealthy revival of Fascist values by exercising its influence in Catholic societies such as Brazil. There can be no doubt that Duarte Costa saw in 'Land and Freedom' a motto representing forceful popular opposition to authoritarian, right-leaning Catholic culture. In expanding the motto to 'God, Land and Freedom' he indicated that this opposition would now be galvanized in the form of a rival, left-leaning Catholic Church. Furthermore, the Fascist-tendency 'Integralist' movement in Brazil – which Duarte Costa opposed and which was not short of conservative Catholic members – had taken a similar motto – 'God, Fatherland, Family' – to which 'God, Land and Freedom' provided a subtle contrast. But Carlos Duarte Costa had been born into a world of contrasts.

Notes

[1] This quotation does not refer to ICAB but rather to the state of mainstream Catholicism in nineteenth-century Brazil; taken from Sister Mary Crescentia Thornton, *The Church and Freemasonry in Brazil, 1872-1875*, Catholic University of America Press, Washington DC, 1948, pp 36-37

[2] Carlos Duarte Costa, 'Manifesto á Nação' [Declaration to The Nation], published in several newspapers including *O Diário de São Paulo*, 19th August 1945, and later in Duarte Costa's own journal *Luta!* issue 12, September 1950, [pp 7-15] – see p 9 – http://diocesedecabofrio.blogspot.com/p/revista-luta.html [accessed 23rd May 2018]

[3] Canon 751 of the 1983 Code of Canon Law – see John P. Beal et al (eds), *New Commentary on the Code of Canon Law*, Paulist Press, New York / Mahwah NJ, 2000. The previous, much older corpus of Canon Law, eventually codified in 1917, contains a near-identical definition.

[4] Cf. John Henry Newman, 'IX. Catholicity of the Anglican Church', [pp 1-73], in *Essays Critical and Historical, 3rd Edition, Volume II*, Basil Montagu Pickering, London, 1873, p 26

[5] Yves Congar, *Challenge to the Church: The Case of Archbishop Lefebvre*, Collins Liturgical Publications, London, 1978, p 35

[6] Daniel M. Bell Jr., 'State and Civil Society', Chapter 29 in Peter Scott and William T. Cavanaugh (eds), *The Blackwell Companion to Political Theology*, Blackwell, Oxford, 2004, [pp 423-438], p 425

[7] Bell, p 430

[8] Duarte Costa, 'Manifesto', in *Luta!* issue 12, September 1950, [pp 7-15] pp 14-15

[9] *New York Times*, 7th July 1945, p 11

[10] Cf. Thomas C. Bruneau, *The Political Transformation of the Brazilian Catholic Church*, Cambridge University Press, London and New York, 1974, pp 15-16

[11] A comprehensive summary of the whole period, from the colonization of Brazil up to the First Republic and beyond, can be found in Thomas C. Bruneau, *The Political Transformation of the Brazilian Catholic Church*, Cambridge University Press, London and New York, 1974

[12] Cf. Bell, p 425

[13] Bell, p 425

[14] The Conciliar Movement opposed the idea of centralized, universal jurisdiction exercised by the Pope and argued for a conciliar or council-based understanding of power in the Church.

[15] Thomas C. Bruneau, *The Political Transformation of the Brazilian Catholic Church*, Cambridge University Press, London and New York, 1974, pp 15-16

[16] Bruneau, p 17

[17] Sister Mary Crescentia Thornton, *The Church and Freemasonry in Brazil, 1872-1875*, Catholic University of America Press, Washington DC, 1948, pp 36-37

[18] Bruneau, p 22

[19] Brazil became an independent monarchical state; it was not a yet an independent republic.

[20] Roman Catholic Bishops of Brazil, quoted in João Dornas Filho, *O Padroado e a Igreja Brasileira [Patronage and the Brazilian Church]*, Companhia Editôra Nacional, Rio de Janeiro, 1937, p 289

[21] Cf. *The Catholic Herald*, London, 9th March 2018 – 'Married priests likely to be on 2019 synod agenda' – http://www.catholicherald.co.uk/commentandblogs/2018/03/09/analysis-married-priests-likely-to-be-on-2019-synod-agenda/ [accessed 22nd April 2018]

[22] 560,781 (in 2010), Source: IBGE – Instituto Brasileiro de Geografia e Estatística [Brazilian Institute of Geography and Statistics], *Censo Demografico 2010: Características Gerais da População, Religião, e Pessoas com Deficiência,* [Demographic Census 2010: General Characteristics of the Population, Religion, and People with Disabilities], IGBE, Rio de Janeiro, 2010, Table 1.4.1. This figure is possibly conservative as it does not include dual affiliates, *occasional* or *undeclared* dual affiliates, or non-respondents.

[23] Cf. Frank K. Flinn, *Encyclopedia of Catholicism*, Checkmark Books, New York, 2008, p 119

[24] Cf. Julie Byrne, *The Other Catholics: Remaking America's Largest Religion*, Columbia University Press, New York, 2016, p 98

25 The original cities making up Grande ABC were Santo André, São Bernardo, and São Caetano. It is a major center of manufacturing, especially automobiles, and is considered a hotbed of left-wing politics.

26 Cf. *Diário do Grande ABC* newspaper, 10th March 2013, 'Eles são católicos mas ignoram o papa' [They are Catholics but they ignore the pope] by Fábio Munhoz −[accessed 20th May 2018] http://www.dgabc.com.br/Noticia/91241/eles-sao-catolicos-mas-ignoram-o-papa

27 Readers may also see parallels between some aspects of ICAB's agenda and the later Liberation Theology movement; however, a conjecture that ICAB's founder was possibly the 'first liberation theologian', though not without appeal, is devoid of substance.

28 The title *Dom* is used in Portuguese-speaking countries to address bishops, and, less frequently in modern times, distinguished laymen. It is an abbreviation of the Latin *Dominus*. The Italian title *Don*, by comparison, is used for diocesan priests, not usually bishops, and, less frequently also, distinguished laymen.

29 Umbanda is a syncretic Afro-Brazilian religion with links to former slave communities.

30 Presbyterians reject the idea of bishops.

31 *New York Times*, 28th March 1961, p 35

32 Cf. *New York Times*, 3rd August 1973, p 4

33 Henry St John OP, in Peter F. Anson, *Bishops at Large*, Faber and Faber, London, 1964, p 15

II

"THE COURAGEOUS AND DEMOCRATIC ROMAN CATHOLIC BISHOP OF MAURA"[1]
— Genesis of a dissident bishop —

At the dawn of the country's First Republic, Catholicism in Brazil existed amid deep contradictions. Opinions of the Church were divided. While it had certainly contributed to bringing about the end of the old regime it was still widely regarded as part and parcel of that regime and therefore ripe to be consigned to history along with it. Most lawmakers and prominent members of society were either Positivists, Liberalists, Freemasons, or followers of other ideologies – very few of them were Catholic. With the national motto *Ordem e Progresso* decorating the flag, anticlericalism had become the State-endorsed norm.[2] It is a Positivist slogan attributed to Auguste Comte (1798-1857), whose 'Positivist Church' is still active today in Rio de Janeiro. The new Constitution imitated those of the United States and France; separation of Church and State being fundamental to the former, with the latter aiming to suppress the Church, which represented the *Ancien Regime*. Generally though, the Brazilian bishops appreciated the increased independence from the State. As Beatriz V. Dias Miranda wrote:

> "If, on one hand, the emerging religious doctrines heralded the advent of the Republic as a safeguard of religious freedom in practice, equally Catholicism was presented with new [and favorable] conditions for its dissemination. In effect Catholicism was now free of the State's shackles imposed during Patronage and was now able to fully imbue itself of its 'Romanness.' The Church was now able to decide strategy autonomously, without State interference."[3]

But the bishops also contradicted themselves, often saying that they repudiated the separation and demanding reunion of the two powers. Church influence had always been understood in tandem with State power and it was generated and expressed through State mechanisms. Without this superstructure there *was* no influence. The bishops still believed in some form of establishment and continued to aspire to having political influence. Meanwhile, relations with the Holy See became normal for the first time – appointments and promotions now came from Rome and there was direct communication, not passing through State intermediaries. This was in harmony with the ethos of increased centralization after the First Vatican Council (Vatican I) and resources and personnel could now be channelled into Brazil. In 1901 a Nuncio – the diplomatic representative of the Vatican – was finally appointed after a mere 400 years. But in terms of organizational structure the Church faced the new era with virtually nothing. In 1889 there were still only 12 ecclesiastical jurisdictions (11 dioceses and 1 archdiocese) in the vast territory, an increase of just three since the independence period of the eighteen-twenties. Suddenly though, organization became rapid: by 1900 there were 17 jurisdictions; by 1910 there were 30; by 1920 there were 58, and by 1964 there would be 178 ecclesiastical jurisdictions. This represents a remarkable 1500% increase in dioceses and archdioceses in 70 years.

The drastic shortage of clergy and the near non-existence of vocations also began to be addressed, with the sending from Europe of religious orders and priests who opened institutions of formation and reopened the closed ones. By 1946 there would be 6383 priests in Brazil, 3419 of whom were members of religious orders; two-thirds of these were foreign-born.[4] The Brazilian Church began to look like a contiguous, coherent body of structures and people for the first time – in short, like an actual Church. Predictably, it also began to resemble the European Church in many respects, and many new features were deliberately intended to imitate, rather than to address an actual need – the Brazilian Church adopted Rome's values wholesale in a spirit of denationalization. It copied

Rome's tough stance against Socialism and Protestantism because these were perceived as the most serious threats to the Catholic Church in Europe, even though they had an insignificant presence in Brazil at that time. Meanwhile, rapidly mounting challenges to Catholicism such as Spiritualism, Theosophy, and Freemasonry were not addressed – and the continuing general lack of Church influence in Brazilian society was overlooked. The Brazilian Church proved incapable or unwilling to reconcile its new-found autonomy with a distinctly Brazilian character. Contradictions abounded – national identity was abandoned in the name of Romanization while the hierarchy still pined for State endorsement; autonomy did not mean more freedom to be Brazilian, but rather to be more Roman. With the end of royal patronage the Church was no longer a mere subordinate function of a monarchical state. However, this also meant that the Church's religious monopoly and privileged status in Brazilian society were gone. At the same time, the adoption of European values, the increasingly European clergy, and dizzyingly rapid organization did not really get to the heart of the fundamental problems of the Brazilian Church.

Into this confused situation the future founder of the schismatic Brazilian Catholic Apostolic Church was born. Carlos Duarte Costa[5] was six months old when the last vestiges of Portuguese colonialism were cast off and the First Republic of Brazil was created. He was born in Rio de Janeiro on 21st July 1888. Catholicism in Brazil, and Brazil itself, were rapidly approaching a major turning point in their history. Duarte Costa's family were well-placed in society, and they also enjoyed excellent ecclesiastical connections – his maternal uncle was Dom Eduardo Duarte e Silva (1852-1924).[6] Eduardo Duarte e Silva was a highly respected cleric whose career coincided with Rome's consolidation of power after Vatican I. In addition, he counted among his friends the powerful Archbishop Joaquim Arcoverde de Albuquerque Cavalcanti of Rio de Janeiro, then without question the most senior person in the whole Latin American Church. Cavalcanti would later become not only Brazil's first Cardinal in 1905 but also the first Cardinal ever

41

to be born in the southern hemisphere. When Carlos Duarte Costa was eighteen months old, his uncle Eduardo, while visiting Rome, was personally invited by the Pope to become bishop of Gôias. Aged just 37, he was consecrated bishop right there in Rome, rather than having to wait the many weeks that would be required to return to Brazil, wait for a written nomination to arrive by sea, and eventually make the trip to Gôias. Even though the circumstances may have demanded it, it is still extremely rare in modern times for a Pope to appoint a bishop personally, face-to-face.

From his earliest infancy, therefore, Carlos Duarte Costa had an influential and well-connected protector in uncle Eduardo, the popular young bishop, and a successful future in the Church seemed to be mapped out for the youngster. Aged just nine, he would accompany his uncle to Rome, where Dom Eduardo was able to secure a seminary education for his nephew at the prestigious Latin American College that he himself had attended. Ill health appears to have brought young Carlos back to Brazil early, and he completed his training for the priesthood at the local seminary run by the Augustinians. Sources suggest that Duarte Costa's academic career never recovered from this interruption and that he even failed his Theology, balancing out his grade average with a better performance in Apologetics. He was only ordained, it was said, "thanks to the benevolence"[7] and direct intervention of his uncle Eduardo. What is certainly true is that occasional mentions of Carlos Duarte Costa having completed a doctorate at the Gregorian University in Rome are not substantiated by the university archives.

Bishop Eduardo personally ordained his nephew and protégé as a priest in 1911. Privileged positions awaited him, working under his uncle's friend Cardinal Cavalcanti in the secretariat of the Rio de Janeiro Archdiocese, where he gained a reputation as a conscientious young priest.[8] Visionaries within the Church were starting to promote education as the key to developing lasting Church influence in society. They began to push for increased focus on the formation of young Catholics, and Duarte Costa keenly tuned in to this mindset, authoring a new catechism for children. Cardinal Cavalcanti recognized that Duarte Costa was not simply treading water and living off his good connections – he rewarded the young priest's hard work with the title of Monsignor and a promotion to General Secretary. By the beginning of the nineteen-twenties the old Cardinal's health was deteriorating. Monsignor Duarte Costa, whose career had been blessed so far, nurtured hopes of being appointed auxiliary bishop, so as to take over ever more duties on behalf of the ageing prelate. But in 1921 the decision that came from Rome left him disillusioned. Sebastião Leme da Silveira Cintra, the dynamic Archbishop of Olinda and Recife, only six years older than Duarte Costa, would be appointed as the Cardinal's coadjutor and successor. The title of coadjutor bishop, rather than auxiliary bishop, is used to indicate that the new appointee will effectively take over the position of bishop from an elderly or infirm superior, with right of succession once the top job sadly becomes vacant. Duarte Costa felt distinctly snubbed, describing the event as "[the] Holy See ... taking advantage of my nature."[9] It was his first major setback since his frustrating underachievement as a student, which had nearly blocked his path to ordination, and it set the scene for the long series of disappointments ahead. It was the beginning of the end of Duarte Costa's love affair with the Church.

At the same time that power was being redistributed in the Archdiocese of Rio de Janeiro, Duarte Costa's protector, his uncle Dom Eduardo, was also now seriously ill. He had successfully gone on to become bishop of Uberaba, but in 1923 he was forced to retire on health grounds – though he did still have considerable influence. Having missed out on the big promotions, Duarte Costa was now available to be moved somewhere new. Silveira Cintra, the Cardinal's new regent, was well-inclined towards the young Duarte Costa. It was Silveira Cintra who, since 1916, had been most vocally campaigning for greater focus on Catholic education, and Duarte Costa had been supportive of the campaign. Both Silveira Cintra and the Cardinal himself were confident in promoting Duarte Costa to the rank of bishop the following year, 1924.

Although gratified by the token of appreciation, Duarte Costa was again disappointed, being assigned to the thoroughly uninviting backwater of Botucatu in São Paulo State. Botucatu, like so many Brazilian dioceses at the time, was relatively new, remote, and underdeveloped. Even at its best the Brazilian Church sorely lacked organization, infrastructure, and resources, but rural areas like Botucatu lagged behind all the rest. It must have been distinctly underwhelming for this able, city-dwelling priest to find himself as a kind of pioneer bishop in such an unencouraging outpost. A further disappointment added sadness to Duarte Costa's daunting new task. His uncle Eduardo did not live to see his nephew become a bishop – he died just weeks before the ordination.

Duarte Costa chose as his episcopal motto *O Senhor é a Minha Luz* – The Lord is My Light – and took control of the diocese of Botucatu in 1925. He seems to have initially managed to muster considerable energy in leading the then-remote rural diocese. Administratively there were several boundary changes to oversee in the early years, as the evolving structure of the Brazilian Church took shape. He also dedicated attention to pastoral work, founding movements for the laity and encouraging missionaries to set up in the diocese. Botucatu was to see the foundations of a new cathedral laid in 1927. However, its construction was to be very protracted – resources were inexpertly diverted away from building work, and Duarte Costa would not see the cathedral anywhere near finished by the end of his almost thirteen-year tenure in Botucatu (it would finally be inaugurated, still unfinished, in 1943).[10]

The following year was another major turning point for Brazil, for the Church, and for Duarte Costa. In 1930 the pragmatic politician Getúlio Vargas seized power in a coup, overturning the democratic constitution of the First Republic. Vargas, known as a harsh authoritarian, was also a complex character whose life would eventually end in suicide. He had a cold, almost neutral opinion of the Church, regarding it as a potential ally to be courted, much as he viewed the military. Senior figures within the Church now faced serious challenges both in the practical and moral orders.

Practically, what modest influence the Church did have must be preserved, especially as the constitution that had freed the Church had now been suppressed. Morally, the Church now faced the challenge of an authoritarian and undemocratic force in charge of civil society, which had the potential to become hostile (as soon came to pass in Italy and in many other parts of the world as the century progressed). The new regime was not without strong anticlerical elements. 1930 was also the year that the ailing Cardinal Cavalcanti of Rio de Janeiro died and the dynamic Sebastião Leme da Silveira Cintra took over the top post in the Brazilian Church. Though aware of people's fears, Silveira Cintra shrewdly grasped that the new political situation presented an opportunity for the Church to make its role and position clear. In October 1930 he personally and physically intervened in one of the most dramatic moments of the coup itself, by going to persuade the incumbent President to peacefully withdraw and flee with his life, just as the revolutionary forces surrounded the presidential palace. Silveira Cintra is credited with saving the deposed President's life and avoiding further bloodshed. But Silveira Cintra's most brilliant move was to come the following year. He mobilized all the forces of the archdiocese to organize two enormous mass religious celebrations in the same year – one for the patron saint, Our Lady of Aparecida, and one to coincide with the inauguration of the 98-foot tall statue, *Cristo Redentor*, unmistakeable symbol of Rio de Janeiro (then the capital city) and of Brazil. There was, crucially, absolutely no political flavor to these events, but the public response was so overwhelming and so total that Silveira Cintra left no-one in any doubt as to the awesome popular power that the Church could marshal. He had successfully harnessed national identity, community spirit, and religiosity – which are arguably different aspects of the same phenomenon. The entire city had taken to the streets at the new Cardinal's prompting, and the show of force was not lost on the astute Vargas. Relations between the President and the Cardinal, which were already fairly good, became even better, and the Church's voice would not be ignored again.

Silveira Cintra may justly be regarded as the 'man of the hour' of the Catholic Church in Brazil. Determined to address the Church's lack of influence in many areas of society, he founded the Catholic University of Rio de Janeiro and the Catholic Electoral League. Even prior to his appointment to the Rio de Janeiro job his forward thinking was well known. He was acutely aware of, among other things, the lack of real engagement with the faith of the great masses of the Brazilian people. Furthermore, he was instrumental in linking this deficiency to the paucity of Catholic education, especially in childhood. The Catholic Church was simply failing to form Catholics in the crib and then nurture them through their formative years. But thanks to Cardinal Silveira Cintra the Church was now recognized as a major mover of the people's mood and opinion, and it would actually be consulted on future social and policy issues. The Church under Silveira Cintra had thus formulated a robust response to the Vargas takeover. We do not know Duarte Costa's immediate reaction to Silveira Cintra's clever political manoeuvring in Rio de Janeiro, but we do know that his own gambit in Botucatu was much less diplomatic. In the State of São Paulo, opposition to the Vargas regime and support for the now-suppressed democratic constitution were so considerable that separatism was seriously debated. São Paulo State, of which Duarte Costa's Botucatu was a part, looked set to secede from the federation of Brazilian states. Events culminated in the Constitutionalist Revolt of 1932, effectively a short Brazilian Civil War. Duarte Costa took the extraordinary step of raising and arming a battalion to fight the government. Known as 'The Terror of Botucatu' or 'The Bishop's Battalion' with Duarte Costa as its colonel, the unit wrote a less than glorious chapter of military history. According to Father Florence M. Dubois, as the troops stood listening to Duarte Costa's setting-off speech, laden down with outdated equipment and antiquated weaponry, the bishop-colonel lost his nerve and stammered all the way through his oratory. Bungling his speech was said to be "one of the greatest sorrows of his life"[11] but worse was to come for Duarte Costa. His

46

battalion arrived too late for the battle – General Klinger, the leader of the revolutionary forces, had already thrown in the towel. The Terror of Botucatu turned around and went home "heads down."[12] Although it was yet another profound disappointment for Duarte Costa, the fact that the inept Bishop's Battalion failed to arrive at the front on time no doubt saved their lives to a man. Added to his shame and humiliation, Duarte Costa had unwisely diverted funds from other causes to finance the battalion, and the mistake would catch up with him. As well as sacrificing his pectoral cross in gold with precious stones, he had also dug into the diocesan treasury to fund the failed revolution.[13]

By contrast, Cardinal Silveira Cintra's diplomatic approach was having a marked effect on the new regime. In the constituent assembly elections of 1933 most of the candidates backed by Silveira Cintra's pressure group the LEC – Catholic Electoral League – were elected. The following year *all* the LEC's demands were included in the new Constitution, which was even prefaced with the phrase 'putting our confidence in God ....." Separation of Church and State was to continue, but the State could now assist the Church financially 'in the collective interest." The rights and reach of the Church were expanded considerably – religious marriage was recognized, chaplaincy to the armed forces was permitted, religious brethren could now vote, divorce was prohibited, and religion was set to return to the classroom. The price of these considerable concessions was effectively the Church's tacit cooperation with an undemocratic, authoritarian regime, but in fairness the LEC and Silveira Cintra himself successfully avoided the even more extreme political alternatives. For example, even though the fascist Integralists supported the Church and won numerous Catholic adherents, including some priests, Silveira Cintra ignored them completely. Similarly, he promoted a 1937 collective pastoral letter opposing Communism – Duarte Costa, in spite of his later pro-Stalin pronouncements, was a signatory. Deeply perturbed by the Church's lack of influence, Silveira Cintra focused on orienting and mobilizing the Brazilian Church, rather than party politics. His own influence on Duarte Costa is evident – Silveira Cintra made it the norm for bishops to be daring innovators and courageous activists. He set the agenda for the Church of a generation, an agenda which would find its extreme, abstract expression in ICAB.

The Church faced a paradox – Brazil was then, as today, the largest Catholic country, though adherence ranged from nominal and marginal, to popular and cultural, to deep and devout. But Catholicism had little influence or impact. Catholics were invisible in the arts, politics, among the intellectual elites, and social structures. Internally, the Church lacked vocations, resources, and organization. For Silveira Cintra this was the real problem facing the Church, and he managed to remain somewhat above the political upheavals of the day – regimes would come and go but the Church would remain, and it must position itself to weather the storms. It was necessary, Silveira Cintra believed, to organize and unite in order to pressure the State – whoever may be in charge of it – for the Church's rightful place in public affairs, schools, and society. In short, the Church must cover all aspects of daily life once more, as it had during the Christendom age. In order to achieve this renewed comprehensive and monopolistic vision, it would be necessary to regain the support of the State. Throughout his career in the hierarchy Silveira Cintra mobilized sectors of the Church with the goal of gaining privileged status for it. Against all odds it worked. In other countries where the Church has been forced out of the public domain (Mexico, Chile, Cuba, France, etc.) the institution never re-entered it on its own terms. Generally, after a period of exclusion the Church has developed new strategies and promoted a different, subtler, more modern model of influence. In Brazil, however, Silveira Cintra's strategy worked, and the Church again entered the public domain on a privileged basis. He convinced statesmen that excessive secularization and ignoring the religiosity of the people were mistakes, but the government still failed to fully grasp the potential benefits of supporting the Church.

The Cardinal's accomplishments left a decidedly bitter taste in some mouths. Appeasing an undemocratic regime was a far from perfect compromise. As the decade of the nineteen-thirties progressed, Duarte Costa was still riding on a wave of disappointments. Though well-disposed towards Silveira Cintra personally, Duarte Costa was consistently more combative than the Cardinal, even though he never seemed to win any of the fights he picked. The Cardinal had been clear in his disapproval of the extreme fascist Integralist movement, but Duarte Costa went one better; he offered refuge to anti-Integralist activists, hiding them in his residence – this included future bishop Hélder Câmara. As a young priest, Câmara had at first supported fascist Integralism, and when he dared to repudiate the movement they targeted him for persecution. Duarte Costa became "a great friend of Hélder"[14] in the mid-thirties, but he was less appreciated in his diocese. His poor management affected the Church's work, and his diverting of funds for causes like the Constitutionalist Revolt raised questions about his priorities. Unlike the Cardinal, Duarte Costa had difficulty balancing the pastoral and the political. Botucatu's modest cathedral project, starved of funds, approached its tenth anniversary as a construction site. Cardinal Silveira Cintra had won enormous concessions from Getúlio Vargas by agreeing to live side-by-side with the authoritarian regime. Duarte Costa, on the other hand, continued to adopt a hostile attitude to the government.

By 1935 Costa had forged an excellent friendship with the local Constitutionalist Governor of São Paulo State, Armando de Sales Oliveira (1887-1945), a committed opponent of Getúlio Vargas. Oliveira was a partner in the *O Estado de S. Paulo* newspaper, which was critical of the Vargas regime and which would eventually be suppressed after raids by the political police. Duarte Costa and Oliveira, who were the same age and politically like-minded, made a perfect partnership of local political and religious power in São Paulo. The official Italian diplomatic diary offers a revealing detail in this regard. Immigration into São Paulo State had diminished by 1935, at a time when increasing industrialization called for more workers. Oliveira was threatened with unrest at the hands of badly overstretched Anarchist and Communist labor unions.

Knowing that his bishop friend could command a certain amount of respect in Italian circles, he asked Duarte Costa to appeal for more immigrant labor in order to avert social strife:

> "The bishop of São Paulo [sic], Monsignor Carlo [sic] Duarte Costa, accompanied by his Secretary, an Italian Passionist Father, came to tell me, on behalf of the President of the State of São Paulo, that in his territory a resumption of Italian immigration would be very favorably looked upon."[15]

The São Paulo team of bishop and governor had high hopes for the future. At the close of 1936 Oliveira stood down as governor, but only in order to run for President of Brazil. The country was ready for democracy and elections had been planned for January 1938. But Vargas changed his mind, and 1937 was to be the year in which the strongman tightened up his regime instead. A new coup d'état in November brought in Vargas's rigid *Estado Novo* – the 'New State' – and democracy was to remain shelved. The opponent Oliveira had shown his hand too soon. He was placed under house arrest for a year before going into exile, first in France and then the USA. Duarte Costa no longer had a friend in the State governor's office, and 1937 presented an opportunity to push the politicized bishop out of office too. There was perhaps every reason to force Duarte Costa to resign. It was becoming widely known that his beliefs were moving towards the extremely liberal, and that he questioned Church discipline on matters such as clerical celibacy and divorce. His financial mismanagement of the diocese and his unusual behaviour could have been enough, but his combative political positions also conflicted with Cardinal Silveira Cintra's more subtle, strategic approach. The Cardinal's cautious political manoeuvring and his friendship with the authoritarian Vargas had so far positively transformed the Church's standing in society. Duarte Costa had shaped up to be the antithesis of Silveira Cintra. While the Cardinal courted the President, Duarte Costa befriended the arch-opponent Oliveira. So when Vargas got rid of Oliveira he wanted the Church to get rid of Oliveira's turbulent bishop friend too – it was a small concession to the President who had reinstated Church power. The Church could not risk one of its own endangering the long-term strategy for the revitalization of the Church in Brazil. Duarte Costa was therefore out of office. From his own 'exile', however, he was to begin hatching a plan of his own for renewing the Church.

Not for the first time, a major milestone in the history of Brazil was to coincide with a major milestone in the life of Carlos Duarte Costa. 1937 was the year Getúlio Vargas consolidated his power with a new coup d'état and a new, uncompromising constitution. Vargas called it the 'New State.' For Duarte Costa, 1937 marked the end of his career in the Roman Catholic Church. It had started so promisingly a quarter of a century earlier, under the tutelage of his uncle, the revered bishop Eduardo. Now he was shown the door. A bishop does not expect to 'be retired' aged forty-nine when the conventional retirement age is 75 (and many bishops serve beyond this age). The Church can be an unforgiving mistress – then, as now, there is rarely any bouncing back from an early, ignominious withdrawal from office. As is the custom when any bishop retires, Carlos Duarte Costa was given an honorary or 'titular' diocese – that is, in title only, with no actual jurisdiction. Titular dioceses are extinct or obsolete dioceses whose names have fallen into disuse due to demographic or boundary changes. It would be incorrect to interpret the assignment of a Titular title as an insult or punishment in itself, as is occasionally inferred. It is merely a necessary formality, because according to Canon Law a bishop must be the bishop *of* somewhere.[16] Duarte Costa thus became Titular Bishop of Maura – a historical diocese within *Mauritania Caesariensis*, a Roman province located in modern-day Algeria. Duarte Costa and others would encourage the shortening of his title to 'Bishop of Maura', thus unintentionally, perhaps, giving the impression of being a working diocesan bishop with an actual jurisdiction. This also caused confusion with the similar-sounding Mauá, which is in São Paulo State – as is Botucatu, Duarte Costa's former diocese. This led the *New York Times*, for example, to describe him as

51

'Bishop of Maura in Sao [sic] Paulo State' on 6th July 1945, after the publicizing of his excommunication. But Duarte Costa was surely under no illusions that as of 1937 he was totally without jurisdiction, power, or standing in the Church.

Once deposed, Duarte Costa became dependent on the generosity of Cardinal Silveira Cintra. The two men's résumés were by now very different; the Cardinal's manoeuvres tended to meet with spectacular success and he was a gifted bishop, while Duarte Costa tended to orchestrate disasters and mismanaged Church funds in order to finance them; Silveira Cintra had responded to the first Vargas coup with a mixture of personal courage, diplomacy and cunning, while Duarte Costa had recruited his own battalion and armed them with museum pieces for a civil war; the Cardinal tackled President Vargas by appealing to reason and common ground, while Duarte Costa befriended and supported politicians who directly antagonized Vargas. There was also a sharp contrast in their handling of the fascist Integralist movement – Silveira Cintra refused to acknowledge or engage with the Integralists while Duarte Costa was directly hostile to them and inadvertently gained publicity for them. More recently the *Estado Novo* coup had signalled the successful culmination of Silveira Cintra's efforts to re-establish the Church, while for Duarte Costa it marked his entry into obscurity. He had no desire to remain kicking his heels in São Paulo State, the scene of his disgrace, and wanted to return to his native home in Rio de Janeiro. Silveira Cintra, as Cardinal Archbishop of Rio de Janeiro, showed himself to be eminently reasonable in accommodating this request and allowed him to maintain for personal use a "tiny blue-walled chapel"[17] at home, in order to celebrate Mass. As a further fraternal gesture the Cardinal sometimes invited Duarte Costa to visit parishes and gave him permission to administer Confirmations. Later, he was invited to take part in the consecration of an Italian-born bishop. This is interesting considering Duarte Costa's growing dislike of foreign-born clergy. Eliseu Maria Coroli was not only foreign-born, but a foreign-born Barnabite priest, as was Padre Dubois, a leading critic of Duarte Costa.

While this was surely a humdrum sort of existence for Duarte Costa, Silveira Cintra was no doubt in his element. The Church and the Vargas regime had reached a perfectly amicable and lasting cohabitation. This would not change even after the ousting of Vargas in 1945. The authors of the 1946 Constitution would see no reason to meddle with a satisfactory working relationship and simply formalized it. Under Silveira Cintra the Church's goals converged with the State's, and their values appeared largely similar and compatible. Broadly Christian principles seemed to be reflected in the State vision, and the State saw no conflict with the social tenets of the Church at that time. The common good of the nation was widely held as the shared objective of Church and State. 'Order and Progress', the Secularist-Positivist slogan which adorns the national flag, was seen as completely in harmony with the Church's aims: to be Brazilian was once again to be Catholic. But no-one could ignore the obvious problem – the Church was in alliance with an authoritarian and undemocratic regime, a dictatorship. This arrangement would end up doing lasting damage to the people's perception of the Church throughout Latin America, but Catholics at the time approved of elements of the Vargas regime such as stability, order, and anti-Communism. For Silveira Cintra the *Estado Novo* regime was a minor evil trumped by a greater good – the regime had conceded the Church a privileged status which amounted to "a return to an influence model similar to that of the Christendom form."[18] As Thomas C. Bruneau explained:

> "[The] institution had prevailed: the Constitution was declared in the name of God, religion was taught in public schools, government funds were used for Church structures and the symbols [of Catholicism] were used by the political elite."[19]

But even with its victories the Brazilian Church was hardly catching up to the modern age. This neo-Christendom Church-State model was at least a hundred years out of date, and it was totally reliant upon State structures and State endorsement. Silveira Cintra's successes left the Church to face the immense challenges of the twentieth century with an antiquated conception of itself. Self-managed resources were non-existent. The Church amounted to a sort of elaborate, external appearance of Catholicism, with all the trappings in place, but little substance behind the façade. Furthermore, the Church's emphasis was towards the powerful, wealthy classes. Primary education was given scant attention – only about 2% of primary schools were Catholic, even though primary education was the most widely accessed, and was most likely to constitute the only experience of education for the poor. Primary education is also the most effective means of combating illiteracy (Brazil's literacy rate was about 50% and would remain so even into the 1960's). Compare this to secondary education, attended by the better-off: between a third and a half of secondary schools were Catholic; and as for university, the preserve of the rich and influential, a third of universities were Catholic. The conclusion was obvious to many – the Church still predominantly focused on the middle class and upwards.

From his enforced vantage point on the ecclesiastical side-lines Carlos Duarte Costa was privileged in one sense – he was able to observe the state of the Church's affairs and see Silveira Cintra's failures as well as his successes. These issues would also begin to make up Duarte Costa's own list of desired reforms and became the foci of ICAB's future agenda. He had shown a genuine interest in education as far back as Silveira Cintra's influential campaign in the 1910's, when Duarte Costa had won acclaim for his new children's catechism. He would later try to insist on every ICAB church having a free school attached. This would be Duarte Costa's way of trying to accomplish what Silveira Cintra never did. Furthermore, Duarte Costa would insist that ICAB should not foist upon the faithful an image of Catholicism imported from afar, but would recognize, respect, and accommodate the many and varied beliefs of the Brazilian people as authentic and holy callings. ICAB's Christianity was to be no façade and no wish list of what *should* be, but a true and complex collage of what Brazilians really believed and practised – what you saw was what you got, in contrast to the superficial window dressing of the Roman Catholic religion. The mainstream Catholic religion was widely regarded as a sort of veil of Catholicism without real substance – it had never actually been assimilated by the people. The paraphernalia was in place but it was superficial, a "Catholicism of pretty words and exterior acts"[20] as a 1950's government study phrased it, not really beating in the hearts of the people. This would be recognized by many people today as the curse of the traditionally Catholic countries such as Italy, Spain, and Ireland – nominally Catholic majorities but with empty pews, flatlining birth rates, rocketing annulments, plummeting marriage numbers, and no vocations. People just do not seem to espouse Catholicism in its entirety when it is presented to them in an all-or-nothing format. This marks another difference between Silveira Cintra and Duarte Costa. Romanization, promoted by Silveira Cintra, required people's adherence to a model of religion presented to them as a sort of constitution – the faithful must conform their beliefs and practices to the religion that the Church expresses. As Duarte Costa saw it, the true task of the Church is to draw together the beliefs and practices of religion as the *people* express it. He would argue that this was both more realistic and more catholic. The Church could not expect from people worship that was a 'right' expression of belief, as though both the belief and the form of expression could be divorced from their culture and customs. This all sounds much less revolutionary in the post-Vatican II Church of course, but this was the 1940's.

Aside from all and any deserved criticism, Duarte Costa may at least be credited with wanting to address genuine problems. He decried the superficiality and ineffectiveness of mainstream Catholicism and the bland hypocrisy of the lip-service paid to it. Duarte Costa began to envisage a Church that would at last address the terrible paucity of basic education for the poor Brazilian working class and took steps to achieve it. He became captivated by the idea of a Church that would be a more authentic expression of people's faith, in harmony with the Afro-Brazilian religions, Freemasonry, the Occult, and Protestantism, with which he saw no incompatibility either in principle or in practice. ICAB would be true to what Brazilians believed, whereas Romanization could only ever achieve a veneer of external rites, appealing mainly to the comfortably-off. Duarte Costa foresaw a more authentically catholic – universal – Christian religion; perhaps only broadly Christian, but as Brazilian people really believed and practised it, and in this sense a National Catholic Church.

It is out of this and similar reasoning that one of the least edifying of Duarte Costa's fixations emerged – hostility to foreigners, which would descend into self-contradiction and hypocrisy. There is clearly some truth in the idea that foreign clergy, by and large, could never understand Brazilian people and culture like Brazilian clergy could, but Duarte Costa now began to portray foreign clergy as wholly and deliberately malignant. They were instruments of Rome (or worse, Berlin, or Franco's Spain) hell-bent on Romanization, which was both detrimental to and impossible to fuse with Brazilian religion. Duarte Costa believed that the Vatican's agenda was effectively, if not in name, fascist. He thought that since most foreign clergy came from Italy, Spain, and Germany, these clergy were unavoidably fascist in values, culture, and mindset, even if involuntarily. They came to Brazil immersed in experiences of State cohabitation with fascist regimes. The true purpose of these 'Axis' priests in Brazil, whether they knew it or not, was to further the worldwide fascist agenda and promote its value system, even if innocently dressed-up as Roman Catholicism. The process was already underway in Brazil, where the Church had slipped comfortably into bed beside the Vargas dictatorship. Despising foreign clergy and religious was something of a turnaround for Duarte Costa; it will be remembered that he had an Italian priest of the Passionist order as his secretary in Botucatu; he had also encouraged the Italian Passionist sisters to set up in Botucatu, providing a convent for them.[21] Duarte Costa may have later suspected his Passionist secretary of colluding in pushing for his forced resignation, which could certainly have soured him towards foreign priests. Even so, he did not refrain from participating in the ordination of an Italian Barnabite bishop in 1940. Anyone can change their mind of course, but Duarte Costa himself was to disregard all his own objections to foreign clergy when it came to staffing ICAB. His original line-up of clergy was a mishmash of different nationalities, as well as a variety of denominations, trendy philosophies, sects and cults – hardly any of it having anything to do with the ordinary people and culture of Brazil.

Duarte Costa probably feared, as many indeed did, that the Vargas regime's political affinity with the fascists would lead Brazil to join the Axis in World War Two, and there was widespread surprise and relief when this did not happen. Brazil maintained an uneasy neutrality at first, but as the importance of its trading relationship with the USA and Great Britain increased, the Allies became a more likely partner and the Axis became a very real enemy. Brazil broke off diplomatic ties to the Axis in January 1942. Duarte Costa began to see Axis spies everywhere in the Catholic clergy, though he made less fuss when German Lutheran preachers were actually caught in the act of passing information to the enemy.[22] Duarte Costa's fears were not entirely groundless, however. Some German Catholic religious were caught operating clandestine radios for espionage purposes.[23] He continued to campaign for the 'nationalization of the clergy' through the combined efforts of current clergy, seminaries, educators and those involved in vocations ministry.[24] By the middle of 1942, neutral or not, Brazilian shipping was suffering heavy losses at the hands of the German U-boats, and on 22nd August President Getúlio Vargas declared war. Duarte Costa sent a telegram to Vargas, ostensibly pledging solidarity, but he soon started calling for concentration camps and expulsion for priests born in Axis countries.[25] Understandably perhaps, a bishop making such petitions to an allied government reached the international press. With the United States having joined the war at the end of the previous year, Americans were anxious to ascertain where loyalties sat among the vast communities of European immigrants in the New World. The *New York Times* reported Duarte Costa demanding that 'Axis' clergy be deported.[26] Many of Duarte Costa's incisive observations on the problems in the Church were praiseworthy and valid, especially his sensitivity to the need for education, attention to the poor, and making Catholicism relevant to the Brazilian context. But even as he developed this constructive analysis, it was overshadowed by his obsessive and unhelpful attacks on foreign clergy, which would also prove utterly inconsistent. He merely succeeded in making more enemies in the hierarchy and looked increasingly unstable to outsiders. His actions did not go without receiving some acclaim – religious commentators in the US lauded him as "the antifascist Bishop"[27] but popularity among American Protestants was not going to win him fans at home.

Disappointments continued to accumulate for Duarte Costa. The great Cardinal Silveira Cintra died of a heart attack in October 1942, aged 60. He had been the last member of the hierarchy to tolerate Duarte Costa, allowing him a limited ministry in Rio de Janeiro. He had therefore lost his second powerful protector, who had in turn replaced his uncle, Bishop Eduardo. The Church hierarchy in Brazil were infuriated with Duarte Costa for his headline-grabbing outbursts and sensationalist diatribes against 'Axis priests', but the following year he compounded it further. In 1943 the Communist publishing house Calvino was set to publish the Portuguese translation of the Reverend Hewlett Johnson's *The Socialist Sixth of The World*, an unreserved apologia for the Soviet Union. It would be published under the alternative American title *The Soviet Power (O Poder Soviético)*. By 1943 Stalin had mobilized the entire international Communist movement to go on the offensive in support of the USSR, to persuade the Allies to launch the Second Front. Hewlett Johnson, the Anglican Dean of Canterbury, who would later win the Stalin Peace Prize no less, was notoriously lavish in his praise of the USSR, evidently without ever jeopardizing his position in the Church of England. The 'Red Dean' had even visited Moscow during the 'Moscow Trials' of the nineteen-thirties, and reported neither seeing nor hearing of anything remotely untoward. For the Brazilian edition of Johnson's book there was an obvious candidate to provide a foreword – the nearest thing to a Brazilian equivalent of Johnson. Duarte Costa's foreword offers little more than a glowing endorsement of Johnson's eulogy for Stalin and praises a Soviet Union in which, according to Duarte Costa, "freedom of religion exists without limitation"[28] and "respect for human dignity is increasing remarkably."[29] Had there been any doubt up to then as to Duarte Costa's espousal of Communism, there was none now. But was he really a Communist at heart, or did he just embrace another clear opportunity to enrage the Church hierarchy?

Whether it was simple provocation or not, his increasingly fierce and public espousal of Stalinist Communism repulsed any fellow bishops who might otherwise have overlooked his frenzied criticisms about the Church and 'Axis clergy.' In July 1944 Duarte Costa was placed under house arrest by the regime and questioned about his Communist sympathies and links. There was a danger of actual imprisonment, and forced exile was also mooted.[30] His mystifying behavior aroused ever greater concern among the bishops' conference. Under house arrest on his 56th birthday, 21st July 1944, he was visited by Dom Antônio dos Santos Cabral and Dom José Mauricio da Rocha, the bishops of Belo Horizonte and Bragança Paulista respectively:

> "Dom Cabral wanted to find out what Dom Carlos's intentions were, should [an ecclesiastical] penalty be imposed upon him and whether he would submit to it. His Most Reverend Excellency Dom Carlos replied that he would not submit and that he would found [his own] Church. Dom Cabral told Dom Carlos that he would never succeed in planting his own church in Brazil. Dom Cabral was deluding himself."[31]

Interventions by the press and pressure from Allied diplomats saw Duarte Costa released by the government in September, but the Church finally imposed its penalty and suspended him from even occasionally exercising his ministry. He was no longer a working bishop of the Church. But in terms of challenging the hierarchy Duarte Costa was still only getting himself warmed up.

Notes

1   Kenneth Leslie, '*Protestant Digest*', Vol. 6, Issue 7, Protestant Digest Inc., New York, 1945, p 14

2   Cf. Gregory D. Gilson and Irving W. Levinson (eds), *Latin American Positivism – new historical and philosophic essays*, Lexington Books, Plymouth UK, 2013, p 128 (note 25), and Cf. Heiko Spitzeck et al (eds), *Humanism in Business*, Cambridge University Press, Cambridge, 2009, p 41

3   Beatriz V. Dias Miranda, and Mabel Salgado Pereira (Eds), *Memorias Eclesiasticas: Documentos Comentados [Ecclesiastical Memoirs: Commentated Documents]*, Editora UFJF / Centro da Memoria da Igreja de Juiz de Fora – Cehila / Brazil, Juiz de Fora, 2000, pp 96-97

4   Collated from data in Thomas C. Bruneau's *The Political Transformation of the Brazilian Catholic Church*, Cambridge University Press, London and New York, 1974

5   A note on Duarte Costa's surnames: 'Duarte Costa' conforms to the Portuguese double surname custom, keeping both the mother's and father's surname, Maternal+Paternal. In everyday use, the first (maternal) surname may be dropped, so that Carlos Duarte Costa may usually be called Carlos Costa. For maximum clarity this book uses 'Duarte Costa.' The hyphenated 'Duarte-Costa', occasionally found in English-language texts, has nothing to do with Portuguese or Brazilian custom, and is avoided here completely. Duarte Costa's first name occasionally appears, erroneously, as 'Carlo', especially where a source may be Italian in origin.

6   The biographical details in this chapter are collated from a variety of sources including the records of the Diocese of Gôias, the now *Arch*dioceses of Uberaba and Botucatu, entries in the *Annuarium Pontificium*, and the work of the Belgian-born Barnabite Father Florence Marie Dubois (1878-1964), who wrote the contemporary study *O Ex-Bispo de Maura e o Bom Senso*.

7   Irmã [Sister] Maria Regina do Santo Rosário [Laurita Pessôa Raja Gabaglia], *O Cardeal Leme [Cardinal Leme]*, J. Olympio, Rio de Janeiro, 1962, p 467

8   Cf. Irmã [Sister] Maria Regina do Santo Rosário [Laurita Pessôa Raja Gabaglia], 1962, p 467

9   Padre Florence Marie [Florêncio Maria] Dubois, *O Ex-Bispo de Maura e o Bom Senso [The Ex-Bishop of Maura and Common Sense]*, Editora Vozes Limitada, Petrópolis RJ–Rio de Janeiro–São Paulo, 1945, p 40

10   By comparison, the 635-ton Christ the Redeemer statue watching over Rio de Janeiro took a 'mere' nine years to complete.

11   Dubois, p 88, and Cf. pp 85-88

12   Dubois, p 88

13   Cf. Oswaldo Faustino, *A Legião Negra: A Luta dos Afro-Brasileiros na Revolucão Constitucionalista de 1932 [The Black Legion: The Struggle of Afro-Brazilians in the Constitutionalist Revolution of 1932]*, Selo Negro Edições, São Paulo, 2011, p 156

14   Nelson Piletti and Walter Praxedes, *Dom Hélder Câmara: entre o poder e a profecia [Dom Hélder Câmara: between power and prophecy]*, Editora Atica, São Paulo, 1997, p 142

15   Commission for the Publication of Diplomatic Documents (Commissione per la Pubblicazione dei Documenti Diplomatici): Ministry of Foreign Affairs (Ministero degli Affari Esteri), *I Documenti Diplomatici Italiani [Italian Diplomatic Documents]* 28th April 1936, Libreria dello Stato, Rome, 1992

16   When Bishop Jacques Gaillot was removed from his post as bishop of Evreux, France, in 1995, he was given the titular see of Parthenia (coincidentally not far from Duarte Costa's see, Maura). Some inferred that this was intended as an insult to Gaillot, that he was being symbolically banished to the North African desert. Some also inferred that this was meant to mock Gaillot's work with (largely North African) migrants and refugees in France.

17   *Time Magazine,* 23rd July, 1945, p 64

18   Bruneau, p 47

19   Bruneau, p 50

20   Thales de Azevedo, *O Catolicismo no Brasil [Catholicism in Brazil]*, Rio de Janeiro: Government of Brazil, Ministry of Education and Culture, Rio de Janeiro, 1955, p 21

21   The Passionist sisters of San Gabriele were at least equally impressed too, and Monsignor 'Carlo' Duarte Costa's visit and foundation for them in Brazil is even today proudly recorded on their website – it is not clear whether they ever became aware of Duarte Costa's subsequent schism and excommunication.

22   Dubois, p 92

23   *New York Times,* 22nd September 1942, p 8: "Several German priests and nuns, who have been operating clandestine radio transmitters hidden under altars and in cemetery chapels, were arrested in five different localities, dispatches from the State of Santa Catalina reported today.

24   Dubois, p 53

25   Dubois, p 52

26   The article reads – "The Bishop of Sao Paulo [sic], Mgr. Carlos Duarte Costa, in a telegram to President Getulio Vargas today, urged that priests with Fascist and Falangist tendencies be forced to retire 'in order to prevent in Brazil what happened in France.'"

27   Kenneth Leslie, *Protestant Digest*, 1945, p 14

28   Carlos Duarte Costa in the Foreword [*Prefacio*] to Hewlett Johnson, *O Poder Soviético*, (4th Edition), Editorial Calvino Limitada, Rio de Janeiro, 1943, p xi

29   Carlos Duarte Costa, in Hewlett Johnson, *O Poder Soviético*, pp xi-xii

30   Cf. Dubois, p 91

31   *Luta!* issue 6, July 1948, p 30

III

A "REBEL IN RIO"[1] AND
A SCHISM IN BRAZIL
— ICAB in its early years —

The year is 1945 and the major turning point of our story approaches. Our protagonist is suspended *a divinis* – from ministry – by the Church, but he is now at least no longer under house arrest. What else do we know about ICAB founder Carlos Duarte Costa at this point? He is in his mid-fifties, but photographs of the time show that he looks around fifteen years older. He has lost his hair and his face is sagging and grey. He is small in stature and tubby around the middle. His expression is tense and harried. His teeth look in a poor state. Repeated disillusionments have shattered his nerves. He can appear stern at times and is said to have a booming voice, though his gifts of oratory are hampered by losing his thread, fluffing his lines, and stammering. Nevertheless he continues to find the energy and courage to stand up for his extreme views, and in terms of clashing with the ecclesiastical establishment he has so far merely presented an *hors d'oeuvre*.

World War Two was drawing to a close. The Brazilian Expeditionary Force had acquitted itself well, but as hostilities in Europe reached their conclusion there was an uncomfortable paradox at home: Brazil itself remained under an authoritarian dictatorship, though it had just helped to defeat similar regimes in Europe. As the troops returned from defeating Nazism, President Vargas was forced to concede moderate reforms and promise democratic elections by the end of the year. Duarte Costa felt compelled to participate. As a communist sympathizer he was less at risk after the reforms, but he was considered an outcast by the Church and was on the brink of excommunication. Suspension had done nothing to rein in his increasingly vocal criticisms of Church discipline and his open support of Communism. These were almost sufficient to expel him from the Church completely and he had no bishop friends left to defend him. His intention to found his own Church was well-known. Nor had his attacks mellowed – in May he even accused the Nuncio of being a Fascist spy and his views were now being enthusiastically reported on the radio in Moscow.[2] His next move was to start his own political party. The Christian Socialist Party (PSC) was founded on 20th June 1945 with Duarte Costa as its president rather than leader – it was not his intention to run for office personally. Critics observed a note of hypocrisy – Duarte Costa would soon be reiterating that he objected to bishops involving themselves in things like the Catholic Electoral League. It seemed that "[the] only one who has the right to participate in party politics is Dom Carlos."[3] The late Cardinal Silveira Cintra had preferred pressure groups and his Catholic Electoral League (LEC) rather than founding a Catholic political party, as some senior Catholics had wanted. Silveira Cintra had rejected this idea, being wary of highlighting factionalism within the Church. Since a party would have to adopt positions that could be perceived as left-wing, centre, or right-wing, this could alienate portions of Catholic voters and would only succeed in splitting the 'Catholic vote.' The Catholic political viewpoint should be first and foremost Catholic, not partisan, Silveira Cintra had argued. A further danger with a Catholic political party was that it would reflect very badly on the Church if the party proved a flop at the ballot box. This in fact ended up being the fate of Duarte Costa's PSC and the venture only succeeded in moving him closer to his own fate – excommunication. It was at this moment that he made known his next, definitive strike – the foundation of his own Church.

A BRAZILIAN BISHOP IS EXCOMMUNICATED
RIO DE JANEIRO, JULY 6 [1945]

"The Most Rev. Don [sic] Carlos Duarte da Costa, Catholic Bishop of Maura in Sao Paulo State [sic], was excommunicated today, the Vatican asserting that he had violated canon law tenets by raising the pennon of rebellion and preaching discord to the faithful.

"The Most Rev. Jaime de Barros Camara, Archbishop of Rio de Janeiro, authorized by the Vatican, circularized the excommunication in all the Brazilian churches. [...]

"Bishop Duarte declared that today was founded the 'Brazilian Catholic Church.' He added that it had many followers and would continue to fight 'Roman church fascism.'"[4]

The Tablet in London reported:

"We understand that Mgr. Carlo [sic] Duarte Costa, Bishop of Maura, who is resident in Rio de Janeiro, has been excommunicated by the Holy Office and has declared his intention of setting up a schismatic "Brazilian Catholic Apostolic Church."[5]

What did Duarte Costa and the Brazilian Catholic Apostolic Church stand for, according to the press of the day?

"Bishop Duarte has been regularly advocating the moulding of the present Catholic Church under more liberal foundations and doing away with practices which he said, worked when the church was founded but which had no part in the modern world. [...]

"The revision of the Brazilian laws on divorce, which the Catholic Church has fought regularly every time in the past when some lawmaker in Congress here brought up the matter for the Government to enact laws making divorce legal, was one of his favourite topics. [...]

"He has been championing the abolition of celibacy. Priests, he has said, should be married and raise families. He has been condemning the present status of priests as immoral. [...]

"Apparently realizing that he was fighting a losing battle, he recently launched a campaign calling on priests to marry, leave the church and form a 'national Christian church' in which all priests would have wives and in which divorce would be allowed."[6]

Critics were ready to spot historical contradictions. Duarte Costa called for Brazilian Catholicism to return to the tradition of the third-century Church: "Note the originality of Brazilian Catholicism in the third century, twelve centuries before Pedro Alvares Cabral [founded Brazil]."[7] Duarte Costa was accused of throwing together

"elements picked from here and there. Divorce, clerical marriage, Mass in Portuguese, recruitment of ex-clergy, reaching out to protestant pastors, hatred towards the Pope, disdain towards the [Church] hierarchy, the arbitrary selection of articles of faith, individual whim, a spirit of contradiction."[8]

Time Magazine described Duarte Costa's move as 'heretical' though they used the term loosely to mean dissident or dissenting. This was actually textbook schism – a new, separate Church – not heresy. In an article titled 'Rebel in Rio' *Time* reported that ICAB mainly consisted of alterations in discipline and devotional practices. Priests "would be permitted to marry (and hold regular jobs in the lay world), confessions and rosaries would be abolished, bishops would be elected by popular vote."[9] *Time* said that Duarte Costa had been "associated with political criticism of the Holy See, and his views have been quoted on Moscow wireless."[10] It went on to say that he took

"an increasingly critical view of what he considered [the Catholic Church]'s political leanings. He became increasingly outspoken and unpopular with his superiors. [...] He accused Rome of aiding and abetting Hitler."[11]

"He also said that he would continue to use priestly cassock and all his episcopal insignia, but would no longer use the title Bishop of Maura, 'because now I am the Bishop of Rio de Janeiro.'"[12]

Time quoted him 'blandly' adding: "I consider today one of the happiest days of my life." The Vatican, *Time* reported, "appeared undisturbed by its latest rival." *O Globo* newspaper published a response by a Vatican spokesperson, acknowledging reports of Duarte Costa's attempt to found a new Church in opposition to the 'strong and united' Roman Catholic Apostolic Church in Brazil. They pointed out the fact that Duarte Costa held no position of authority, having been 'forcibly retired' – an interesting admission. The situation would certainly have been more complicated for the Vatican if he had still held any official position in the Catholic Church, which he did not. He was not only retired but also suspended from ministering. While it is theologically true that a bishop remains a bishop for all time, without actually holding office he has no effective power. Under Canon Law a retired bishop loses seniority and is subordinated to those holding proper office, while of course being afforded all the courtesy and dignity due to his rank. It is much the same as a retired army officer who continues to enjoy the title of Major or Colonel, but can hardly turn up at an army base and start giving orders. Undaunted, the former Constitutionalist 'colonel', the excommunicated Bishop of Maura, awoke the following day as the Bishop of Rio de Janeiro.

Thus, on 6th July 1945, Carlos Duarte Costa officially declared the foundation of the *Igreja Católica Apostólica Brasileira* – the Brazilian Catholic Apostolic Church. ICAB was unequivocally an organic separation from the Roman Catholic Church, a schism. "After that", *Time* commented the same month, "his excommunication was inevitable."[13] In fact, his excommunication was automatic, or *latae sententiae*. Roman Catholic Canon Law states that certain offenses such as schism, by their very commission, incur excommunication and no declaration or fanfare is needed. You are absolved of the need to wait for the letter of excommunication to arrive – there is no need for one. The Archbishop of Rio de Janeiro, after dutifully consulting the Vatican, simply made this legal point public.[14] Duarte Costa himself claimed that he learned of his excommunication from the newspapers of 6th July – making it appear that his announcement of the launch of ICAB was in *response* to what he called his "blessed excommunication."[15] He had known perfectly well that it was coming, however, and he had been openly planning to launch ICAB for some time. A year previously he had told his two fellow bishops that he would rather start his own Church than bow to Rome. Then on 4th May 1945 he had set out his plans in an interview with *O Globo* newspaper.[16] It was deliberate schism, and it would seem that this first public declaration was considered the culmination of the offense. The CNBB – *Conferência Nacional dos Bispos do Brasil* (the National Roman Catholic Bishops' Conference of Brazil) records the date of excommunication as 7th May 1945[17] – three days after Duarte Costa set out his plans in *O Globo*. It is therefore most likely that neither party took the other by surprise by going public with their actions in July. Since his arrest for communist activism the previous year Duarte Costa had been fully suspended from functioning as a cleric – a classic 'shot across the bows' in the lead-up to excommunication. Besides, Duarte Costa's plan to launch ICAB was not the only factor in his excommunication – the impact of founding his own socialist political party is not to be underestimated. In any case he dismissed excommunication in his *Manifesto* as a "political weapon of the middle ages", stating that

"[The] Bishop of Rome, Eugenio Pacelli, does not have the power to excommunicate me, and [...] I am more Bishop of Rio de Janeiro, having been elected by popular acclamation, than he is Bishop of Rome [having been] elected by Italian Cardinals."[18]

ICAB, the *Manifesto* went on, aimed to "centralize the person of Christ, seeking harmony and concord between all religions [...] Within the amplest educational and scientific freedom." ICAB was to allow divorce "within the [parameters of the] Gospel." It abolished celibacy for being "contrary to the laws of nature." It rejected auricular confession for being "absurd." It allowed priests to have a civilian or military profession. All services would be done in the vernacular.[19] "Separating myself from the Roman Church, in order to re-establish the Church of Christ in its purity, correcting its errors, I aim to centralize the figure of Christ so that all Christians, in the true Christ, may have their model and advocate before God the Father."[20]

There seems to have been confusion on all sides, however, over which specific Christians, apart from Duarte Costa himself, would actually make up the new Church. The legal registration documents of ICAB, officialized later that month (July 1945) list a variety of roles – Treasurer, Legal Advisor, Tax Advisor, etc. – shared out among about twenty laypeople, some of whom appear to have multiple roles. Some of them share the same surnames and are presumably related. Several of them appear on the foundation documents of the Christian Socialist Party as well, in the roles of Treasurer, Procurator, Publicist, etc. But the only cleric appears to be the former Bishop of Maura, now declared Bishop of Rio de Janeiro. It does not appear that any other priest or bishop was ready to join ICAB at the outset. In spite of Duarte Costa's fervent campaigning for the "Brazilification of the clergy" however, he soon hoped to ordain an unnamed Mexican as his co-bishop, and a Polish bishop would apparently soon be joining as his auxiliary.[21] Back on 4th May 1945, in *O Globo* newspaper, Duarte Costa had outlined a slightly different team:

> "[Salomão Barbosa] Ferraz, of the Free Catholic Church, Aleixo Alves de Sousa,[22] head of a Catholic Church, and Leão [Leon] Grochowski, founder of the Polish Catholic Church."[23]

Whichever the true line-up was to be, it already started to appear that the new *Brazilian Catholic* Church was to be something less than 100% Brazilian, so how Catholic would it be? Aleixo Alves de Souza, described vaguely as the 'head of a Catholic Church' was in reality a leading Theosophist and later the author of the *Catecismo Teosófico* – the Theosophical Catechism – published in 1949 by the Theosophical Society. His so-called 'Catholic Church' was the 'Liberal Catholic Church', a small esoteric offshoot of the wayward and short-lived British branch of the Old Catholics, though repudiated by them and never recognized by any major Church. The Liberal Catholics aimed to combine Theosophy and various occult ideas with a few broadly Christian elements.[24] Regarding Bishop Leon Grochowski of the Scranton, Pennsylvania-based Polish National Catholic Church (PNCC), it seems quite unlikely that he would be in a position to have any practical involvement with Duarte Costa's new Church.[25] It is not clear whether Grochowski ever even visited Brazil, though another Polish bishop, Jan Piotr Perkowski (1901–1963) certainly did, and later had some minor involvement with ICAB. Perkowski was part of a breakaway faction that had split from the PNCC (itself a break-off from Roman Catholicism, of course) to become the short-lived 'Polish Old Catholic Church." As their Churches were therefore rivals it seems unlikely that Bishops Grochowski and Perkowski would have cooperated on the ICAB venture. It does not appear that the Theosophist Alves de Souza or Bishop Grochowski of the PNCC ever did play a part in ICAB and Bishop Perkowski does not seem to have been more than a supporter. The other name in Duarte Costa's announcement, Salomão Barbosa Ferraz, would indeed become the first bishop ordained in ICAB. Ferraz certainly was Brazilian, but not Catholic. He was also an (almost) lifelong Freemason, a practice considered incompatible with Catholicism. Duarte Costa's second bishop would also be a Freemason, and ICAB would go on to attract many members of that fraternity.[26] Duarte Costa declared in his *Manifesto á Nação* (Declaration to the Nation) published in *O Globo*, *O Estado de São Paulo* and elsewhere, that ICAB aimed to offer "[an] absolute guarantee of civil, political, philosophical, and religious liberty, not allowing that any person be probed under any pretext, with respect to their beliefs."[27] The *Manifesto* came to be regarded as "the most important confessional document of ICAB."[28]

A Belgian-born Barnabite priest, Father Florêncio (Florence) M. Dubois accepted the task of demolishing the credibility of Duarte Costa and ICAB. Father Dubois published *The ex-Bishop of Maura and Common Sense* in 1945. He aimed to debunk Duarte Costa's claim to have founded a truly national church, which Dubois called "the dream of the Pharisees, the Anglicans, Mussolini and Hitler."[29] Duarte Costa, Dubois wrote, "follows in the footsteps of Henry VIII, Luther and Calvin."[30] Duarte Costa argued that the early Church was composed of 'national churches' which enjoyed exactly the kind of autonomy he advocated. He announced a return to choosing bishops, priests, and deacons by a vote and full lay participation in councils and synods – "true religious democracy."[31] Father Dubois mocked Duarte Costa's supposed innovations of Church reform:

> "He thinks he has discovered America. Founders of human religions are like parrots. The devil does not have the gift of originality, but his skill in plagiarism dates back to the great flood."[32]

But was this fair? Duarte Costa did not really claim originality. In his *Manifesto á Nação* he stated that ICAB was named in honor of a previous organization of the same name, which had been founded in 1913 and ground to a halt. Its founder, according to Duarte Costa, had been murdered. Duarte Costa's ICAB of 1945 was to be a revival, rather than a continuation, of the earlier schism. This earlier schism had been launched by Father Manoel Carlos de Amorim Correa "who appointed himself patriarch of the Brazilian Church, despite being Portuguese."[33] There were various attempts to compare Duarte Costa with leaders of previous renegade church movements – Châtel in France, Gavazzi in Italy, Jacinto Loyson in France, Reinkens in Germany, and not forgetting Henry VIII – with varying accuracy. "In Brazil itself", Dubois wrote, "Dom Carlos has half a dozen predecessors."[34] It is true that there were ample precedents in Brazilian history for the rejection of celibacy, for priests being involved in politics, for affirming the national character of the Church, and for resisting interference by Rome. In all these respects Duarte Costa proposed a new Church more in keeping with the historical reality of Christianity in Brazil, rather than the Romanized, centralized Catholicism that had been promoted since the pontificate of Pope Pius IX and the First Vatican Council. Father Diogo Antônio Feijó was one example of a priest and politician who, during the Regency period, advocated Church separation from Rome to go hand-in-hand with national independence, along with the suppression of celibacy. As early as 1828 Feijó tried to unite his supporters in a 'Congregation of Married Priests', but Feijó did not get as far as founding his own Church. In 1835 the statesman Estevão Rafael de Carvalho proposed controversial legislation to separate the Church from Rome and place it under complete State control. A century later in 1935, João de Minas[35] attempted to start a national church – the Brazilian Christian Scientific Church (IBCC). De Minas, an accomplished writer and lawyer, awarded himself the title of Head of the Church in Brazil, and called Pope Pius XI his 'colleague' rather than rejecting him outright. The short-lived IBCC had an eclectic, nationalistic doctrine, combining popular Catholic devotions, spiritualism, Umbanda, and esoteric practices. De Minas obviously thought along similar lines to Duarte Costa. But the real precedent for ICAB was that of 1913, from which Duarte Costa took the name Brazilian Catholic Apostolic Church.

This first incarnation of ICAB arose in a small town rather than a metropolis. On the eastern border of São Paulo State a settlement began to form around the chapel of Nossa Senhora da Penha (Our Lady of Peñafrancia) in about 1820, and thirty years later the town officially took its name from the chapel. During the process of founding the First Republic, when the issue of abolishing slavery caused mounting tensions in rural areas, the town became notorious when a local abolitionist was beaten to death by a mob. After this bad publicity the town appealed to have its name changed, and adopted the local indigenous name 'Itapira.' The religious life of the town was simple, poor, and spontaneous at first, according to historian Arnaldo Lemes Filho, but this changed with the Catholic Church's gradual organization and establishment of parishes during the nineteenth century. The class system – through the big landowners and the military – began to impose itself upon Church life. "Religion clearly shifts [after the 1840's] to become the domain of an elite, and the people are left outside."[36] With the dawn of

72

the twentieth century the separation of Church and State made it legally possible for a priest "to challenge the diocesan bishop and start his own church. In reality, the religious arena was no longer so clearly dominated by the Catholic Church."[37] Into this scenario for potential conflict a new parish priest arrived at the Nossa Senhora da Penha chapel in 1909. Canon Manoel Carlos de Amorim Correa was born in Portugal in 1873. He was "young and full of new ideas," Filho wrote, "he introduced feasts, motivated the associations of the faithful, [and] organized, with aplomb, the Holy Week solemnities [...] receiving eulogies from everyone."[38] With the benefit of coming from the outside, without the jaundiced view of an insider, Amorim Correa was able to recognize, circumvent, and oppose some of the problematic characteristics of Brazilian Catholicism – he bluntly waved elitist and class prejudices aside. Like Duarte Costa a quarter of a century later, Amorim Correa lacked the subtlety and diplomacy needed to successfully challenge established conventions, but clearly did not lack the chutzpah. Like Duarte Costa, Amorim Correa made powerful enemies, for example with the 'Mãozinha Church." This was an unofficial, local religious devotion centered around *A Mãozinha* – 'The Little Hand' – a supposedly miraculous piece of wood shaped like a human hand. The sophisticated European-educated young priest had no time for such primitive superstitions. Furthermore, Amorim Correa objected to all types of religious events and feasts taking place off church premises, in ranches and other places, without his authorization. "There was a tendency by the parish priest to monopolize all the worship and devotional practices", Filho wrote. But Amorim Correa was nevertheless extremely popular, as witnessed by the consternation caused by his eventual dismissal. He was energetic and committed, opening up parish life to all and challenging the elites' grip on the Church. By 1912, however

"[Criticisms] of the parish priest began to surface, mainly with regard to his moral conduct, as it was said that he lived with a woman. Even if this were true, the criticisms also had political motivations, as his popularity and some of his actions did not please the agrarian elite – the dominant class – very much."[39]

Other aspects of the priest's lifestyle were gaining negative attention. Between morning Masses, it was noticed "the bizarre priest downed two or three beers"[40] and he seemed prone to various mysterious bouts of ill-health.[41] Amorim Correa insisted that he lived utterly alone without so much as a cleaner or housekeeper, but the local bishop was inclined to think that there was probably some substance to the accusations and decided on a strategy. In October 1912 he sought to pave the way for the indirect removal of Amorim Correa. The bishop announced that from the following year the diocesan seminarians would start spending their holidays in Itapira, and therefore the parish priest should in all fairness be someone directly involved in seminary formation, meaning that Amorim Correa should be prepared to step down. Amorim Correa refused to comply with this ploy and the conflict quickly escalated when the new priest arrived to take possession of the parish. Amorim Correa was suspended, first from ministry and then from the priesthood altogether.

Amorim Correa ignored all the suspensions and on 30th January 1913 began celebrating Mass at home, founding the Brazilian Catholic Apostolic Church (ICAB) and nominating himself as First Patriarch. He won some supporters, especially among fellow outsiders such as Portuguese traders, and among fellow 'underdogs' such as small landowners. He also had support from anticlerical groups and Masonic lodges in São Paulo[42] who were always keen to see someone take on the Catholic Church. He travelled to other cities drumming up support and recruiting ex-priests. Among the parishes to join the movement were São Roque in Juiz de Fora. Unaccustomed to seeing the Church being challenged, people across the diocese were thunderstruck by the revolt and the bishop received messages of solidarity from all over Brazil. Amorim Correa's actions also revealed deep divisions between different groups in society. He appealed mostly to the small business community, immigrant merchants, traders, and those who struggled to live off smallholdings. He appealed to the classes which felt largely ignored by the Roman Catholic Church at that time, which was to be an enduring problem of the Church in Brazil. Carlos Duarte Costa would eventually focus his efforts in this direction too.

Just eight months after the foundation of ICAB however, Amorim Correa died aged 40, of unclear causes. Some linked his death to the disordered nature of his lifestyle. "The sins of the throat and of the flesh were the twin hounds which the devil used against that soul. They ended up choking him."[43] Others, like Duarte Costa, insisted that he had been poisoned by forces working for the Catholic Church.[44] Father Francisco Federico Arditi of the ICAB-linked São Roque chapel proclaimed himself the new Patriarch – an Italian priest to succeed a Portuguese priest as Head of the Brazilian Church. The chapel of São Roque in Juiz de Fora had defected to ICAB, though the chapel building itself was owned by a lay religious fraternity – an *irmandade* – as many chapels were. Divided over the ICAB issue, the fraternity collapsed due to squabbling, outside pressure, and financial problems. The chapel was donated to the Redemptorists in 1920, ending ICAB's tenure in Juiz de Fora.[45] The press summarized the first years of ICAB as an "unhappy gesture of rebellion" but somehow it kept on going. The *A Cidade de Itapira* newspaper of 6th February 1916[46] recalled that Amorim Correa had been "blinded by vanity" and that the ICAB headquarters was by now "a sordid ranch in ruins" with a chapel for the adoration of "a piece of wood shaped like a human hand" – referring to *A Mãozinha* – the miraculous Little Hand. During his lifetime Amorim Correa had railed against this popular cult, wanting a monopoly on all local worship. After his death however, his followers took charge of the Mãozinha chapel, causing even more conflict with the Catholic Church. The police had to intervene to make sure the two churches' religious processions did not cross paths. Amorim Correa's remaining followers still came under great pressure from the Catholic Church, which was looking out for an opportunity to finally extinguish ICAB.

After 1920 the ICAB of Itapira started to diminish, but the local press still carried announcements of their events and a small Sunday commentary. After 1930 the conflicts between ICAB and the Catholic Church got worse. Salomão Barbosa Ferraz, the protestant pastor and Freemason who would later become Duarte Costa's first bishop, visited Itapira in 1933 to look at ways to reinvigorate ICAB, but without success. A new parish priest was then appointed to Nossa Senhora da Penha, Amorim Correa's original Roman Catholic parish. The new priest arrived with the express intention of putting an end to ICAB once and for all. He did succeed, largely by revitalizing the parish, creating new activities, and re-launching local associations, much as Amorim Correa had initially done. In 1935 internal disputes divided the remaining members of ICAB and they failed to pay the required association levy to the Prefecture. As a result, ICAB not only lost its juridical status, but pressure from faithful members of the Catholic Church also led to the imposition of a fine. The ranch property was seized by the Prefecture in settlement and the miraculous Mãozinha – the magical Little Hand of wood – disappeared one night. Local rumor had it that three members of the Catholic parish, under the dynamic new priest, took the poor Mãozinha home and burnt it. As late as 1938, however, even though ICAB was left without clergy, some followers still remained. From 1940 onwards, attempts to re-energize ICAB were fruitless, even with the potential support of Salomão Barbosa Ferraz or Duarte Costa. The story of Amorim Correa's ICAB was a sign of increasing secularization, liberalization of belief, and a rejection of class divisions in religion. It was also a precursor, an example of what was possible now that all religions were on an equal footing:

> "Father Amorim's dissidence in 1913 was only the starting point of contesting the authority of the Catholic Church, revealing a distinct secularization of society, collective conflicts between colonists and combines against the big landowners."[47]

Salomão Barbosa Ferraz reappeared in Itapira in 1945, attempting to "re-establish the sect of the Mãozinha."[48] But it was apparently the death-knell of ICAB in Itapira and that was the last anyone ever heard of the short-lived Church. By that time Ferraz was set to become the first bishop consecrated in the *new* incarnation of ICAB.

In mid-July Duarte Costa, "calling himself 'Bishop of Rio de Janeiro', told reporters that he hopes soon to ordain ten married lawyers and professional men as priests in his new church."[49] On 18th July, as a prelude to making Ferraz a bishop, Duarte Costa ordained him priest. Three days later Duarte Costa turned 57. The following day he ordained another committed Freemason, Jorge Alves de Souza, who was set to become ICAB's third bishop just six months later. Salomão Barbosa Ferraz, though head of something called the 'Free Catholic Church' which he had founded in 1936, was not then and never had been a Catholic. Aged 65, he was eight years older than Duarte Costa, married and a father of seven, and had spent his career moving steadily from church to church. Elected bishop by his Free Catholic Church, he awarded himself the title of Monsignor and started celebrating Catholic-style Mass in Portuguese, despite not being a Catholic priest. "He does not approve of celibacy", Father Dubois wrote mischievously, "but let us not dwell on the fact that he accumulated about as many lady-friends as Salomão [his namesake, Solomon] of the Bible."[50] Ferraz was born in Jaú on 18th February 1880. He was raised in the Presbyterian Church, to which his father, impressed by the local missionary, had converted in his youth. In the Ferraz family, father, son, and more than one brother would end up serving as Presbyterian ministers. Between 1902 and 1917 Ferraz began his ministry, married, and had seven children. In 1917 he quit the Presbyterians for the Episcopal Church. Ferraz switched churches four times in his long life, spending an average of 13 and a half years each in the clergy of five different denominations.[51] While with the Anglicans Ferraz launched the 'Order of Saint Andrew', which, although named for the patron saint of the Scots Presbyterians, was meant to be Catholic in style.[52] Within the Episcopal Church his initiatives were not always popular – he introduced 'Catholic' elements such as candles and a crucifix on the altar, encouraged parishioners to make the sign of the cross and refer to the 'Mass' rather than the 'service.'[53] On one hand he was idealistic about the possibility of bringing the Catholic and the Protestant closer together through these initiatives and on the other hand he simply had a passion for all things ceremonial and pompous.[54] The Episcopal Church was focused on expansion and actively sought to welcome Roman Catholics to convert to its ranks. Ferraz, it seems, refused to get involved in poaching members from the Catholic Church, and his flock noticeably dwindled.[55] All of these things won him esteem, appreciation, and friends in Roman Catholic circles, and the increasing displeasure of the Episcopalians. In 1936 Ferraz organized a conference on the subject of launching a 'Free Catholic Church' and was duly voted its bishop, thus breaking with the Episcopal Church. His hope was to have one of the Polish Old Catholic[56] bishops, Władysław Marcin Faron (1891–1965) or Jan Piotr Perkowski (1901–1963), consecrate him bishop, and it is not clear what difficulty intervened.[57] While some sources suppose that World War Two made it impossible for Bishop Perkowski to travel to Brazil, in fact Ferraz was elected bishop in 1936 – there were nearly three years between Ferraz's election as bishop and the Nazi invasion of Poland. Other sources suggest that Perkowski was already *in* Brazil because the Polish Old Catholics had a mission there. Bishop Perkowski was certainly in Brazil some years later to assist Ferraz in consecrating a successor for the Free Catholic Church, Manoel Ceia Laranjeira. Whatever the truth, Ferraz would end up being consecrated – first priest, then bishop – by Duarte Costa in 1945.

It was unclear, and is still unclear, how that union was supposed to work – as far as Ferraz was concerned the Free Catholic Church was not being dissolved, but for Duarte Costa, Ferraz was becoming 'his' man in São Paulo. Ferraz may have interpreted his consecration as a good deed on the part of Duarte Costa, whereas Duarte Costa expected complete fealty to him and his cause. Ferraz had been elected bishop of his own Church and all he wanted from Duarte Costa was consecration. Ferraz assumed the title of *Bishop of Brazil* no less, "leaving his comrade with the title of [mere] Bishop of

Rio de Janeiro."[58] It will be noticed that both in ICAB and in Ferraz's Free Catholic Church, bishops avoided distinctions such as Archbishop, Metropolitan, or Cardinal, in keeping with Duarte Costa's vision of adhering to the simple 'threefold ministry' of the early Church. Consequently, even bishops of the larger cities or territories would be simply 'Bishop.' This has broadly remained the case in dioceses still faithful to ICAB, while the modern offshoots of ICAB have generally ignored both the principle and the practice of moderation in the use of titles.[59]

The relationship between Duarte Costa and Ferraz, which sounds like it was founded on a misunderstanding, would quickly deteriorate – "since the moment of his 'episcopal consecration' Salomão Ferraz began a quarrel with Carlos Duarte Costa."[60] Ferraz's priorities would always be his Free Catholic Church, his Order of Saint Andrew, and his Freemasonry (up to 1959). It will be noticed that in these first months of the great Brazilian-Catholic experiment, Freemasonry and Protestantism were well represented along with, it was initially planned at least, Mexicans and Poles. The previous incarnation of ICAB in 1913 had a Portuguese and then an Italian 'Patriarch.' In the coming years, as we will see, the supposedly Brazilian National Church would welcome Venezuelan, Spanish, and Italian priests – a far cry from Duarte Costa's demands for a Brazilified clergy for Brazil. But there was a significant intake of Brazilians too. Jorge Alves de Souza[61] – Brazilian, Catholic, Freemason – was one of the 'professional men' who Duarte Costa had announced were about to become priests in ICAB. Alves de Souza was born on 2nd April 1912 in Corumbá, Mato Grosso State, on Brazil's western border with Bolivia. He began studying to become a Franciscan Friar but left before completion, and managed to secure a desk job somewhere inside the vast machinery of law enforcement under Getúlio Vargas's *Estado Novo* regime. In July 1945 he became one of the first men to be ordained priest by Duarte Costa, around the same time as Ferraz. At 33 years of age, Alves de Souza was half the age of his fellow newly ordained priest Ferraz. Following ordination, Alves de Souza was appointed pastor of the ICAB parish in Ribeirão Pires in São Paulo's 'Grande ABC' Metropolitan Region. He was soon elected as ICAB bishop of Campos in the State of Rio de Janeiro (on 12th December 1945) and consecrated bishop the following year on 2nd February, again by Duarte Costa. He took control of the fledgling diocese on 2nd April 1946 (his 34th birthday) and remained there just under a year. On 12th March 1947 he was transferred to São Paulo for some reason – possibly personal preference. As already stated, Alves de Souza was a committed and rising member of Freemasonry alongside working in police administration.[62] Freemasonry and Police contacts were to prove a combination of attributes that would make him a very valued member of ICAB, garnering various forms of support from fellow Masons and even securing free flights around Brazil for fellow bishops through a Lodge contact.[63] Alves de Souza would thus prove to be one of the most useful and, apart from a brief defection, loyal ICAB bishops.

With the first anniversary of ICAB come and gone Duarte Costa had by this time been formally excommunicated at the level of *Vitandus* by the Vatican on 3rd July 1946. This meant that the Catholic faithful were officially forbidden to have anything to do with him for the good of their souls, *Vitandus* meaning 'to be avoided.' Undeterred, Duarte Costa was getting ready to consecrate a third bishop for ICAB. On 8th December 1946 Antídio José Vargas would become bishop for the new diocese of Lages in Santa Caterina State. Unlike the first two bishops, Vargas was already a Roman Catholic priest who, like Duarte Costa, had fallen out with the Catholic Church. Duarte Costa had previously attacked the Roman Catholic clergy as a malevolent force on humanity, but he was now engaged in a letter-writing campaign to convince more of them to join his revolt.[64] Vargas was drawn to the announcement of the new independent Church like a fly to honey, convinced that the way forward had suddenly been revealed to him. Vargas was born in the tiny town of Tijucas, Santa Caterina State on 19th December 1906, the youngest of eight.[65] Two of his siblings died in infancy and the rest married and left home. So when the young

Antídio was made an orphan he was sent to the Roman Catholic junior seminary in Curitiba and then the major seminary in São Leopoldo, Rio Grande do Sul – a Jesuit-run seminary, giving rise to a later misunderstanding that Vargas was a Jesuit. ICAB's *Luta!* journal stated that Vargas had been ordained priest on 6th November 1938 aged nearly 32, but there is no explanation as to why there was a gap of a decade between seminary and ordination. Quite possibly this is an error. Vargas was ordained by Bishop Daniel Hostin OFM, who had become Bishop of Lages in 1929 and would remain in the post until 1973, thus becoming not only Vargas's first bishop but also his long-term adversary. *Luta!* describes Bishop Hostin as being from the German branch of the Franciscans and having Nazi tendencies – yet another "foreign bishop"[66] sent to oppress Brazil – neglecting to point out that he was in fact Brazilian and born nearby. Vargas – under the persecution of the 'German Franciscans', according to *Luta!*[67] – was drawn to ICAB and elected bishop in October 1945. He was not actually ordained bishop until December *1946* – another significant gap which is left unexplained. Years later, an Orthodox bishop visiting Brazil recorded an overwhelmingly negative and disturbing first impression of Vargas:

> "From the first moment, 'Bishop' Antídio [José Vargas] gave me the impression that he was mentally ill. My observations and conversations with him later confirmed this impression. He could not even formulate one word calmly; one moment he darts about the room debating violently until foam comes out of his mouth; then he starts to laugh wildly for no reason; then he starts to cry and threaten people."[68]

As worrying as this picture sounds, 'Padre Antídio' already had a following in Lages and quickly developed an active ministry as an ICAB bishop. Page after page of early editions of *Luta!* are taken up with news and photographs of church growth and church building flowing out of Santa Caterina State, with local people praising ICAB's "work of Christian revival."[69] But there was no doubt that

ICAB was attracting an eclectic range of characters. "The mixture of heterogeneous elements was vast: Masons, Kardecists, followers of [Annie] Besant, bible-thumpers of various sects, would-be popes, communists, atheists and malcontents."[70] Padre Dubois found it absurd that this conglomeration of diverse individuals was all supposedly in the name of restoring the 'Church of the third century.' Surely, a revived third-century Church could not hope to unite

> "Marxist materialists, with professed atheists, with Masons, with Spiritualists, with Protestants, with free-thinkers, with anti-clericals and other religion-haters who live hating Christ, mocking bishops, and persecuting the clergy. [...] Dom Carlos expects to find friends and associates [among suchlike], while these people, in the bottom of their hearts, consider the rebel prelate to be ridiculous, simply making use of [their] guile and artfulness in order to better denigrate the Christian religion. The only one who fails to understand this is the ingenuous head of the Brazilian Catholic Church."[71]

The diversity inside ICAB was deliberate. A later bishop would consider himself, and his wife and family, still Jewish after joining the ICAB clergy.[72] People of any religion were welcome to join, provided they were Brazilian of course – a rule not to be enforced on the clergy, however, without apology or explanation. Furthermore, the definition of 'religion' was broad:

> "[Any] organized manifestation [of belief], be it philosophical or temporal, which upholds the two basic precepts of the National Catholic Apostolic Churches: 'Love one another' and 'Do not, nor allow to be done unto others, that which you would not want done unto you.'"[73]

Note that the first 'precept' is a truncated Gospel quote, emptied of Jesus's intended meaning, i.e. 'love one another *as I have loved you*' (Mt. 12:15).[74] ICAB's all-comers formula was surely vulnerable to criticism, but as with Bishop Vargas in Lages the new Church was not without appeal – *Luta!* reports that by the end of the decade

ICAB had several bases in each of eleven states.[75] Successes were always interspersed with problems – page two of January 1947's *Luta!* warned against individuals circulating in the name of ICAB asking for donations. On page 32 of the same edition, though, *Luta!* reports the launch of a similar movement in Venezuela, inspired by ICAB. The Venezuelan Catholic Apostolic Church (ICAV) claimed to already have 50 priests under its juvenile leader Luis Fernando Castillo Mendez, who would go on to become a central figure in the ICAB story. As we shall see in the next chapter, Castillo Mendez's new movement became entangled in the political upheavals of his country and he would pay a hefty price.

In Rio de Janeiro work began on the construction of the 'Mother Church' at 54 Rua do Couto, Penha district,[76] but organizational problems continued to plague Duarte Costa, slowly but surely chipping away at his nervous composition. His Christian Socialist Party (PSC) had sunk without a trace by now. At its foundation the party had a president (Duarte Costa), a VP, two secretaries, two treasurers, two legal advisors, two procurators, a campaign director and a publicity director – an ample line-up for a very small new party. Their presidential candidate was a criminal lawyer called Stélio Galvão Bueno who, once the campaign was underway, turned out to be broke and unable pay the deposit for his candidacy. He joined forces with Luís Carlos Prestes, the main left-wing candidate, and the Party, as they say, was over. Could Duarte Costa rely on no-one? By 18th August 1948 Duarte Costa was publishing a 'warning' about his bishop Jorge Alves de Souza, the police department official and prominent Freemason. De Souza had recently abandoned his diocese to act as Auxiliary Bishop to his companion of ordination Salomão Barbosa Ferraz, thereby snubbing ICAB in favor of Ferraz's 'Free Catholic Church.' The so-called 'Bishop of Brazil' – Ferraz – and de Souza, Duarte Costa wrote, had "used and abused" his good name and were clearly in the service of the Vatican, which had set out to crush ICAB. "Dom Jorge Alves de Souza is in league with the Cardinals of São Paulo and Rio de Janeiro, though in public he pretends to be a friend of the ex-Bishop of Maura."[77] (This would turn out to be the last edition of *Luta!* for some time due to subsequent legal action.) In what was to become standard procedure over the coming years, de Souza would find himself silently rehabilitated and accepted back into the ICAB fold without explanation or fuss. But there was more to worry about, much more.

On 27th September 1948 ICAB was forced to close its doors. The Roman Catholic Archbishop of Rio de Janeiro, Dom Jaime de Barros Câmara, lodged a legal complaint with the President, Eurico Gaspar Dutra. He argued that ICAB's rites, liturgy, vestments, and insignia were identical to those of the Roman Catholic Church, with the aim of hoodwinking and confusing the faithful.[78] Cautiously, the government accepted that there was at least a case to look into and ordered the closure of ICAB's churches and the suppression of *Luta!* Duarte Costa, understandably, launched a counter-complaint, describing the closure as the "violation of common and certain rights guaranteed by the Constitution, namely the freedom of religious worship."[79] It would take over a year for the gavel to fall:

> "According to the judgment of the Consultor-General of the Republic, approved by the President of the Republic, the worship of the Brazilian Catholic Apostolic Church has been prohibited in public spaces, as these authorities believe that this Church has no rites of its own; their religious practices, priestly vestments and insignia give rise to confusion with those of the outward solemnities of the Roman Catholic Apostolic Church, constituting an imitation of these, consequently violating the freedom of this latter Church, which must be avoided for the sake of public order."[80]

What are we to make of the case – did the Roman Catholic Archbishop wield an unfair amount of clout over his smaller rival? It is worth remembering that while the Constitution in theory still placed all religions on an equal footing, since the days of Cardinal Silveira Cintra and President Vargas the Roman Catholic Church had regained a special place in society. It was always by far the biggest religion of course, and the Catholic hierarchy had the ear of the government. But it is also worth noting that until this judgment the rites, liturgy, processions, prayers, vestments, and symbols of ICAB really *were* identical to the Roman Catholic Church. The differences would have been minute – obvious examples would be that the Pope would not be mentioned in the Mass, and the signboards outside the churches would have read *Igreja Católica Apostólica Brasileira* instead of *Igreja Católica Apostólica Romana*. Easy to miss? It depends whether the observer knows what to look for. The same could perhaps be said of SSPX churches today – they do not mention the local diocese on their signboards, which a recognized diocesan parish, chapel, or sanctuary would do; SSPX do not use the term 'parish' at all; they *do* display the words Catholic Church. The informed and watchful Catholic could tell at a glance, while the passerby or less-than-expert observer would be hard-pressed to spot the difference.

The court's ruling suggested that it did agree with the Roman Catholic Archbishop, that ICAB's aim was indeed to be a 'cuckoo's egg' church, to undermine and supplant the Roman Catholic Church through mimicry. Supposing that this were not the case, just why did Duarte Costa insist on using the same rites and vestments as the Catholic Church when ICAB had rejected so much else? All the external characteristics had been maintained, while the content that really distinguishes a religion – the theology, the ecclesiology, the communion – had been thrown out. Could the bottom line be that the 'Rebel in Rio' was really just out to antagonize the Roman Catholics? Whatever the explanation, Duarte Costa now faced the permanent closure of ICAB unless he made sufficient changes to differentiate it from the Catholic Church – a straightforward if not-so-simple solution. Most noticeably the priests' cassock changed from black to an attractive 'ash gray' with matching fabric buttons – ten times better-looking in fact than Roman Catholic black (if ICAB were cuckoos then the Romans were a bunch of old crows). ICAB bishops would wear the ash-gray cassock with scarlet piping and scarlet fabric buttons with matching silk moiré biretta. These are typically the embellishments reserved for Roman

85

Catholic Cardinals, a rank which ICAB did not have. This touch was a masterful riposte to the Roman Catholics, effectively saying 'if my bishops are not allowed to dress like your bishops, I will dress them like your Cardinals.' To this day all ICAB bishops are 'Cardinals' as far as buttons, sash, and biretta are concerned. Originally the sash was intended to be in yellow-gold and green like the Brazilian flag, but in the end this carnivalesque touch was judged going too far, and the bishops' sash is also scarlet. Duarte Costa had already decreed that ICAB clergy on principle would not wear clerical attire outside of church, a measure which seemed acceptable to the Courts, but in reality this was not adhered to.[81] The clergy of the Venezuelan Catholic Apostolic Church were also by this time part of the ICAB extended family, its first international 'ramification.' They would continue, for the time being, to wear Roman Catholic black cassocks, though its juvenile 'Patriarch' already preferred papal white.[82]

The rites of ICAB also had to change – now Duarte Costa would have to make good his promise to switch to the vernacular. This would worryingly mean translating the sacramental rites too, including ordination, as long as these were held publicly – as properly they must be. This threatened Duarte Costa's original intention that the unadulterated Roman Rite should always be used for ordinations[83] so as to preemptively quash queries over validity. The Roman Rite in 1949 had no official vernacular translation for liturgical use. Any vernacular translation produced on one's own initiative, even by a bishop and however expertly done, would cease to be the Roman Rite – the Roman Rite meant the authorized Rite, which meant Latin, period.[84] ICAB's arch-critic Father Dubois seized on this, stating only partly correctly that "The Church spoke Latin in the cradle and it will speak Latin until the grave."[85] He pointed out the incongruity of a supposedly Brazilian Catholicism raising the tongue of the colonial oppressors to a sacred language. He labeled the whole thing "misdirected patriotism."[86] The switch to Portuguese was neither particularly Brazilian nor national, Dubois wrote, having little to do with the land of Brazil and its indigenous peoples, nor was it at all original as it was simply copying again – this time from the Protestant reformers.[87] But these attacks had surely become tiresome by now. They were also small potatoes compared to the battering ICAB had received in court. Bruised maybe, Duarte Costa had nevertheless come through it in one piece. The ICAB churches could now reopen with a 'new look' resulting from its court-imposed makeover. At the start of 1950, a broiling Rio de Janeiro summer welcomed the dawn of a new decade full of promise for Brazil – and after five years of incubation the cuckoo finally hatched, proudly displaying its new feathers; they were ash-gray and scarlet.

Notes

1   *Time Magazine,* Monday, 23rd July 1945, p 64
2   Cf. *Time Magazine,* Monday, 23rd July, 1945, p 64
3   Padre Florence Marie [or Florêncio Maria] Dubois, *O Ex-Bispo de Maura e o Bom Senso [The Ex-Bishop of Maura and Common Sense],* Ed. Vozes Limitada, Petrópolis-Rio de Janeiro-São Paulo, 1945, p 93
4   *New York Times,* Saturday, 7th July, 1945, p 11
5   *The Tablet,* Saturday 14th July 1945, p 18
6   *New York Times,* Saturday, 7th July, 1945, p 11
7   Dubois, p 7
8   Dubois, p 22
9   *Time Magazine,* Monday, 23rd July 1945, p 64
10   *The Tablet,* Saturday 14th July 1945, p 18
11   *Time Magazine,* Monday, 23rd July, 1945, p 64
12   *New York Times,* Saturday, 7th July, 1945, p 11
13   *Time Magazine,* Monday, 23rd July, 1945 p 64. The article seems to have reversed the order of events – the excommunication came first, followed by the official announcement of ICAB's launch.
14   Cf. Circular letter of the Ecclesiastical Chamber of Rio de Janeiro, 6th July 1945, published in 'Revista Eclesiástica Brasileira', September 1945, pp 709-712
15   *Luta!* issue 6, July 1948, pp 3-4
16   Cf. *O Globo,* 4th May 1945, quoted in Dubois, pp 41-2
17   Cf. CNBB – Conferencia Nacional dos Bispos do Brasil [National Conference of Bishops of Brazil], 'Comunicado Mensal' [Monthly Communiqué] Number 252, September 1973, p 1221

18 Carlos Duarte Costa, 'Manifesto á Nação', [Declaration to the Nation], published in *Luta!* issue 12, Sept. 1950, [pp 7-15] – see p 7 – http://diocesedecabofrio.blogspot.com/p/revista-luta.html [accessed 23rd May 2018]. At the Conclave which elected Pope Pius XII, just over half the Electors were Italian.

19 Cf. Duarte Costa, 'Manifesto' – all the reforms mentioned here can be found on pp 14-15

20 Duarte Costa, 'Manifesto', pp 14-15

21 Cf. Dubois, p 42 and pp 86-87. Neither event came to pass – no Polish or Mexican bishop would be involved with ICAB during Duarte Costa's lifetime.

22 Actually *Souza*.

23 Cf. *O Globo*, 4th May 1945, quoted in Dubois, pp 41-2

24 Aleixo Alves de Souza was ordained for the Liberal Catholic Church in 1926, the first of its priests in Brazil. He died in 1970. The surviving LCC in Brazil has named its seminary after him – http://www.catolicaliberal.com.br /seminario.php [accessed 11 April 2017]. The Brazilian census does not report a current membership for the LCC specifically, but gathers several 'Esoteric Traditions' together for a total of 74,013 adherents.

25 Grochowski was not, as stated, the founder of the Polish Catholic Church (PCC), which is based in Poland, but the second Prime Bishop (not the founder) of the Polish National Catholic Church (PNCC), a separate body based in the USA.

26 Cf. Obispo Alejo Pelypenko, *Infiltración Comunista en las Iglesias de América, [Communist Infiltration in the Churches of America]*, Pia Sociedad de San Pablo, Buenos Aires, 1961, p 136

27 Duarte Costa, 'Manifesto', pp 14-15

28 Dom Gerardo Albano de Freitas, *Igreja Brasileira – Abençoada Rebeldia [The Brazilian Church – Blessed Rebeliousness]*, Centro de Estudos Teológicos ICAB, São Paulo, 1987, p 10

29 Dubois, p 8

30 Dubois, p 10

31 Duarte Costa, 'Manifesto', pp 7-8 in *Luta!* 12 http://diocesedecabofrio.blogspot.com/p/revista-luta.html

32 Dubois, p 19

33 Dubois, p 21

34 Dubois, p 20

35 One of the pseudonyms of writer and lawyer Ariosto de Colona Morosini Palombo.

36 Arnaldo Lemes Filho, *Os Catolicismos Brasileiros [Brazilian Catholicisms]*, Editora Alinea, Guanabara, Campinha, SP, 1996, p 46

37 Lemes Filho, p 46
38 Lemes Filho, p 54
39 Lemes Filho, p 55
40 Jácomo Mandatto, *Relíquias da Terra Natal [Relics of One's Native Land]*, Gr. Pedra, Itapira, 1959, p 99
41 Lemes Filho, p 54
42 Beatriz V. Dias Miranda, and Mabel Salgado Pereira (Eds), *Memorias Eclesiasticas: Documentos Comentados [Ecclesiastical Memoirs: Commentated Documents]*, Editora UFJF / Centro da Memoria da Igreja de Juiz de Fora – Cehila / Brazil, Juiz de Fora, 2000, p 89
43 Jácomo Mandatto, p 99
44 Cf. Duarte Costa, 'Manifesto', in *Luta!* issue 12, Sept. 1950, pp 9-10 http://diocesedecabofrio.blogspot.com/p/revista-luta.html [accessed 23rd May 2018]
45 Dias Miranda and Salgado Pereira, p 89
46 Cf. quote in Lemes Filho, p 59
47 Lemes Filho, p 60
48 Lemes Filho, p 62
49 *Time Magazine*, Monday, 23rd July 1945, p 64
50 Dubois, p 22
51 Ferraz was a Presbyterian minister for 15 years between 1902 and 1917; an Episcopalian minister between 1917 and 1936, when he founded the Free Catholic Church; after 9 years he became involved with Duarte Costa's ICAB; after a further 14 years he joined the Roman Catholic Church, where he remained for the 10 years until his death in 1969. A total of 67 years as a man of the cloth, in five churches.
52 Gestures such as this won Ferraz long-lasting appreciation in Roman Catholic circles. The accumulated goodwill would come back to serve Ferraz well later on, in spite of his intervening association with ICAB.
53 Cf. Dom Raimundo Augusto de Oliveira, *Dom Salomão Ferraz e o Ecumenismo [Dom Salomão Ferraz and Ecumenism]*, Feira de Santana, Bahia, undated, pp 48-49. Hereafter 'Oliveira.'
54 Cf. Oliveira, p 49
55 Cf. Oliveira, pp 48ff
56 The Polish Old Catholics were a breakaway faction in Europe of the Polish National Catholic Church.
57 Cf. Henry R.T. Brandreth, *Episcopi Vagantes and the Anglican Church*, SPCK, London, 1961, p 110
58 Dubois, p 22
59 Cf. Bishop Manoel José da Rocha Neto, Administrative Secretary, 'Declaração Acerca do Arcebispo David Bell' [Declaration Regarding Archbishop David Bell], 12th July 2013 [accessed 20th May 2018]

http://noticiasicab.blogspot.com.br/2013/07/declaracao-acerca-do-arcebispo-david.html?m=1

60 Obispo Alejo Pelypenko, *Infiltración Comunista en las Iglesias de América*, p 190

61 Cf. Câmara Municipal de São Paulo, Seção de Protocólo, [São Paulo Municipal Chamber, Protocol Section], case number 3779 of 1963, "Naming after Dom Jorge Alves de Sousa [sic] of the current planned street between […]." No apparent relation to *Aleixo* Alves de Souza, the leading Theosophist of the Liberal Catholic Church mentioned above. Biographical details of *Jorge* Alves de Souza found in a dossier of São Paulo City Hall, and also from Alejo Pelypenko's research.

62 Pelypenko, p 140

63 Cf. Pelypenko, pp 123-124

64 Cf. Dubois pp 91-2

65 *Luta!* issue 1, January 1947, p 23 contains a biographical sketch of Vargas, with omissions.

66 *Luta!* issue 7, August 1948, p 24

67 Cf. *Luta!* issue 7, August 1948, unnumbered page coming immediately after page 12

68 Pelypenko, p 130

69 *Luta!* issue 2, November 1947, p 8

70 Dubois, p 13

71 Dubois, p 94

72 Pelypenko, p 122

73 Dom Estêvão Bettencourt OSB, in the journal founded by him in 1956, *Pergunte e Responderemos, [Ask and We Will Answer]*, No. 55, July 1962, http://www.pr.gonet.biz/revista.php [accessed 19th April 2018]

74 The result is reminiscent of Aleister Crowley's reworking of Augustine's phrase 'Love, and do what thou wilt' into the Hedonist motto 'Do what thou wilt.'

75 Cf. *Luta!* issue 8, July 1949, p 2

76 Cf. *Luta!* issue 2, November 1947, p 2

77 *Luta!* issue 7, August 1948, p 31

78 Cf. CNBB – Conferencia Nacional dos Bispos do Brasil [National Conference of Bishops of Brazil], 'Comunicado Mensal' [Monthly Communiqué] Number 243, December 1972, p 91

79 Minister Lafayette de Andrada, 17th Nov. 1949 'Revista Archivo Judiciário' Vol CI/6-15, Jan.-Mar. 1952.

80 Minister Lafayette de Andrada, 17th November 1949

81 Cf. Pelypenko, p 125

82 Cf. Rodrigo Conde Tudanca, 'Un Incidente Olvidado del Trienio Adeco: La Creación de la Iglesia Católica, Apostólica, Venezolana'

['A Forgotten Incident of the Adeco Period: The Creation of the Venezuelan Catholic Apostolic Church'], in *Boletín CIHEV,* No. 8, Yr, 5, Jan.-June 1993, [pp 41-81]. p 110

[83] Cf. *Luta!* issue 2, November 1947, p 32

[84] See Chapter Seven for a discussion of the theology and sacraments of ICAB.

[85] Dubois, pp 72-73

[86] Dubois, p 20

[87] Dubois, p 72

IV

"PRIESTHOOD-MANIA"[1]
AND "BISHOPS GALORE"[2]
— ICAB in an age of revolution —

With the 1950's, the age of the 'Brazilian Revolution' had dawned. This decade would witness the start of extraordinary growth in Brazil's agriculture and industry. A process of massive urbanization would ensue, accompanied by fresh waves of immigration from European countries still recovering after World War Two. Traditional ways of life soon began to give way to a new type of society. Like most revolutions, the process was both irreversible and difficult to keep pace with, resulting in political instability. The people at the helm of this fast-changing society were still largely the same lawmakers of the 1930's, 1920's or even earlier – professional men from well-off families born around the turn of the century or in the later decades of the previous one. Being broadly conservative, the sudden upheavals of a rapidly modernizing society caught them on the back foot. The Roman Catholic Church, too, had maintained a conservative outlook in order to survive fifteen years of Vargas's secularist authoritarian dictatorship. It had taken as its inspiration the pre-nineteenth-century way of doing things – a rehashed Christendom relying on a stable Church-State symbiosis. This left the Catholic Church ill-prepared to engage with the new industrialized working class. Wars, depressions, and dictatorships had robbed modern Catholics of their former innocence and meekness. They were now more savvy, cynical, ambitious, and less inclined to passively accept hierarchies, unquestioningly assimilate the values commended to them, and swallow myths and superstitions. It was also a golden age for the Left. In supposedly Catholic Italy, the Vatican had forbidden Catholics to vote for the Italian Communist Party in the first big post-war election, under pain of excommunication,[3] but this had not stopped the Communists coming a close second and building the largest Communist party in Western Europe. The more or less equal stand-off between Communists and Christian Democrats would characterize Italian politics for more than a generation. If that could happen in Italy then the Vatican was unwilling to risk burning its fingers again by forcing the working class to choose between 'them or us' elsewhere.

The Catholic Church in Brazil had a little communist thorn in its own side. They may have hoped or expected Duarte Costa and his ICAB rebellion to quickly founder and be forgotten, once his point had been made and he had enjoyed his moment in the sun (and in the press). Now they saw that this new renegade and rival Church was not going away, and that it was actually growing. Duarte Costa celebrated by increasing the pages of *Luta!* from 32 to 44. But although ICAB had survived the Romans' legal challenge, its early years were marred by internal disorder, as a mixed bag of individuals with varying motives swelled its ranks. Duarte Costa's most enduring and tiresome bugbear would be conflict with his own churchmen. The first big character clash, as we have seen, was the one with the sixty-five year-old Protestant pastor Salomão Barbosa Ferraz. Ferraz was the first bishop Duarte Costa consecrated without papal permission – a grave offense in Canon Law. This deed alone could have led the Church to consider excommunicating Duarte Costa. Canon Law was subsequently amended to make this offense grounds for *instant* excommunication – at the time only a suspension was automatic, and Duarte Costa was already suspended. In fact the deed was overshadowed by the more shocking offense of Schism, namely the foundation of ICAB itself. Ferraz's consecration sent out an additional clear message that the rupture with the Roman Catholic Church was final and total. It demonstrated that Duarte Costa really did intend to continue exercising his powers as a bishop. ICAB was not just a tantrum or a protest – he meant business. For these reasons 'The First ICAB Bishop' was not a casting choice that Duarte Costa should have got wrong – but he did.

Ferraz already had his own independent Church, the Free Catholic Church (*Igreja Católica Livre*) which he had founded back in 1936.[4] Duarte Costa envisaged this being merged into the larger ICAB; Ferraz would become one of 'his' bishops, and while Duarte Costa ruled Rio de Janeiro he entrusted the other fast-spreading metropolis, São Paulo, to Ferraz. But Ferraz evidently did not see himself and his Church being thrown into the ICAB melting pot of gregarious groups, Spiritualist sects and questionable characters. Duarte Costa publicly denounced this obstinate refusal to submit to his authority.[5] Ferraz retorted by poaching Duarte Costa's *second* bishop, Jorge Alves de Souza. This infuriated Duarte Costa – the first bishop he consecrated leading astray the second bishop he consecrated. There is more than just a whiff of schoolyard politics here, but it was perhaps slightly deeper than petty squabbling. Both Ferraz and De Souza were active and committed Freemasons, and it is understandable that they should have experienced an affinity based on this. Predictably, the Ferraz side of the story is all quite different – he never agreed to 'join' Duarte Costa's ICAB or saw himself as one of ICAB's bishops.[6] Since the day he founded the Free Catholic Church, Ferraz had been a 'bishop elect' in search of a benevolent bishop to formally consecrate him, and Duarte Costa had finally stepped forward. In contrast to those first two turncoats, Costa's third choice of bishop in December 1946[7] would stand out as a beacon of loyalty and commitment. Antídio José Vargas held fast to the ICAB cause and never aimed for more than the appointment Duarte Costa gave him – Bishop of Lages in Santa Caterina State. In fact Vargas was already based there and ministering there, so Duarte Costa's 'appointment' was a simple recognition of reality. Vargas was the bishop who one eyewitness described as mentally ill after watching his theatrical behavior – he described Vargas frothing at the mouth as he snarled, shrieked, sobbed, and screamed with laughter in a tirade against ICAB's enemies.[8] Vargas spent his entire career in Lages pitted against his Roman Catholic counterpart and rival, his own former superior Bishop Hostin, who presumably somewhat regretted having ordained Vargas a priest a decade earlier. But Vargas remained loyal to Duarte Costa.

Much of the criticism directed at ICAB over the years has had to do with inconsistency, both in the sense of disparity between words and actions and in the sense of it being organically inconsistent, fragmented, and incoherent. In later decades, as we shall see in detail, the Roman Catholic Church's various reports on ICAB would accuse it of being not one Church at all but rather a collection of loosely-connected (and sometimes mutually hostile) sects, cliques, groups, and individuals. The Roman Catholic authorities derided the absence of unity in thought, practice, or worship. Each fiefdom seemed to operate singly – frequently under a charismatic local leader – for its own sometimes questionable benefit. Furthermore, there has clearly been inconsistency over time. ICAB jettisoned much of its early content after the passing of Duarte Costa – the strong religious pluralism, the socialist and communist sympathies, the focus on politics and education. When the opportunity arose, ICAB re-branded itself as conservative and traditionalist. Before all this was to unfold, however, even in the very early days the idea of 'Brazilian-Catholic' was denounced as a contradiction, with Catholicism being fundamentally international in character, not national. But Duarte Costa may not necessarily have meant for national to mean nationalist, or for Brazilian-Catholic to mean isolationist. He said from the start that "the movement which is now getting underway in Brazil [will have] possible ramifications in other nations of the American Continent and other continents."[9] There was an international aspect to ICAB from very early-on.

Of the main characters in the early years of this Brazilian Catholic Church, Duarte Costa was almost in the minority for being both Brazilian and Catholic; of the first four bishops consecrated by Duarte Costa, only two were both Catholic and Brazilian since birth. Duarte Costa also planned to involve Polish and Mexican bishops in ICAB, and one of his eventual successors as overall leader would be an Italian. To say the least, this all sharply contradicted Duarte Costa's previous attacks on foreign clergy and his condemnation of priests from 'Axis' countries as fascists. Even with such inherent contradictions the trials and tribulations of ICAB's first five years did not prevent it from expanding. The 1950's were to be years of growth, though the Roman Catholic Church would forever afterwards try to play it down. It would be the first and last full decade entirely under the leadership of ICAB's founder, though he would increasingly lose control of his movement and seek to wrest back control up to the last moment.[10]

Duarte Costa was eventually able to more or less patch things up with his two wayward Freemason bishops De Souza and Ferraz, but worse heartache was to come. Duarte Costa's most explosive and fractious relationship was to be with his fourth bishop, Luis Fernando Castillo Mendez, who he would soon be accusing of a variety of crimes, duplicities and disorders. He would not be the first to conclude that Castillo Mendez's obsession with the priesthood – or "priesthood-mania"[11] – was pathological rather than spiritual in origin. Their warring would contribute to the fossilization of internal wrangling, dissent, and schisms as permanent features of ICAB. It would also tarnish the final years of Duarte Costa's life and leadership. Amazingly, Castillo Mendez would not only survive all the disputes and remain in ICAB, he would also eventually succeed Duarte Costa and lead the Church into the current century. Castillo Mendez would become a relentless and prolific consecrator of priests and bishops, lending his ordaining services to many – and any – sect, church or individual. When Padre Dubois criticized ICAB's intention of ordaining "Bishops galore"[12] he could not have imagined that Duarte Costa's final tally of eleven bishops would be dwarfed by Castillo Mendez's eventual hundreds. The 1950's began, incidentally, with Duarte Costa's discovery that Castillo Mendez was in prison – not for the first time.

Luis Fernando Castillo Mendez,[13] who would reshape and then dominate ICAB for over forty years, was not Brazilian but

Venezuelan. He would become Duarte Costa's fourth bishop aged only 25. Castillo Mendez was born into a humble and pious Catholic family in Ureña, Táchira State, on 4th December 1922. By the time he reached his teens he appears to have developed some sort of pathological fixation with the priesthood and an extraordinary level of cunning and creativity in his determination to achieve it. This assertion is deliberately understated and readers will make up their own mind; but as we will see from contemporary documents, much harsher conclusions were reached by the authorities at the time. Castillo Mendez's priestly odyssey, in fact, is an extraordinary story. Let us consider some key facts from his *curriculum vitae*:[14]

~ *September 1936 – Estado Táchira, Venezuela* ~

Luis Fernando Castillo Mendez is a thirteen year-old would-be seminarian from Ureña, Táchira State. Even today, Ureña is a very small and unimposing frontier town, perched right on Venezuela's western border with Colombia. In the Táchira state capital, San Cristóbal, Castillo Mendez is admitted to St. Thomas Aquinas Seminary, run by the Eudist Fathers. The Eudists are a French religious congregation dedicated to nurturing vocations in areas where it has so far been difficult to access a seminary education. After one semester, however, Castillo Mendez is expelled from the seminary on account of his extremely poor grades. The enterprising fourteen year-old does not miss the opportunity to demonstrate his ingenuity: he doctors the grades on his report card in order to show his parents, parish priest, and others that his expulsion was unjustified.[15] Clearly, they all thought, the Eudist Fathers must be unreasonably harsh, and Bishop Enrique María Dubuc Moreno of Barquisimeto is persuaded to agree. Castillo Mendez is admitted to the Bishop's *Divina Pastora*[16] Seminary (conveniently very far away from any possible interference by the Eudists). He does not last much longer than he did in San Cristóbal, however, and is this time expelled "for having an erroneous concept of priestly vocation"[17] – typically evasive ecclesiastical language that leaves much to the imagination. The version of Castillo Mendez's seminary days published ten years later in the ICAB journal *Luta!*[18] – the version furnished by Castillo Mendez – tells a different story. According to Castillo Mendez he was first expelled from the Eudists' seminary for being too poor – he could not pay the board and lodging exacted by the miserly French missionaries. In Barquisimeto, Castillo Mendez told *Luta!* he was expelled because he did not belong to that diocese. Neither excuse holds much water. If he did not meet the requirements for enrolment to the seminaries, fair or unfair as the requirements may have been, why was he admitted in the first place? In the case of the *Divina Pastora* Seminary, it is not remotely out of the ordinary for seminaries to take in students from neighboring dioceses. In any case, surprisingly, both versions do concur that just two semesters were quite enough for Castillo Mendez. "At this point", *Luta!* Reports, "the young Castillo Mendez had concluded his Minor Seminary studies."[19] Indeed. He is now all of 15 years old and getting ready to celebrate his first Mass.

~ *January 1938 – Valencia, Venezuela* ~

Castillo Mendez has chosen not to be fazed by the ominous wording of the *Divina Pastora* Seminary's assessment and heads east to Valencia (midway between Barquisimeto and the capital Caracas – even further from home than before). From there he applies to join the Congregation of the Sacred Hearts of Jesus and Mary, known as the French Fathers,[20] based in Palo Alto to the east of Caracas, but they are tipped off and reject him. Castillo Mendez is now a robust just-turned-fifteen-year-old who can pass for considerably older. Taking the various knock-backs on board he has decided to dispense with the need for seminary training altogether, and has taken to wearing a cassock and calling himself Father Otero. His claims to be a priest are apparently taken at face value in small towns around Valencia and he meekly accepts favors, gifts, and donations. His offers to substitute for priests at

Mass are accepted in Turmero and Choroni. After several months this little racket is uncovered and he is arrested.

~ 18th November 1938 [21] – Caracas Prison ~

From his cell in Caracas jail, Castillo Mendez writes pleadingly to Monsignor Miguel Antonio Mejía, auxiliary bishop of Caracas: 'I have been detained for seventeen days already, let us say unjustly, because the one who should be punished is the priest who allowed a young lad as I am to officiate as an ordained priest, without asking me for the necessary credentials to identify me as such.' He then pleads that he should be punished according to Church law rather than civil law – the ploy works, and he is released. From Caracas, Castillo Mendez's adventure takes him to Cumaná, where, in the temporary absence of the local bishops Monsignor Sixto Sosa and his auxiliary Monsignor Rafael Arias, he returns to masquerading as a priest. The charming 'young priest' (he is still aged just 16) ingratiates himself with the Carmelite Sisters and basks in their hospitality. Bishop Arias soon hears about it and this time Castillo Mendez is forced to hand over his vestments and priestly accoutrements. Stripped of the tools of his trade, he flees to Margarita with the aim of becoming a teacher – he is going straight, for now. He makes friends with the Carmelite Fathers and teaches for them. Some years pass and he drifts back to Caracas, where he somehow manages to save a sum of money.

~ January 1944 – Embarkation for Spain ~

Now just turned 21, Castillo Mendez sets off on the next leg of his odyssey and sails for Europe. The priesthood is in the cross-hairs again and this time he will try his luck in Spain. There he is admitted to, but promptly expelled from, the Novitiate of the Carmelite Fathers in Tarrasa, and then the same story at the Diocesan Seminary in Barcelona. This time, it really is his last flirtation with seminaries; there is to be no more messing about. Castillo Mendez has come to Spain with several carefully crafted cards up his sleeve: false documents with seals, stamps and signatures, all acquired, borrowed and copied from here and there over recent years. His papers identify him as a seminarian of the Diocese of Coro, fully trained and ready to be ordained. A year later the bishop of Vich, Monsignor Juan Perelló y Pau, recalled:

> "On May third last year, a person telephoned the episcopal palace calling himself Luis Fernando Castillo Mendez, seminarian of the Diocese of Coro (Venezuela), whence he had just arrived, requesting to receive Holy Orders before the shrine of the Blessed Anthony Maria Claret. After examining the documentation and consulting with my Vicar General, albeit with some revulsion, though trusting in the authenticity of the documents presented, I conferred upon him Tonsure and Minor Orders on the 5th, 6th, and 7th of the said month of May and Major Orders (Sub-diaconate and Diaconate) on the 14th and 21st of the same month.

> "The individual wanted to be ordained up to the Presbyterate, but, providentially, shortly before the agreed date, I learned via a letter from the Rector of the Seminary of Barcelona to his counterpart in Vich that this same Castillo had been expelled from his seminary and from the Novitiate of the Calced Carmelite Fathers in Tarrasa."[22]

Now rumbled, 'Deacon' Castillo Mendez hotfoots it to Solsona. There, the elderly and infirm bishop receives a mysterious telephone call purporting to be from the Archbishop Primate of Caracas. The 'Archbishop' asks the near-blind Bishop of Solsona, Monsignor Valentín Comellas y Santamaria, to ordain a man called Luis Fernando Castillo,

> "to which request [the] Bishop initially refused, telling him that because of his age and ill-health he was unavailable, and to look for another Bishop who might be able to help. The supposed Archbishop [on the telephone] continued to insist, begging him

before God and all the saints of heaven to do him this favor, and assuring him on his honor that the individual had all his documents in order..."[23]

The elderly bishop continued to protest – could the Archbishop not do it himself? What about another bishop? But the arm-twisting 'Archbishop' on the telephone had a smart answer ready for every objection. Never suspecting anything more sinister than bad protocol, the bishop ordained Castillo Mendez on 10th August 1944. Only afterwards, the warnings flying around Spain about Castillo Mendez finally reached Solsona. The tricked bishop, mortified, reported everything to the Apostolic Nuncio, who replied:

> "Now we have to find a possible remedy to this lamentable case: for my part I will telegraph Rome and send a circular to all the bishops of Spain that under no circumstances are they to permit him to exercise sacred ministry in their dioceses."[24]

With a time-honored combination of exaggerated politeness and thinly concealed impatience with an old man's gullibility, the Nuncio went on:

> "But I should be interested to know, so as to duly inform the Holy See, how this thing unfolded in your diocese and with regard to Your Excellency; that is to say, what documentation was presented?
>
> "I would be grateful therefore, if Your Excellency could furnish me with detailed reports and updates about the case."[25]

Bishop Valentín Comellas y Santamaria, who was 83, passed away the following March. Castillo Mendez had his wish, priesthood, but all doors were now closed to him in Spain. It had taken him eight years of tricks and schemes to reach ordination, much longer than it would have taken by the orthodox route, but that door too had been closed to him. He could take satisfaction in having reached ordination with only the inconvenience of two semesters spent in Minor Seminary. But in the absence of theological studies he was perhaps unaware that dubious and illicit Holy Orders obtained by deception could never be recognized by the Church. He was either unaware of this or perhaps did not care, but after all that effort he could not really be considered a priest at all. The whole of Spain was alerted to the case of the phony priest. Castillo Mendez was briefly held by the National Guard[26] and then agreed to repatriate voluntarily. Aboard ship, the *Cabo de Hornos*, the ship's chaplain later recalled the young priest in his cassock. Castillo Mendez had adopted a new look – glasses and a quiff. He said Mass on board but news of the case had reached fellow passengers – some of whom were missionaries and clergy themselves – and he was regarded as *Vitandus*.[27] During the voyage Castillo Mendez claimed to have two doctorates from Rome (despite having just recently turned 22 and having never been to Italy) – an absurdity that he did not dare repeat to Duarte Costa and *Luta!* Nevertheless, myths about Castillo Mendez's degrees from the Gregorian University would occasionally resurface.

Castillo Mendez returned to Venezuela at a crucial moment in its history. In 1945, Venezuela – not unlike Brazil – emerged from a period of dictatorship into a precarious era of democracy. There was a comparatively stable government with one party – Democratic Action – holding power, and the Constitution was scheduled to be updated. As in many parts of Latin America, an era of great modernization and social transformation was dawning. 1945 to 1948 would become known as *El Trienio Adeco* – the 'Three-year Adeco *(Acción Democrática)* Period.'[28] The Church in Venezuela also saw opportunities for expansion and development, and it was determined not to be left out of this period of modernization and social improvement. Peacetime had reopened lines of communication with the European Church, meaning renewed possibilities of material assistance; besides which the Church was already a major player in education and social work in Venezuela. But the new ruling party, supported by the Venezuelan Communist Party, harbored a distinctly anticlerical element. In retrospect it is believed that the Church overestimated this, equating *Acción Democrática* (AD) with Communism. Anticlericalism – not unknown across Latin America – was misread as Marxist atheism, and AD's social program was misinterpreted as class war, when in fact the party plotted neither.[29] The Church, in self-defense, promoted a new party which was to become AD's chief rival, the Christian Social Party *(Partido Social Cristiano)*. The Church and ruling party were therefore pitted against each other. It was at this point that Castillo Mendez stepped off the boat from Spain.

The well-informed Church hierarchy in Caracas awaited his return in order to clip his wings without delay – he was outlawed and disowned, and preparations were made to have him formally reduced to the status of layman by the Holy See. Prior to Castillo Mendez's return, the Venezuelan Church, treading with extreme caution, decided to follow the prescribed process for 'reduction to the lay state' – *laicization* as it is called – "in case a valid priestly ordination is detected in this individual."[30] But there was no chance of recognizing Castillo Mendez as a priest and his was regarded as a "fake ordination."[31] The decree from Rome came through in June 1945, and on 8th August – very nearly a year to the day since he knelt before a blind, confused, and unwilling Spanish bishop to be 'ordained' – Castillo Mendez gave his formal assent to the laicization. The document was read out in the chamber of the Archbishop's Palace in Caracas, before Castillo Mendez signed it alongside two witnesses.[32] Case closed? Not quite. While the Catholic Church had no use of him, Democratic Action did. The ruling party cynically saw in Castillo Mendez an opportunity to embarrass and divide the Church, raise controversial issues, and distract Catholic voters' attention away from anti-AD politics. In no time the Communist and AD-aligned newspapers fanfared his arrival onto the national stage. He was, they reported, part of an international anti-celibacy movement,[33] the leader of the Venezuelan Church's 'reform wing' alongside thirty-three other priests[34] in favor of elected bishops, married priests, and abolishing Latin.[35] The reaction was predictably one of scandal and horror, but there was some sympathy too. If the Church was not exactly divided over these outrageous statements, apparently coming from within its own ranks, it may well have looked that way from the outside – which was of course the desired effect. And while Catholics were debating Castillo Mendez's claims and the activities of the alleged 'reform wing', they were not taking the Church seriously as a major player in the new society. If the Church could not keep its own house in order on basic disciplinary matters, could its Christian Social Party ever be trusted with power? Castillo Mendez's actions seemed to be working in the anticlerical government's favor, but the question arises as to whether he received only moral support and newspaper space from his AD "comrades"[36] or financial aid as well. The Venezuelan historians of the period Rodrigo Conde Tudanca and Aureo Yépez Castillo are in agreement – Castillo Mendez was subsidized by mid-ranking activists from both Democratic Action and the Communist Party of Venezuela.[37] In return he acted out a farce which, these activists felt, aided the left-wing populist parties' agenda. The newspapers which reported Castillo Mendez's spurious declamations were those partly or wholly controlled by the parties themselves and openly hostile towards the Catholic Church.

By this time Castillo Mendez had found a long-distance mentor in Carlos Duarte Costa. His personal agenda from now on would be set by the developments of ICAB.[38] The next step therefore was for Castillo Mendez to start his own renegade Church of which he could be the bishop. At the close of 1946, by way of provocation, he wrote casually and rather offhandedly to the Papal Nuncio:

"Dearest Brother,

"I think it best to inform you, so that you can bring it to the attention of Pope Pius XII, Bishop of Rome, that we, a group of priests, have legally established ourselves and formed the Venezuelan Catholic Apostolic Church, aimed at vindicating our suffering and cheated people.

"In a few days we will send you collectively [sic] a fuller, more substantial and more detailed report of an official nature for any legal eventualities.

"Furthermore we will announce the 'good news' to our country in a collective letter, subject to certain legal formalities..."[39]

The influence of Duarte Costa is easily detectable – the Bishop of Maura's brand of chutzpah is there, though perhaps not his mastery of language. Thus the *Iglesia Católica, Apostólica, Venezolana* (ICAV) was born.[40] *Luta!* of January 1947 proudly reported the launch of ICAB's Venezuelan branch, and Duarte Costa was now quite justified in having predicted 'ramifications in other nations of the American continent.' In addition to ICAV's *50* initial priests *Luta!* reported that a further *200* were ready to join but currently terrorized into obedience by the Vatican.[41] ICAV planned to launch a journal called *Lucha!* (Fight!) in obvious homage to ICAB's *Luta!* but in the end they opted for the name *Liberación*.[42] With his 'group of priests' (there were three of them at one point)[43] Castillo Mendez set to work, having little lean-to chapels quickly erected and traveling around to ingratiate himself with the 'suffering people', funded as ever by activists from the Communist and AD parties.[44] These activists' unsophisticated plan was to further discomfort and discredit the Catholic Church, but it seems that the real leaders of AD and the government were not directly involved. The leadership may have been amused by the ICAV farce, but this did not save Castillo Mendez from being arrested on 28th February 1947 for masquerading as a bishop (the same day he and his little band were excommunicated) nor from being arrested again for the same offense on 13th April.[45] He was not detained for very long however (it is not clear whether Party friends intervened on his behalf) and he was free to celebrate the accession to the presidency of AD's candidate – "my great friend (…) and *compañero* Rómulo Gallegos."[46] Castillo Mendez continued founding chapels and went to discuss the launch of a counterpart National Church in Colombia. Other successes included a pact of cooperation with 'The Enlightened One' of Sarría – a famed medium in the Sarría district where ICAV had a chapel. The Enlightened One had for years pinned her hopes on finding a priest to lend credibility to her work and extend her appeal to the more wary and devout Catholics. Castillo Mendez was happy to oblige.[47] Curiously, around this time, Castillo Mendez admitted to the press that he had been expelled from the seminary in Barquisimeto in 1937, saying that he was expelled "for having a *very clear* concept of priestly vocation and for having fully understood Christian Socialism."[48] (The seminary's actual wording had been "for having an *erroneous* concept of priestly vocation."[49]) What did he now mean by "a very clear concept of priestly vocation" and what exactly had the seminary meant with its sinister phrasing in the first place? As the full picture of Castillo Mendez's complex personality becomes clear, consider the version of events suggested in the 'Opinion' column of *El Universal*, Caracas: "he is [sic] expelled for poor grades and for dressing up as a woman, which earned him – among the other seminarians – an epithet which we will not repeat here."[50] The truth is impossible to verify at a distance of some 80 years, but Castillo Mendez's admission that he was expelled from seminary is as bizarre as it is defiant. Perhaps he intended to taunt the seminary that had – with considerable discretion, under the circumstances – ejected him. He threw the seminary's words back in their faces, ten years on. The young Castillo Mendez was not averse to these little demonstrations of his 'I'll show *them!*' attitude.

And nothing would 'show them' like Castillo Mendez being consecrated bishop by his new mentor, Duarte Costa. Neither Brazil nor Venezuela wanted the spectacle of this potentially notorious schismatic consecration on its soil however, and both governments refused the other party a visa (no *compañeros* in the Venezuelan government stepped in to assist, obviously). Consequently, Duarte Costa and Castillo Mendez met on US-protected soil – in Balboa, Canal Zone, Panama – and on 3rd April 1948 Castillo Mendez was consecrated bishop.[51] It was possibly the first sacramentally valid ordination he had received, or at least the one which he employed the least deception in order to obtain. *Luta!* proclaimed him "the world's youngest bishop. He is, just, 25 years old."[52] The new bishop could not contain his joy, immediately sending this bizarre postcard to the Archbishop of Caracas:

"Esteemed Brother,

"Today I was consecrated Bishop by Bishop Carlos Duarte Costa. Get this straight: I am now a bishop for all eternity. Oh yes, now ICAV will make some progress."[53]

Recruiting new priests now became easier – he could simply ordain them himself. On his return home he ordained the plumber, Ildefonso Nuñez, and an odd-job man, a 35-year old Italian immigrant called Stefano Corradi (later consecrated bishop) – although officially, like its Brazilian patron, ICAV was opposed to the 'interference' of foreign clergy. ICAV aimed to mirror ICAB in every way.[54] ICAV recruited Father Francisco José Verde, a defrocked Roman Catholic priest "who was well-known for having more than half a dozen screws loose."[55] But the glory days of the Adeco period were coming to an end, and with them would end Castillo Mendez's free ride courtesy of the Communist and AD party purses. ICAV was by this time banned from some districts,[56] which was a shame because Castillo Mendez now needed to develop new sources of income. As the pursuit of funds became increasingly unscrupulous, ICAV's apparently sincere second in command Father Ramón Cortada Battle resigned along with a number of other clergy, realizing that:

"this has not been an attempt to create a more authentically Christian Venezuelan Church, free of fanaticisms, imbued with a social sensitivity that corresponds to modern needs, with a freedom that begins with that of its own priests, but rather one that surpasses the Roman Church in all its defects, with exaggerated ceremonies, superfluous and every-day-more-abundant devotions, luxuries and comforts of all types, and cheap mysticism to trick the poor."[57]

By 1950 nearly everyone else had deserted ICAV too. The AD government had fallen and given way to instability, which in turn led to a military takeover. Eager to appease the much-maligned

Catholic Church, the junta imprisoned Castillo Mendez on 11th August 1950, this time for nine months, until May 1951. As a prisoner he was apparently as much of a nuisance as when free, even managing to rack up charges of "corruption and immorality"[58] while jailed.[59] On the outside, the Italian handyman remained loyal – Castillo Mendez had raised Stefano Corradi (aka Esteban Corradi Scarella) to the rank of bishop before going to jail, and Corradi in turn consecrated Albert A. Steer (who had previously been consecrated as an 'Old Catholic' bishop in the US), who then tried to launch the Panamanian Catholic Apostolic Church. Corradi's progeny would eventually amount to around 150 bishops, mostly in the USA. Castillo Mendez also attempted to start the Guatemalan Catholic Apostolic Church.[60] None of these fledgling Churches lasted much longer than the time it took for the ink to dry on the acts of consecration, but the precedent for spawning offshoot Churches was now established. Castillo Mendez, for his part, was done founding Churches and, invited by the junta to leave Venezuela for ever, he made his way to Brazil.

With the addition of 'the world's youngest' and now exiled bishop, Duarte Costa had made four bishops, and two more indirectly through Castillo Mendez. They were a rag-bag of characters and he would continue to fall out and then make up with them all for the rest of the decade. Ferraz, now over 70, was doing his own thing again by this time. On 29th June 1951, assisted by the Polish 'Old Catholic' bishop Jan Piotr Perkowski (1901–1963), Ferraz consecrated a bishop for his own 'Free Catholic Church.' He poached the lucky candidate from among Duarte Costa's most able priests – Manoel Ceia Laranjeira, who had been ordained priest by Duarte Costa in 1947 and had soon risen to become Secretary General of ICAB.[61] This increased the episcopal descendants of Duarte Costa to seven, but he wanted nothing to do with this new defection and merely fumed from a safe distance. The first two issues of *Luta!* of the 1950's roundly denounced Ferraz and his gang. On 12th May the following year, 1952, Ferraz finally quit.[62] Castillo Mendez, meanwhile, had arrived in Brazil on 21st July

1951[63] (Duarte Costa's 63rd birthday) but by the following March he was already suspended for disobedience.[64] With his fingers thus well and truly burnt, there would be a gap of several years before Duarte Costa would consecrate any more bishops.

ICAB continued to grow steadily as the 1950's progressed, but the coming and going of bishops would gradually become a sign that Duarte Costa was losing control of the movement – he would desperately attempt to wrest back control right up to the end. He ordained a fifth bishop after a six-year abstinence in 1954 – Diamantino Augusto Pereira da Costa[65] for Pernambuco (Recife). A sixth bishop was consecrated on 29th June 1955 for a new Bolivian National Church. Pedro Luis Hernandez was a Roman Catholic priest from Bolivia and was due to lead ICAB's planned branch there, hoping to take advantage of a wave of popular nationalism and anticlericalism. Hernandez went to Brazil to receive episcopal consecration but died of a heart attack not long after his return to La Paz. In Argentina, meanwhile, June saw the first of 1955's two coup d'états, and for the first time hopes were raised for founding an ICAB branch there.[66] By this time Duarte Costa had sufficiently made peace with Ferraz to invite him to ICAB's tenth anniversary celebrations[67] at the mother church, Saint Ana, 54 Rua do Couto, Penha, Rio de Janeiro, but Ferraz was no longer numbered among the ICAB clergy.[68] Duarte Costa by now acknowledged Ferraz as the leader of the Free Catholic Church, but in fact Ferraz would soon start looking internationally – towards Rome – for the next stage of his career. Duarte Costa felt the need to begin consolidating his power base at home. In 1956 he appointed a coadjutor bishop for his own territory; Pedro dos Santos Silva was consecrated bishop on 4th November for Rio de Janeiro, and later became diocesan bishop of Barra de São João in Rio de Janeiro State. Silva was a former Roman Catholic priest who had married, eventually having two daughters and a son. As 'coadjutor' he would be expected to take over from Duarte Costa when the latter went to his eternal reward – Dom Carlos was beginning to prepare for his *adieu*. Later that month Duarte Costa consecrated a bishop for another planned satellite Church in Chile, Orlando Arce Moya, whose defection would not last very long and who, the misinformation mill persists to this day, was to be graciously taken back into the clergy of the Roman Catholic Church. This rumor, utterly unfounded, goes that the Vatican 'recognized' his status as bishop. This could mean many things – they would perhaps be bound to accept, theologically, that he may have been validly consecrated; it would be difficult to prove or disprove. But in fact the Roman Catholic Church did not consider him a bishop – or a priest – to any effects. Arce Moya has, of course, never appeared in the *Annuarium Pontificium* list of recognized bishops. It is beyond doubt that he did not 'return to Rome' as a bishop, as the *annuarium* of hearsay insists.[69]

One bishop who would not go away, as much as Duarte Costa may have wished it, was Luis Fernando Castillo Mendez. In the March 1956 issue of *Luta!*, Duarte Costa thoughtfully provided readers – and posterity – with a warts 'n' all summary of Castillo Mendez's career so far,[70] unapologetically leaving himself out of Castillo Mendez's backstory:

"Rio de Janeiro, 6th January 1956

"Dom Luiz [sic] Fernando Castillo Méndez — Venezuelan Bishop — Dangerous Character — Con Artiste — Forger.

"He arrived in Brazil, claiming to be persecuted by his government for being the founder of the Venezuelan Catholic Church.

"Welcoming him in a Christian and tender way, aiming to alleviate his exile, I entrusted him to the people of Uberlândia, who are very dear to me, ever since the days of the late Father Pio [Dantas Barbosa], whom my uncle, Dom Eduardo Duarte Silva, greatly respected. These are memories of my youth, tied up with my priestly ordination. This spiritual affinity inspires a very special fondness for the Triângulo Mineiro.

"A perturbed soul, such as Dom Luiz must have been, would find there – as in fact he did find – comfort for the open wounds in his spirit.

111

"The liberal, deeply Christian people of Uberlândia understood my gesture and opened the doors of their homes completely.

"The directors of the Central Brazil College found him some classes to teach, so that he would not go without an income, and they went above and beyond for him.

"The Brazilian Catholic Apostolic Church is National, just as the Venezuelan Catholic Apostolic Church is National, and as all the Churches arising out of the liberation movement of 6th July 1945 will be National, in order for Christianity to return to the early days when the Churches were national. Without jeopardizing this basic principle of the Brazilian National Church, I sought a way to give jurisdiction to Dom Luiz, since, being a foreigner, he could not have Brazilian subjects. I arrived at the decision to endorse and validate all his actions, lending him my authority in the sense that actions taken by him would be as if I had taken those actions. As long as Dom Luiz kept within these principles, everything went well. It came to pass, however, that human passions which he could not contain took control, and with them a spirit of independence. Dom Luiz quit the role of 'exile' in order to reinvent himself as a Chief of the Brazilian National Church. He began to act on his own initiative accumulating errors upon errors, and ended up betraying me and ICAB along with me.

"In short, he established a culture of lies and indiscipline. He began to ordain priests without justification, merely creating difficulties for them in the future. Finally, he made himself 'Diocesan Bishop of Central Brazil' – in order to gain people's support, he uses and abuses my name and ICAB.

"What is more, he extracts money from the gullible, tricks the authorities and entangles himself with mercenary individuals trading on people's faith. He falsifies a document and uses my name, so that priests and faithful sign it, making them believe that he is acting in accordance with my wishes. He engaged the Notary to authenticate the signatures of the individuals who he had persuaded to sign that document for a supposed meeting in order to launch a supposed branch of ICAB in Uberlândia. He caused trouble in Goiás which ended up reaching the ears of Parliament. Newspapers and radio programs report on all these things as if

112

they are carried out by ICAB. I then approach the newspapers and deny the involvement of ICAB in these scandals. Only then was I able to comprehend the full reality of Dom Luiz in Brazil, which is as follows:

1) He is exiled; 2) He is permitted to return to his country; 3) The Venezuelan Government would pay his airfare; 4) He would not be allowed to involve himself in religious matters; 5) This injunction was accepted, with the proviso that the Government of Venezuela pay him X amount of money for the real estate owned by the Venezuelan Catholic Apostolic Church or owned by individuals – him or his family; 6) This proviso of Dom Luiz raises the question of which is real estate owned by the Venezuelan Catholic Apostolic Church and which is his own and that of his family; 8) That of the Venezuelan Catholic Apostolic Church he cannot concede [to the government], because it was bought with money donated by the public; 9) Looking at the issue from the economic point of view, it is evident that the OBJECTIVE of Dom Luiz is money, and not the religious liberation of the people of his country; 10) The resolution of the case is the concern of the competent authorities.

"A failure in his own country and a failure here, Dom Luiz has no right to disrupt the life of peaceful cities in the Goian area, using and abusing my name and ICAB's. I declare my objection to the way of doing things of this individual – who is not connected to ICAB – and, with me, the officially existing dioceses declare their objection; they are Santa Catarina and Pernambuco and all the adherents of the National Brazilian Church, in the whole of the National territory.

"Let the police of the States of Minas Gerais and Goiás examine Dom Luiz's record, establish whether these things are true or not, whether Dom Luiz is or is not a Dangerous Individual, Con Artiste, and Forger. The trouble caused by Dom Luiz cannot go unpunished, for the good of society.

"Acting with sincerity and loyalty, this is what duty demands, I say to you Brazilians worthy of Brazil.

"+ Carlos Duarte Costa, Bishop of Rio de Janeiro, of ICAB"[71]

Perhaps it goes without saying by now that Castillo Mendez, though ejected from ICAB and publicly condemned, would soon return without ceremony and crawl back under the wing of Duarte Costa, whose power of forgiveness can surely not be called into question.

It continued to be a trying time for the Roman Catholic Church as well. It had only just adapted itself to the first half of the twentieth century, at whose outset the Church had been woefully underdeveloped in structure and resources of all kinds. It was now faced with a rapidly changing society and challenges to traditional values from all sides. Alternative philosophies and beliefs, which had always been a factor in Brazil's religious make-up, flourished more than ever, while the strict confines of Catholic discipline gave no leeway for dabbling in such things. Population shifts, urbanization, and immigration were bringing people together as never before, which increased situations such as mixed-faith marriages and multi-faith families living in multi-faith communities. Catholic doctrine was utterly unprepared to provide solutions and answers for all this, but it would have to learn and fast. Does the steady growth of ICAB suggest that it was better prepared to deal with the new social reality? In some immediate senses this could be so – ICAB had already branded itself the Catholic Church open to all, and being of mixed faiths or none, or divorced for that matter, were no barriers to official marriage and baptism in ICAB. It already actively reached out to non-Christian faiths – ICAB services were held in Spiritualist centers[72] and at the Positivist Club[73] of Rio de Janeiro. The Umbanda religion would also become an ally.[74] *Luta!* testifies to ICAB's energetic outreach to Freemasons,[75] and boasts of its excellent relations with Protestants.[76] ICAB had also been heavily politicized since its beginning (and Duarte Costa long before that) so Marxists and Anarchists could find a spiritual home in ICAB, if they felt the need for one. Furthermore, given the vastness of Brazil and rapid shifts in population, it was not difficult for an ICAB church community to find itself the only church for miles around. ICAB could therefore be filling an important gap in local life – not that they would be thanked by the Roman Catholics of course.

The Roman Catholic Church itself was still only slowly developing its presence in the national territory. In the post-war period it still had only around six and a half thousand priests, a fraction of the clergy in much smaller countries, and half of these were foreign. By the 1950's the first post-war seminary intakes were beginning to graduate and bear fruit, but it would be a decade-long job for the Catholic Church to really gear up for the modern world. It was not just a question of having priests of course. Perhaps the biggest obstacle was the Catholic Church's traditional alignment to the wealthy and powerful classes in a time of increasing poverty, on the topic of which it had nothing concrete to say. It began to be widely seen as "a church that traded in spiritual verities while ignoring the material plight of the masses."[77] Beyond these 'spiritual verities' it seemed devoid of content, a "Catholicism of pretty words and exterior acts."[78] While ICAB was ready to provide answers to some immediate problems of the day, it was not attempting to develop long-term sustainable ways to address the new range of social problems. This the Roman Catholic Church would eventually do, and by the 1960's Brazilian Roman Catholics would be at the forefront of addressing new urban poverty and a range of new injustices – and dictatorships – across Latin America. Among other things this would lead to the development of Liberation Theology.

Desperate need demanded that the sense of the sacral, culturally innate in Latin Americans, forge new connections to the realm of the practical. The sacral had to refind its place in the secular.[79] This would also mean no longer ignoring the undeniable political dimension of the Church. This did not necessarily mean creating a political role for the Church, as is often assumed. Liberation Theologians generally did not want a return to Christendom "when the church *directly* wielded political power."[80] They generally accepted the modern understanding that politics is the business of the State, and agreed to work within the tendency to "cordon off the church in the apolitical realm of values and ideals."[81] But they would debate how these values and ideals are to be put into action and not just remain as pretty words. Liberation Theology would inadvertently vindicate Duarte Costa's ecumenical approach in a sense, recognizing that "many people of good will from other religions are able to take the option that Jesus took. Thus they follow Jesus in practice much more than those who merely profess a formal ritualistic allegiance to Christianity."[82] In order to successfully reach out to the people the Roman Catholic Church would eventually learn to be more flexible, diverse, and 'all things to all men'; less dogmatic and doctrinaire; more accepting of different values; more accommodating of Brazil's other religions; and also a little more revolutionary. But Duarte Costa could have told them all this ten years previously.

Notes

1.   The Archbishop of Caracas, Lucas Guillermo Castillo Hernández, published in *La Religión*, Caracas, 11th November 1946, an exhaustive report titled 'Abnormal, Fraudulent, Heretical, or Simply Scandalous?' The subtitle to the report read 'The story of a sadly famous case. – The priesthood-mania of a young adventurer.
- Shocking audacity, obstinacy, and stupidity. – Poverty of intellect, sacrilegious fraud. – Theft, falsification of documents, and much much more.' The subject of the article was Luis Fernando Castillo Mendez. Cf. Aureo Yépez Castillo, *La Universidad Católica Andrés Bello: en el marco histórico-educativo de los Jesuitas en Venezuela*, Universidad Católica Andrés Bello, Caracas, 1994, p 106

2.   Padre Florence Marie [Florêncio Maria] Dubois, *O Ex-Bispo de Maura e o Bom Senso [The Ex-Bishop of Maura and Common Sense]*, Editora Vozes Limitada, Petrópolis-Rio de Janeiro-São Paulo, 1945, p 19 – Dubois astutely predicted that a multitude of bishops would become a defining feature of ICAB.

3.   Cf. *Luta!* issue 5, June 1948, p 17

4.   In spite of his Church's name, and in spite of his penchant for all things candle-lit, gilded, and incensed, Ferraz had never been a Roman Catholic. As such it is important to note that he was not subject to Roman Catholic Canon Law, and therefore incurred no censure at all for being ordained bishop. He certainly did not lose the friends he

had cultivated in the Catholic hierarchy, and there was no reason why he should. See Dom Raimundo de Oliveira, *Dom Salomão Ferraz e o Ecumenismo [Dom Salomão Ferraz and Ecumenism]*, Feira de Santana, Bahia, undated, pp 48ff

5   Cf. *Luta!* issue 10, January 1950, p 42, and issue 11, April 1950, p 38. Duarte Costa acquired a habit of using the back pages of *Luta!* to denounce ICAB's traitors and defectors.

6   Cf. Dom Raimundo de Oliveira, *Dom Salomão Ferraz e o Ecumenismo [Dom Salomão Ferraz and Ecumenism]*, Feira de Santana, Bahia, undated, pp 52ff – "Elected bishop of the Free Catholic Church, the problem of the necessary ordination arose (…). … Finally, the opportunity presented itself via agreements with the Bishop of Maura, Dom Carlos Duarte Costa" (op. cit. pp 52-53).

7   It is tempting to speculate about the gap between Vargas's appointment (Oct. 1945) and installation as bishop in (Dec. 1946) – did someone change their mind about making Vargas a bishop, and then relent?

8   Cf. Obispo Alejo Pelypenko, *Infiltración Comunista en las Iglesias Cristianas de América*, Pia Sociedad de San Pablo, Buenos Aires, 1961, p 130

9   Duarte Costa, 'Manifesto', in *Luta!* issue 12, Sept. 1950, pp 14-15

10   Duarte Costa would eventually ordain his last bishop only a week before his death, in a last attempt to finally unite ICAB and provide it with a protégé to restore order.

11   The Archbishop of Caracas, Monsignor Lucas Guillermo Castillo Hernández, in *La Religión*, 11th November 1946, quoted in Aureo Yépez Castillo, *La Universidad Católica Andrés Bello: en el marco histórico-educativo de los Jesuitas en Venezuela*, p 106. Whatever forces guided Castillo Mendez he would go on to minister as a bishop for a remarkable sixty-one years.

12   Dubois, p 19

13   A note on Castillo Mendez's names: 'Castillo Mendez' conforms to the Hispanic double surname (unhyphenated) custom of keeping both the father's surname and then the mother's surname, (paternal+maternal). In everyday use, the second (maternal) surname may be dropped, so that, for example, Luis Fernando Castillo Mendez may usually be called Luis Castillo. In Brazil, the double surname custom is reversed to maternal+paternal, but with the maternal surname *still* being dropped in everyday use. Since Luis Fernando Castillo Mendez was a Venezuelan who settled in Brazil, he is sometimes found in documents referred to as 'Mendez' or 'Dom Mendez' in the short surname form, just as Carlos Duarte Costa becomes 'Costa' in the short form, not Duarte. In his native land, the short form of Castillo Mendez would be 'Castillo.' For

117

maximum clarity the present text uses 'Castillo Mendez.' The hyphenated form 'Castillo-Mendez', occasionally found in English-language texts, has nothing to do with either Brazilian or Hispanic custom and is avoided completely in the present text. Furthermore, Castillo Mendez's first name is here presented in its original form 'Luis' rather than the Brazilian form 'Luiz' which is occasionally found in Brazilian-origin texts.

[14] The story of Castillo Mendez's early years was pieced together between 1944 and 1948 and published in two editions of *Adsum,* journal of the Archdiocese of Caracas, with ample photostats of original and originally-forged documents, Issues 107 of November 1946 and 128 of August 1948. These researches were greatly added to and meticulously verified by Rodrigo Conde Tudanca in 'Un Incidente Olvidado del Trienio Adeco: La Creacion de la Iglesia Católica, Apostólica, Venezolana' [A Forgotten Incident of the Adeco Period: The Creation of the Venezuelan Catholic Apostolic Church], in *Boletín CIHEV (Centro de Investigación de Historia Eclesiastica Venezolana)* No. 8, Yr. 5, Jan.-June 1993, pp 41-81, and in *Boletín de la Academia Nacional de la Historia,* Caracas, No. 302, Apr.-June 1993, pp.87-117) and Aureo Yépez Castillo (Ch. 10 of his *La Universidad Católica Andrés Bello,* 1994).

[15] As all Castillo Mendez's grades were below 10 (out of 30), he added a number '1' before all his grades, so that they seemed neither catastrophically bad nor unconvincingly brilliant – 9/30 became 19/30, 7/30 became 17/30 and so on. Below average grades (the 'amended' versions), certainly, but not warranting expulsion after one semester.

[16] 'Divine Shepherdess', named after one of Venezuela's most important religious icons, which is housed in Barquisimeto.

[17] Yépez Castillo, p 106

[18] *Luta!* Issue 7, August 1948, pp 16-18

[19] *Luta!* Issue 7, August 1948, p 16

[20] Also known as the Picpus Fathers.

[21] Two weeks before Castillo Mendez's sixteenth birthday.

[22] *Adsum,* issue 128 (August 1948), pp 211f

[23] Letter from the Bishop of Solsona's Secretary to the Secretary of the Archbishopric of Caracas in *Adsum,* 128 (Aug. 1948), p 212. Under a cloud due to this affair, Bishop Comellas passed away some months later.

[24] Letter from the Apostolic Nunciature in Spain, San Sebastián, to the Most Excellent and Most Reverend Monsignor Don Valentín Comellas y Santamaria, Bishop of Solsona, 30th August 1944.

[25] Letter from the Apostolic Nunciature at San Sebastián, Spain, 30th August 1944.

26   Cf. Fr. Francisco Maldonado in *El País* (Caracas), 8th November 1946, quoted in Conde Tudanca, p 97

27   Letter from the ship's chaplain, 1st February 1945, in *Adsum*, No. 128 (Aug. 1948), pp 215-216

28   A thorough explanation of the Church's and Castillo Mendez's roles in the Adeco period is found in Rodrigo Conde Tudanca, 'Un Incidente Olvidado del Trienio Adeco: La Creacion de la Iglesia Católica, Apostólica, Venezolana' [A Forgotten Incident of the Adeco Period: The Creation of the Venezuelan Catholic Apostolic Church], in *Boletín CIHEV* No. 8, Yr. 5, Semester Jan.-June 1993, pp 41-81, also in *Boletín de la Academia Nacional de la Historia*, Caracas, No. 302, (Apr.-June 1993) pp 87-117

29   Rodrigo Conde Tudanca, p 89. See also Alberto Micheo and Luis Ugalde, 'Proceso Historico de la Iglesia Venezolana', in Various Authors, *Historia General de la Iglesia en America Latina; Vol VII: Colombia y Venezuela*, Sigueme, Salamanca, 1981, pp 625-627

30   The Bishop of Coro, Francisco Jose Iturriza, in *La Religion*, 18th March 1945, in Yépez Castillo, p 107

31   Yépez Castillo, p 105

32   Conde Tudanca, p 95

33   Conde Tudanca, p 95

34   Some made-up names were cited, alongside the names of unwitting priests, apparently picked at random.

35   Conde Tudanca, p 96

36   The socialist form of greeting used between members of AD – *compañeros* – and used by Castillo Mendez with regard to his party contacts. Cf. Yépez Castillo, p 126

37   Cf. Yépez Castillo, pp 125-126 and also Cf. Conde Tudanca, pp 112-115

38   Conde Tudanca, p 109

39   Letter to the Papal Nuncio, 13th December 1946, Caracas Archdiocesan Archive, 'Castillo Mendez' file.

40   Cf. *New York Times*, 9th March 1947, p 5

41   Cf. *Luta!* issue 1, January 1947, p 32

42   Conde Tudanca, p 99

43   *Luta!* issue 1, January 1947, p 32 claimed 50 ICAV priests while Venezuelan newspapers were claiming 33. Only three priests could be identified for the decree of excommunication. Castillo Mendez may have revived his old technique of adding extra digits, as with his seminary report card.

44   Conde Tudanca, p 112

45   Conde Tudanca, p 98

46 Letter from Castillo Mendez to the Ministry of Justice asking for a pension, 16th April 1975, Universidad Católica Andrés Bello, Caracas – 'Padre Barnola Papers', also quoted in Conde Tudanca, p 116

47 Conde Tudanca, p 99

48 Conde Tudanca, pp 98-99 [emphasis added]

49 Yépez Castillo, p 106 [emphasis added]

50 Omar Estacio, 'Opinion', in *El Universal* (Caracas), 6th February 2006, "Born in 1922, Luis Castillo Mendez attempted, without success, to complete his studies in the seminaries of San Cristóbal, Minor, and Barquisimeto, run by the French Fathers of Palo Grande and San José de Los Teques, from where he is [sic] expelled for poor grades and for dressing up as a woman, which earned him – among the other seminarians – a designation which we will not repeat here, because we do not want anyone to infer an allusion to a third party." http://www.eluniversal.com/2006/02/06/imp_opi_art_06490AA [accessed 26th March 2018] and http://enopinion.tripod.com/salven_al_hermano.htm [accessed 26th March 2018]

51 Conde Tudanca, pp 109-110

52 Luta! issue 6, July 1948, p 18

53 Conde Tudanca, p 110

54 Conde Tudanca, p 109

55 Rodolfo José Cárdenas, quoted in Yépez Castillo, p 122

56 Conde Tudanca, p 100

57 Ramón Cortada Battle, quoted in Conde Tudanca, p 111

58 Conde Tudanca, p 100

59 Cf. Conde Tudanca, pp 100-101

60 Cf. Dom Estêvão Bettencourt OSB, in *Pergunte e Responderemos*, Number 55, July 1962, online version at http://www.pr.gonet.biz/revista.php [accessed 05/04/2018]

61 Cf. *Luta!* issue 9, October 1949, p 36

62 Câmara Municipal de São Paulo, Seção de Protocólo, [City Hall, Protocol Section], case 3779 of 1963

63 Cf. *Luta!* issue 17, October 1952, p 31

64 Cf. *Luta!* issue 17, October 1952, p 31

65 Born 3rd February 1891, joined ICAB in June 1950, was ordained Deacon and Priest a month later. Consecrated Bishop 15th August 1954.

66 Cf. *Luta!* issue 22, July 1955, pp 3ff

67 Cf. *Luta!* issue 23, March 1956, pp 78-79

68 Cf. Pelypenko, p 140, lists six bishops: Duarte Costa, de Souza, Vargas, Castillo Mendez, Silva, Costa.

69   Future Cardinal Archbishop of Santiago, Carlos Oviedo Cavada, confirmed this, writing of the Arce case (they were contemporaries) in 'Obispos Irregulares' [Bishops Irregular], Pontifical Catholic University of Chile, 1986, pp 207-219 – https://repositorio.uc.cl/handle/11534/16821 [accessed 10th April 2018]

70   *Luta!* issue 23, March 1956, p 66 – *'ICAB condemns the crimes of Dom Luiz'*

71   *Luta!* issue 23, March 1956, p 66

72   Cf. *Luta!* issue 10, January 1950, p 42, also Cf. *Luta!* issue 11, April 1950, p 45

73   Cf. *Luta!* issue 10, January 1950, p 39

74   Cf. *Diario da Manha*, Tuesday 12th June 1956, p 8

75   Cf. *Luta!* issue 1, January 1947, p 29

76   *Luta!* issue 1, January 1947, p 29

77   Daniel M. Bell Jr., 'State and Civil Society', Chapter 29 in Peter Scott and William T. Cavanaugh (eds), *The Blackwell Companion to Political Theology*, Blackwell, Oxford, 2004, [pp 423-438], p 430

78   Thales de Azevedo, *O Catolicismo no Brasil [Catholicism in Brazil]*, Government of Brazil: Ministry of Education and Culture, Rio de Janeiro, 1955, p 21

79   Cf. Thomas C. Bruneau, *The Political Transformation of The Brazilian Catholic Church*, p 61

80   Bell, p 430 [emphasis added]

81   Bell, p 430, pp 430-431

82   Michael Amaladoss SJ, *Life in Freedom – Liberation Theologies from Asia*, Orbis, Maryknoll, 1997, p 95

V

"THE CHURCH'S DOORS WILL ALWAYS BE OPEN"[1] BUT "WHAT DOES 'CANONICAL' MEAN?"[2]
— ICAB in a conciliar age —

At the start of 1958 Duarte Costa still saw himself as "relentlessly persecuted"[3] by the followers of his old adversary Pius XII, who was now in the 19th year of his long Pontificate. Duarte Costa, under his own Pontificate, now had five active bishops: Alves de Souza, Vargas, Castillo Mendez, Dos Santos Silva, and Pereira da Costa, only two of whom took advantage of the permission to be married.[4] Castillo Mendez had recently been obliged to join his forgiving sponsor in Rio de Janeiro, where Duarte Costa could keep an eye on him. Castillo Mendez did, however, escape the attentions of Aleksei (Alejo in the Spanish form) Pelypenko, an exiled Ukrainian bishop dedicated to uncovering Communist sympathies in Catholic quarters. Aleksei Pelypenko appeared on the scene at this time and turned his attentions to ICAB, in what would become a revealing first-hand report, published in 1961.

Through Aleksei Pelypenko we enjoy, for the first time, a critical outsider's view into the world of ICAB. We meet the flesh and blood individuals who comprised it, still in its relatively early days. Pelypenko's main contact in ICAB was Michel Von Roeder[5] Michels, a "friendly and likeable"[6] priest in his thirties who was ordained by Duarte Costa around 1955.[7] As well as fashionable ICAB-gray suits Von Roeder Michels claimed degrees in medicine and theology and was well-versed in scripture, according to

Pelypenko,[8] but was in fact a veterinarian.[9] Von Roeder Michels was Duarte Costa's secretary at the time, though he lived 900 km from Rio de Janeiro in Curitiba, Paraná. In Pelypenko's assessment Von Roeder Michels took all the decisions.[10] Pelypenko visited his new friend's house and found it "an old wreck, neglected, needing constant repairs to avoid collapse."[11] The front room contained an altar.[12] Von Roeder Michels was blasé about ICAB, calling it a "Catholic Church, identical to the Roman one, with the only difference that it has no Pope."[13] Did he hope thus to ingratiate himself with the Orthodox Pelypenko? Von Roeder Michels claimed that the 20,000 ICAB faithful in Paraná had elected him bishop (Pelypenko believed the real figure to be "a few dozen"[14]) but he wanted at least two bishops to consecrate him, with at least one bishop in a state of canonical regularity – would Pelypenko assist? "Your wish is in reality a dream, which can never be realized"[15] came the reply. This would become a familiar pattern for ICAB and its offshoot clergies, attempting to 'regularize' or legitimize their status and meeting with failure.

Von Roeder Michels was able to shed light on the reality of life in the ICAB clergy: "all our priests, as also bishops, are under the direct authority of Dom Carlos, of Rio, since Dom Carlos does not trust any of our bishops and does not concede them more authority than to the priests."[16] Von Roeder Michels claimed to have studied philosophy and theology under Duarte Costa[17] but it is not clear how this had been carried out. Nor is it clear whether this was before or after ICAB's seminary in Rio de Janeiro was shut down by the police "for reasons of immorality and counterfeiting of money"[18] according to Estêvão Bettencourt, another keen ICAB observer. Dom Estêvão Bettencourt OSB was a highly respected Benedictine priest who in 1956 had founded a popular magazine aimed at answering people's theological questions in plain language – *Pergunte e Responderemos* – Ask and We Will Answer. "The intellectual and moral formation of [ICAB's] 'ministers' is very substandard,"[19] Bettencourt wrote; "the candidate may, in some cases, obtain priestly ordination within eight days."[20]

Pelypenko also met a priest called Raúl Clementino Smania – an active Freemason, as many ICAB priests were[21] – of Italian descent. Smania was employed as a nurse at the army hospital, but according to Pelypenko he was "illiterate"[22] and "of minimal culture."[23] When asked what he thought about ICAB not being a Church in a canonical sense, Smania asked "what does 'canonical' mean?"[24] Smania was one of Antídio José Vargas's priests, though of course he too reported directly to Duarte Costa. In spite of ICAB's core principle that priests could – and should – have a profession of their choice, Smania was forced to choose between his demanding job with the army and ICAB. When he chose to stick with his day job he was considered a "traitor."[25] Pelypenko and Bettencourt were not the only ones compelled to write about ICAB in this period. Others included the Roman Catholic bishops of the Province of Belo Horizonte. They published their views on 12th April 1958, casting doubt on the validity of ICAB's actions:

> "There is no shortage of eminent theologians who put in doubt the ordinations of the *'Igreja Brasileira'* ... The opinion of these theologians is based on the fact that the 'Bishop of Maura' and his followers lack the intention to do what the Church does. Although they pronounce the right words in slavish imitation of the rites and formulas, in reality they do not want to do what the Church does, because they ordain priests to live outside of and against the unity of the true Church, to teach dogmas different and antagonistic to those which the Church teaches, to administer sacraments whose efficacy they no longer maintain as the Church does. They do *like* the Church does, but they do not do *what* the Church does."[26]

Damning stuff, to which no published ICAB response survives, but Pelypenko did not notice any deceleration in the activity of ICAB's priests. Bishop Antídio José Vargas caused Pelypenko the most anxiety, being in his assessment severely mentally ill. Vargas proudly showed Pelypenko his huge church with adjacent buildings and a seminary – all paid for by donations from the parish, Vargas said.[27] But Fathers Von Roeder Michels and Smania said that Vargas had only about 20 families backing him, and not wealthy ones.[28] Where did the money come from then, Pelypenko wondered. Soon, Vargas inadvertently began to offer Pelypenko an explanation. "I have reliable information that the local Roman Catholic bishop, a damned German, intends to burn down my church ... . It is true, I have proof."[29] As predicted, a few days later, the church burned down. Fortuitously the pews, ornaments, books, chalice, vestments, and everything else of value had been moved to the church hall just before the fire. To Pelypenko's mind this farce had two objectives – to collect on the insurance, obviously, and to provide fuel for further diatribes against the dastardly Roman Catholics[30] – "I was a witness of how 'Bishop' Antídio, foaming at the mouth, goaded his parishioners." Pelypenko wrote,

> "'The Communists – he [Vargas] said – hold no fear for us! In Soviet Russia the Church is flourishing and there the government helps the bishops; who holds fear for us are the Romanists! They burned down our church, they undermine the government, and our Governor is a thief – he is a Romanist and he supports the Romanists!'"[31]

These words convinced Pelypenko that ICAB was secretly a puppet of the Communists – "a subversive and astute work of the enemy of God, of the Holy Church."[32] Vargas's line of argument is certainly very Duarte Costa *á la* early ICAB – pro-Soviet and anti-'Romanist.' It all helped to cultivate the image of being "relentlessly persecuted."[33] Even the Germans had not given up on attacking ICAB, Vargas insisted, but the "damned German"[34] bishop that Vargas referred to was of course the Franciscan Daniel Hostin, a Brazilian, who had himself ordained Vargas in 1938.

"The *igreja brasileira* has no organization, nor definite credo, and each priest gets by as best he can",[35] a disillusioned ICAB priest confessed to Pelypenko; "they promised me mountains of gold when they invited me to take part."[36] This was Father Vasquez, a young *Fidei Donum* priest from Spain. *Fidei Donum* was, in the first place, the title of an encyclical letter by Pope Pius XII which underlined that the missionary task of the Church was not over and done with.

On the basis of *Fidei Donum* – the 'Gift of God' – the Church, especially in Italy and Spain, arranged to send diocesan priests to mission territories. The terms were to be stipulated between the sending and receiving dioceses. After arriving in Brazil, Father Vasquez found himself in a most predictable predicament – he fell in love. At the time Pelypenko met him, Vasquez had a common law wife (not yet divorced), two children, and both health and money problems.[37] ICAB was supposed to have been his salvation as he had few chances of employment, was not well enough to do physical labor, and his religious visa was invalidated as soon as he quit the Catholic Church. Vasquez begged Pelypenko to intervene on his behalf with Von Roeder Michels – who controlled everything in ICAB – in order to secure him a job in Von Roeder's vast parish of 20,000 souls. Pelypenko rudely awakened Vasquez to the fact that there was no such parish. Surely a pitiful state of affairs in which Vasquez felt abandoned by ICAB – "the main foundations of this ecclesiastical movement are lies and deception, trickery and exploitation"[38], he concluded.

ICAB could no doubt give cause to feel despondent, and Bishop Ferraz, by this time 78 years old, began enquiring about the possibility of being accepted into the Roman Catholic Church. Much of his long ministry had been pointing in this general direction – his tastes had always been broadly Catholic and he had won influential Roman Catholic friends. Even so, he had taken sides with the firebrands of *anti*-Roman Catholicism. But Ferraz himself had never been a Catholic – he owed no allegiance to Rome, and was not subject to Canon Law. He had therefore committed no schism, heresy, or apostasy, since only a Roman Catholic can be subject to Roman Catholic Canon Law. There was no impediment to him joining the Roman Catholic Church. However, this was early to mid-1958, the Church of the old days before Ecumenism and Religious Freedom. In order to convert, Ferraz was told, he would have to renounce his status as a bishop and priest – not because of his schismatic past, but because of his Protestant past. He would even have had to submit to being re-baptized – his Presbyterian baptism could not be trusted as valid (norms of Ecumenism after the Second Vatican Council would expressly rule out the need for a second baptism, as long as the first followed the Trinitarian formula). These requirements were unacceptable to Ferraz. His timing was just a little premature though – a new era was about to dawn in Rome too.

At the same time that Ferraz was looking longingly in the direction of Rome, *from* Rome came a young Roman Catholic priest whose future would intertwine with ICAB's. Luigi Mascolo[39] was born in Irsina, a small town in the Basilicata region of Italy. To this day it is the least developed Italian region – the provincial capital, Matera, is the only one in the country that does not have a railway station. Mascolo was born on 7th January 1927 and was guided towards the priesthood from childhood, as was normal in that time and place. His seminary studies were interrupted by the Nazi occupation of Italy in late 1943, when the seminary was requisitioned for military use. The seminarians had to flee on foot at the start of a harsh winter. They were split up and eventually reallocated to other seminaries. The war was going badly for the Nazis – as they retreated north through Italy, the desperate need for labor back home in Germany intensified the practice of *rastrellamento* – 'raking-up' forced labor, press-ganging civilians for deportation. One day, Mascolo and others were apprehended in the street and herded into trucks heading northeast. Mascolo looked for his chance and managed to jump off the truck unseen. He made good his escape and hid in the woods, before eventually reaching the town of Facen di Pedavena in Veneto, where he was taken in by the parish priest until the end of the war. He returned home to Irsina after the war to a rapturous welcome – his family had heard nothing from him and had feared the worst. Italy had been cut in two by civil war, and there had been no way to send news home. His regular schooling as well as his seminary studies had been interrupted by the war, and he remained for several years assisting the parish priest in Pedavena. When he did return home, as he was not at that time a seminarian, he was liable for peacetime military draft service of 12 to 18 months. At some point he returned to continue his seminary studies up to the philosophy years, first needing to finish high school studies. He then went on to study theology at the Angelicum in Rome, studying under the Dominicans Garrigou Lagrange and Raimondo Spiazzi.

This accumulation of delays was such that Mascolo was not ordained priest until 7th December 1957 (aged almost 31, unusually late for his generation) with the consolation that his ordination took place at Saint Paul's in Rome. He celebrated his first Mass the following day, the Feast of the Immaculate Conception, in the Basilica of Saint Mary Major. That same year saw the beginning of *Fidei Donum* missionary service for diocesan priests. Pope Pius XII's encyclical *Fidei Donum* was primarily an initiative aimed at promoting service in Africa, but attention quickly turned to Latin America as well. On this pretext, on 16th September 1959 Luigi Mascolo arrived in Brazil, and seems to have tried out various roles without finding his niche. There was disquiet in the heart of the Italian priest, and he began to feel a calling to something new – and right at that moment he heard about ICAB. He would not be the first *Fidei Donum* priest to jump ship and join ICAB. The ironic fact is that the Pope who excommunicated Carlos Duarte Costa in 1945 wrote the document which would provide Brazil with Duarte Costa's eventual successor, Luigi Mascolo.

In similarity to the new arrival from Italy, Bishop Salomão Barbosa Ferraz had also been experiencing disquiet, as did the married priests of his Free Catholic Church. These latter, balancing work, family, and church life, deserted with regularity, or found other organizations to join.[40] "Dom Salomão was highly criticized, furthermore, for the fact that he preached unity between the Churches while he himself, in fact, had founded a new one, [two in fact – the Free Catholic Church and the Order of Saint Andrew] thus increasing the number of dissident religious institutions."[41] These were the final pushes that he needed to reopen dialogue with the Roman Catholics, and this time he was much more favorably received – it was now the Papacy of John XXIII, and

Ferraz was embraced in the spirit of the age of ecumenism to come. On 8th December 1959, the Feast of the Immaculate Conception, at eight-thirty in the morning, in the Chapel of the Child Jesus, Dom Salomão, before His Eminence Cardinal Carlos Carmelo de Vasconcellos Motta, made a profession of faith and signed a corresponding act of commitment. Many were in attendance. Thus he was received into the Roman Catholic Church as Bishop Superior of the Order of Saint Andrew. The Cardinal spoke about the significance of the event and blessed Dom Salomão's episcopal ring. At nine o'clock, Dom Salomão celebrated his first Mass as a Roman Catholic Bishop, with Father Nicola Rossetti SJ and Monsignor Costa Neves as acolytes. At four o'clock that afternoon the 'new' bishop was received by Cardinal Motta in the *Palácio Pio XII*. The modest Chapel of the Child Jesus had evidently been chosen in order to assure discretion – "either because the event, in the understanding of the organizers, was of no great importance, or in order to avoid any undesirable clamor on the part of the Roman Catholic public."[42] They need not have worried about mass demonstrations calling for the end of clerical celibacy: "as was to be expected, [the Catholic faithful] regretted the Roman Church's having received into its clergy a formerly dissident married bishop, with a wife, in full state of matrimony and with seven children – in short a normal family life."[43] Dom Salomão experienced regrets too – he continued to say Mass every day but now in Latin, and he felt that it had lost meaning. It would be the first of several disappointments. On 30th December he was set to fly to Rome to meet the Pope, and he began preparing a petition to have the Order of Saint Andrew received (along with their wives) into the Roman Catholic Church. He woke up on the first day of 1960 in the *Pensionato Romano* in Rome, hoping to be quickly received by the Holy Father, but was in fact destined to spend the next few weeks doing the tourist rounds in Rome and environs.[44] Ferraz's reception into the Church had come, of all things, amid increasing controversy over the future of compulsory clerical celibacy.[45] Significantly he was not invited to attend the Roman Synod held that January, even though he was staying right there in Rome. At this Synod Pope John XXIII was obliged to vigorously reaffirm the Church's commitment to a celibate priesthood, exceptions notwithstanding and not even mentioned. Obviously, the presence of a married bishop with seven children could only have added an element of farce and embarrassment to the Synod proceedings. Had Ferraz's reception into the Church been a mistake? "In early February [Ferraz's] secretary, acting on superior orders, advised Dom Salomão not to celebrate any further Masses, until his certificate of consecration arrived from São Paulo."[46] The delays unsettled Ferraz – blame fell on the postal service, and the slow-turning wheels of bureaucracy, but was the Vatican having second thoughts? At least one Cardinal seemed to be under the impression that Ferraz was not married, but widowed.[47] It was at least unlikely that the bishop would father any more children – on 18th February, while still 'holidaying' in Rome, Ferraz turned 80. Nine days later a fresh set of consecration papers finally arrived – replacements for those 'lost' in the post, and one further week later he was authorized to say Mass. But it was not all good news from the Vatican – Ferraz was now asked to sign a declaration that, at age 80, his marriage was effectively chaste and inactive – a sort of celibacy. Ferraz refused, saying "There will be no blemish on my family."[48] Regardless, on 25th March he finally had his audience with the Pope – Ferraz later stated that the Pope had personally commissioned him to labor to bring the 'separated brethren' of Latin America – the schismatics and dissidents – back into the fold.[49]

Certainly the Church was changing before everyone's eyes; before returning to Brazil, Ferraz attended the investiture of seven new Cardinals in Saint Peter's – the names of a further three new Cardinals, working behind the Iron Curtain, were not made public. This was not the only sign of the times at the March 1960 Consistory. Three of the seven named Cardinals were non-Europeans: Cardinal Doi of Tokyo, Cardinal Santos of Manila, who was aged only 51, and Cardinal Rugambwa of Tanzania, who was only 47. Compare this to previous investitures – the 1953 and 1958 Consistories included only one Asian between them – Cardinal Gracias of Bombay – and no Africans; the new Cardinals of 1953 and 1958 had an average age of 64 and 68 respectively.

On 8th April 1960, Ferraz headed home to Brazil, shaken and perturbed by his own situation – clearly there was unease about his presence in the Church, both in Rome and in São Paulo.[50] What do we make of Ferraz's handling by Rome? In the climate of increasing debate over clerical celibacy, there was understandable apprehension – a little late in the day – over the sudden appearance of a married bishop. Married *priests,* on the other hand, have always been a feature of the wider Church, and at 80 years old Ferraz was never going to have a 'full' episcopal ministry anyway – he would have a nominal position in the hierarchy, but no executive power. And this would still be dependent on his coming round to the idea of signing that 'chastity' declaration – Ferraz did not appear in the *Annuarium Pontificium* until 1963.

For ICAB, Ferraz's reception into the Roman Catholic Church with his credentials for the most part intact was understandably assumed to be a great precedent,[51] but this was not strictly accurate – in fact, Ferraz's was a unique case and would not precede any other similar one. It was certainly unprecedented. Ferraz had taken part in a schism, clearly, but without being personally guilty of schism. Furthermore, he was not only innocent in the eyes of Canon Law – since only Catholics can be subject to it – he also spent several decades making friends and building up goodwill among the Roman Catholics. Sacramentally, his episcopal consecration in 1945 came before ICAB was legally obliged to create its own rites – Ferraz was therefore a respected (Protestant) Christian, consecrated using the Roman Rite by a Catholic bishop, without incurring sanction under Canon Law.[52] It would be next to impossible for such a precise combination of factors to coincide again. Aleksei Pelypenko opined that Ferraz's departure was no great loss to ICAB – "The defection of Salomão Ferraz from 'ICAB' should not cause it too many problems; on the contrary, it could even benefit 'ICAB.'"[53] After all, Pelypenko explained, all Ferraz and Duarte Costa had ever done was quarrel, and this would probably now mean the end of Ferraz's rival dissident churches, leaving the field clear for ICAB. However, with the supposed Ferraz 'precedent' the seed of doubt had been planted among the priests and bishops of ICAB – the Roman Catholic Church, with its security, eternity and certainties, might take them back with their ordained status intact; that door may still be open. As we shall see, all future attempts to play the 'Ferraz card' would come to nothing. It is crucial to remember that even while Ferraz the newly received married Catholic bishop was being fêted in Rome, the Pope was reaffirming at the January 1960 Synod that clerical celibacy would remain the rule.

Luta! and the municipal archives tell us about more comings and goings of the time – on 15th November 1959 Bishop Alves de Souza had finally been confirmed as Bishop of São Paulo – it seems he had been 'acting Bishop' since 12th May 1952, after the resignation of Ferraz. Exactly six months later, on 12th May 1960 – eight years to the day he took over in São Paulo – Alves de Souza died aged just 48. This time it really was a great loss for ICAB – as well as a loyal bishop the Church also lost de Souza's valuable connections within Freemasonry.[54] A young priest called Milton Cunha, who had only been ordained priest by Duarte Costa on 18th December 1958, took over in São Paulo[55] and was consecrated Bishop the following month, June 1960. Two months later, on 31st July 1960, Duarte Costa consecrated his penultimate bishop, José Barbosa dos Anjos, as the first diocesan bishop of Natal, Rio Grande do Norte.[56] As in Rome, this was most definitely a time when a new guard was forming the ICAB ranks, and in precisely this atmosphere the Italian *Fidei Donum* priest Luigi Mascolo fell in with them. It was almost a case of a revolving door – Ferraz was received into the Catholic Church and heading to the Vatican just three months after Mascolo had arrived *from* Italy. In spite of all the trials and tribulations he had overcome in order to get to the priesthood, Mascolo had been a Roman Catholic priest for less than three years before succumbing to the dual attractions of ICAB and life in Brazil. How can we interpret this turnaround in the pious, Rome-educated young priest? His maturation into a schismatic priest and future bishop did not come out of the blue.

Mascolo had been immersed in a unique theological atmosphere, Rome in the years immediately preceding Vatican II. The Church was gearing up to face the modern world – talk of reform was everywhere, and Mascolo was not detached from it. He had studied theology under Father Raimondo Spiazzi OP, an Italian Dominican whose progressive views reached a climax in 1959 with a controversial article which dismantled the historical bases for priestly celibacy.[57] Spiazzi and this school of thought were unequivocally slapped down by Pope John XXIII at the subsequent Roman Synod in January 1960[58] – from which Ferraz was notably left out – but calls for a debate on the issue would grow louder in the approach to Vatican II.[59] As for Spiazzi himself, the controversy saw him banished from Rome – but how much was his former student, Luigi Mascolo, influenced by the outspoken Dominican? There is surely no doubt that once he arrived in Brazil, faced with the living reality of Catholic (ICAB) priests who were either married or free to find a girlfriend – and not obliged to actually marry – something slotted into place for Luigi Mascolo. His defection then took weeks rather than years to reach fruition. The effect of having been nurtured in the progressive pre-Vatican II atmosphere of Rome under forward-thinking theologians should not be underestimated. Spiazzi's writings would later be quoted, also, in support of theologians' arguments in favor of greater roles for women in the Church, including priesthood.[60]

Reform was very much in the air in June 1960 when Ferraz launched his campaign for the use of Portuguese in the liturgy. It was a low-key campaign because, bishop or not, the 'cathedral' assigned to him was a small chapel in the maternity hospital. He did, however, send a formal request to the Pope. On 3rd August Ferraz led his married priests of the Order of Saint Andrew in making a Catholic profession of faith, as a step closer to drawing them into the Roman Catholic fold. He continued to take his special ecumenical mission seriously – openly attending services in the Presbyterian and Episcopal churches. On 10th August the Nuncio chastised Ferraz for assorted misdemeanors, especially for conducting the marriage of an ex-priest who was already civilly married, leaving Ferraz disgruntled. Five days later he celebrated his anniversary – 15 years since the day Duarte Costa had consecrated him bishop – and with all the quarrels, spats, and clashes going on, Ferraz may have felt that little had changed for him since 1945.

By this time Duarte Costa appeared "elderly, a person with his nervous system destroyed, who after all he lived through, his life and emotions and religious practices led him to psychical anomaly."[61] He reigned over a dysfunctional organization and still found it impossible to delegate.[62] The clergy count at this point, according to Pelypenko, was 10 bishops and 98 priests, and he believed that two new bishops were destined for Bolivia – there is no other record of this, however.[63] Duarte Costa had already named his successor in the Rio de Janeiro diocese – Bishop Pedro dos Santos Silva, his coadjutor. But as the other bishops began to fight over succession, Duarte Costa decided that Dos Santos Silva would become "General Supervisor" as well.[64] Shortly before his death, however, Duarte Costa decided to appoint a co-successor. His final protégé would be his last general secretary, José Aires da Cruz, a thirty-three year-old unmarried bank official[65] (c. 1927-1988). Aires da Cruz was named Auxiliary Bishop of Rio de Janeiro and Bishop of Guanabara. Power was to be divided between him and Dos Santos Silva.[66] Aires da Cruz was duly consecrated bishop on 19th March 1961. Exactly one week later, Carlos Duarte Costa, 72, died of a liver ailment.[67] The following day O Globo reported a "great number of members of the public and no small number of priests of the Brazilian Catholic Church"[68] in attendance at the vigil. Duarte Costa's corpse lay embalmed in an open coffin at the 'National Temple' in Rua do Couto, which would also become his final resting place. The newspaper reported that "Dom Luis [Castillo Mendez], inconsolable, wept."[69] While O Globo called Aires da Cruz the "probable successor",[70] it was Castillo Mendez who was photographed in pole position crying at the head of the coffin. By the following day the official story was that "Bishop Duarte [Costa] died *without* naming a successor"[71] and that one would "be chosen by a conclave of Bishops of the church."[72] By this time Brasilia had become Brazil's capital, and Luis Fernando Castillo Mendez, now aged 38, grabbed the plum role of Bishop of Brasilia before anyone else could – even, he claimed, before the Roman Catholics. It was the beginning of Castillo Mendez's long and ultimately successful campaign to seize control of ICAB.

But in spite of Duarte Costa's failure to secure his overall successor, his choice of successor in Rio de Janeiro, Pedro dos Santos Silva, was respected. Meanwhile, Bishop Antídio José Vargas of Lages, as the most senior bishop both alive and still a member of ICAB, stepped in as caretaker leader. Vargas took the title of "General Supervisor"[73] instead of Dos Santos Silva, as Duarte Costa had intended,[74] and later became "Dean of the National Episcopate" as well.[75] The ICAB Special Council of 1961 recognized the talents of the younger generation – Luigi Mascolo was placed in line for a bishop's job as soon as one became available, thus giving him time to become a naturalized Brazilian.[76] One longer-serving priest, though still only 37 years old – Raimundo Simplicio de Almeida, born in Ceará on 11th June 1924 – was also placed in line for a miter.[77] Before being ordained by Duarte Costa in 1948, Simplicio de Almeida embarked on an ecclesiastical odyssey that almost seems designed to rival that of Castillo Mendez. He went from the Capuchin seminary to the Capuchin novitiate, then switched to the Salvatorian seminary before opting for the Sacramentine order. Then, "persecuted"[78] for undisclosed reasons, Simplicio de Almeida found his spiritual home in ICAB and was ordained deacon and then priest on 17th and 18th January 1948.

Duarte Costa, many felt, had always held down his bishops and priests,[79] but with his passing the bishops were free to exercise their power as they wished. Rather than a power vacuum, everyone could now become a leader. The effect was the *balkanization* of ICAB, which in time would become its prevailing characteristic. The Roman Catholic Bishops' Conference observed that "groups multiply which are alien to the Roman Catholic Apostolic Church, though organized and presented in such a way that they attract the Catholic faithful."[80] Bettencourt tried to explain this multiplication of groups: "[just as] members easily rally to ICAB, they easily turn against it, creating 'internal schisms' or abandoning the movement completely."[81] ICAB clergy "separate from each other, constantly forming new 'churches' under various designations."[82] Bettencourt listed a few offshoots already present in 1962: "Old Catholic Church (Brazilian Branch); Brazilian Orthodox Church; Latin Orthodox Church, and others similar."[83] Compare Bettencourt's modest list to the one compiled by the Catholic Bishops' Conference a decade later:

> "Ecumenical Catholic Apostolic Church; Independent Catholic Apostolic Church; National Catholic Apostolic Church; Christian Catholic Apostolic Church; Trinitarian Catholic Apostolic Church; ... American Orthodox Catholic Church; Free Orthodox Catholic Church; ... Order of the Missionary Messengers of the Divine Word; Congregation of the Missionaries of Christ Eternal Priest; Congregation of the Missionaries of Jesus; Congregation of Saint Joseph; Missionary Society of Saint Mark the Evangelist [and Ecumenical Christian Church of Brazil[84]]."[85]

It is not generally easy to determine which individual ICAB bishops or priests were responsible for these 'internal schisms' as this period also marked the start of ICAB becoming more secretive [86] – membership numbers, for example, were not publicized or perhaps simply not known.[87] In terms of clergy, Bettencourt counted 21 bishops descending from Duarte Costa, and "circa 150 priests"[88] in 1962. So what was the point of ICAB in these years, as far as the clergy saw it? "We have retained everything that is Roman" Von Roeder Michels had told Aleksei Pelypenko frankly, "only our religious services are celebrated not in Latin but in Portuguese."[89] Beyond this, the Roman Catholic Church would lament after Vatican II that ICAB endeavored to keep Catholicism firmly in the dark ages; "in the context of ... conciliar renewal, [ICAB] contradicts and prejudices everything that the Council desires."[90]

137

Dom Salomão Ferraz was certainly focused on his ecumenical objectives – on 18th October 1961 in the Colégio São Luiz he had organized a conference on the 'Unification of the Churches." He continued to attend services with Anglicans and Presbyterians, especially at the Most Holy Trinity church in São Paulo, to the consternation of his fellow Roman Catholics. He was called before the Nuncio, Dom Armando Lombardi, to explain himself, and Ferraz's secretary Father Rossetti SJ expressed his deep misgivings and dissatisfaction. But in May 1962 Rossetti also brought wonderful news – both of them would be going back to Rome that coming October to attend the Second Vatican Council.[91] In July Ferraz's Order of Saint Andrew held its own Council, reforming its constitution in the hope of increasing its chances of being received into communion with Rome. Ferraz, also seeking to better ingratiate himself to Rome, now dissolved the Free Catholic Church (ICL) after 25 years, transferring its patrimony to the Order of Saint Andrew, which in turn subordinated itself to the Holy Father.[92] With the collapse of the ICL, ICAB saw a competitor leave the field, but this was the extent of the effect of Vatican II on ICAB. Its rites and doctrines would remain as they were before the Council.[93] In turn, if ICAB influenced the Brazilian Catholic bishops' approach to the Council in any way, the archives do not show it.

What about Ferraz's own effect on ICAB? It is possible that his 'successful' admission into the Roman Catholic Church inspired other ICAB bishops to angle for a 'free trip to Rome." The 'Ferraz effect' evidently took hold of Dom Raimundo Simplicio de Almeida in 1963. He was 38 and one of the most recently consecrated ICAB bishops when he petitioned for readmission to the Roman Catholic Church. It is not clear whether he even requested recognition as a bishop or priest, but in any case he was readmitted on 10th May 1963 as a layman. This would be the standard procedure put in place for all ICAB 'returnees': "Under no circumstances and never, may schismatic bishops expect to be received as bishops into the Catholic Church."[94] Ferraz, crucially, was never a 'schismatic', as only Roman Catholics can be guilty of schism under Canon Law. Ferraz's example gave abortive hope to other ICAB bishops that they too might be accepted back to Rome. As the rumor persists that *two* ICAB bishops were welcomed back to the Roman Catholic Church as bishops, it is worth looking a little more closely at the case of the Chilean Orlando Arce Moya. We perhaps cannot know who the source of the Arce Moya myth could have been, but we can know the truth of the case itself, from Carlos Cardinal Oviedo Cavada, Roman Catholic Archbishop of Santiago. The Cardinal was a contemporary of Orlando Arce Moya, who was "an ex-seminarian from Concepción",[95] never a priest;

> "Mister Arce ... until several years ago lived in Germany, put up by a Salesian community. He has reaffirmed his episcopal ordination but no particular group of faithful or Church recognizes him as such. In the early Seventies he made some overtures to return to Chile, but his intended return came to nothing, because he requested to be recognized as a bishop of the Catholic Church, a request which was not granted."[96]

On 13th January 1964, 37 year-old Luigi Mascolo became a Brazilian citizen,[97] followed by becoming an ICAB bishop on 5th April the same year. He was consecrated bishop by the General Supervisor and senior bishop Antídio José Vargas, thus underlining the continuity of the direct line from Duarte Costa. Vargas was a thoroughly orthodox ICAB and had never defected, and Mascolo was regarded as a conservative choice as well. Mascolo's consecration was welcomed by the old-guard bishops who sought to dissuade any contenders circling like vultures around the vacant leadership position. The right-wing military coup taking place outside did not dampen the mood.[98] This US-backed coup – or the *Golpe de '64* – ousted the elected President by simultaneously encouraging and exploiting a climate of anti-communist fear. Right-wing and military groups organized mass demonstrations in favor of 'the Family, with God, for Freedom' – *Marchas da Família com Deus pela Liberdade*. This motto was reminiscent of the Integralists' slogan which ICAB's 'God, Land and Freedom' was intended to contrast. Later in 1964 Dom Milton Cunha resigned, leaving the diocese of São Paulo vacant for Dom Luigi Mascolo, who would prove the driving force of ICAB for many years. After 1961 ICAB had resolved to hold regular Councils, starting in February 1965.[99] Eight of the ten active bishops were present and they resolved to consecrate at least four more in 1965 – including Michel Von Roeder Michels, who had been elected bishop seven years earlier. The position of General Supervisor, held by the senior bishop, Vargas, was abolished – Vargas became 'Dean of the College of Bishops.'[100] The change of political mood across the continent would see ICAB move distinctly to the right.[101] This re-branding, "taking advantage of the current trend of nationalism in Latin America,"[102] was seen as a purely opportunist move, considering that "Duarte Costa … had been excommunicated [partly] for his pro-Communist views."[103] But the populist strategy seemed to work; "the period of [ICAB's] greatest growth is post-1965," as Wagner Pires da Silva wrote:

> "The changes of the Second Vatican Council arrived in Brazil and put a check on popular Brazilian Catholicism. The actions of the schismatic church, aimed at the most popular level and sacramentalization, with the emphasis on baptisms, confirmations, and weddings, attracted a large number of converts to ICAB."[104]

In addition, ICAB had always underlined its free and easy compatibility with other beliefs and philosophies, and continued to celebrate Masses and other events in Spiritualist centers, at gatherings of Macumba,[105] Candomblé,[106] Umbanda,[107] and in the company of Freemasons and Positivists.[108] The Roman Catholic bishops would admit that "numerous Catholic faithful seek out the temples of this organization,"[109] but they insisted that

> "They do it, for the most part, in good faith, believing that it is not a different church but the Church of their baptism, the Roman Catholic Apostolic one, given that the ministers of the 'igreja brasileira' use the designation 'Catholic' in a misleading way, they use vestments and rites used by the Catholic Church since

time immemorial, they display icons of saints which [the Catholic Church] traditionally venerates, they give themselves the titles of 'father' and 'bishop.'"[110]

ICAB appealed to the common Catholic faithful, the Roman Catholic bishops argued, "above all those of ardent but simple faith and with little formation ... disorientated by the ambiguities of ICAB."[111] Meanwhile, 1965 also saw Dom Ferraz heading for the fourth and final session of Vatican II, departing on 23rd August from Brazil. He was still pushing for recognition and acceptance of his congregation of married priests, the *Ordem de Santo André*, even though all hope now seemed lost. If Rome would not admit the Order, he reflected, he could try to link them to another 'branch' of the Church – the Anglicans for example – or declare it 'independent' like another ICAB – its actual fate.

ICAB planned to consecrate three new bishops in 1966, including one for an attempted branch in Paraguay during the Stroessner dictatorship. Luigi Mascolo consecrated Antonio Ramon Talavera Goiburu[112] on 21st June 1966, appointing him Primate of Paraguay. Word reached them that the Stroessner government was not eager to have an anti-Roman Catholic movement to upset relations with the Vatican, in spite of ICAB's nationalist credentials, and Talavera contented himself with lurking on the Paraguayan border as auxiliary bishop in Foz do Iguaçu. Similar numbers of new bishops followed in successive years. The second National Council in 1968, with 18 bishops present, elected Pedro dos Santos Silva – Duarte Costa's old choice of successor – as President of the Episcopal Conference of ICAB.[113] The decade began to draw to a close with the news of the death of Bishop Ferraz, aged 89, on 9th May 1969. Until the end he was concerned about the fate of his Order of Saint Andrew, which would never be in communion with Rome now. Ferraz's Free Catholic Church had re-formed on its own initiative, under a new name – the Independent Catholic Apostolic Church in Brazil. Ferraz's behavior had always posed a challenge to his superiors, but no-one could say that he did not try to take ecumenism and Church unification seriously, in his own way. His secretary, Father Nicola Rossetti SJ, deeply moved, celebrated his funeral Mass, and Dom Ferraz was buried in the São Paulo Metropolitan Curia's crypt.

The National Council of 1970 – 4th to 6th July – was in fact the second session of the Council begun in 1968, and it included ICAB's 25th Anniversary celebrations. It was the most comprehensive and sweeping Council yet – 21 bishops attended, five new dioceses were planned, a commission for further liturgical reform was inaugurated, the statutes of ICAB themselves were reformed, and finally, Carlos Duarte Costa was canonized[114] as Saint Carlos of Brazil.[115] Accompanied by prayers to the newly canonized Saint, ICAB prepared for its biggest piece of international expansion so far. ICAB was about to endorse a branch in Argentina that would prove to be almost as successful, as controversial, and as fractious as the mother church (see Chapter VI). The consecration of the Primate of Argentina, Leonardo Morizio Dominguez, was retroactively approved at ICAB's third National Council, which took place from 4th to 6th July 1973 with 19 bishops present. Three new dioceses were announced, and the liturgical reform was completed, resulting in the new Brazilian Missal and Brazilian Ritual.[116]

By the end of the 1960's ICAB had evolved but then fossilized, effectively becoming and remaining the Church we see today. By the time ICAB's thirtieth anniversary approached, it had definitively acquired the form and characteristics that would become its permanent features. To its credit, ICAB survived after Duarte Costa's death in 1961 – in spirit at least, though not as a coherent body – and it more or less successfully avoided a full-on leadership crisis. ICAB was described at this time as "semi-secret,"[117] with masses usually taking place in people's homes. Most sources, even the hostile ones, indicate that this was a period of growth for ICAB, but membership numbers were unclear – some said a handful of people, others claimed 20,000 in one State alone, some said 20,000 members in total.[118] The areas of strongest growth have always seemed to be São Paulo and Brasilia,[119] where the two undisputed leaders (one Italian, one Venezuelan) were based in the two decades following Duarte Costa's passing. The innovation of National Councils saw the achievement of Duarte Costa's canonization,[120] further liturgical reform, constitutional reform, and above all an explosion of bishops.

But ICAB still struggled to really find its place – it had "positioned itself at the head of the campaign to break with the Roman hierarchy, but did not find a way to channel into Brazilian popular religiosity."[121] They certainly did try to tap into *populist* religion, "illegitimately [utilizing] Catholic rites, the names of Saints, vestments and clothes, etc., which are rightly ours,"[122] the Roman Catholic Church complained. ICAB, the great reform movement, now sought to reform nothing, simply setting up in competition with Rome: "After the death of the founder, the model opted for by the *igreja [brasileira]* was that of a vast dispensary of ecclesiastical services for people who cannot obtain them from the Roman Church."[123] This more than anything earned the attention of the Brazilian Roman Catholic bishops, who warned of the "dangers"[124] of ICAB, which seemed to generate confusion quite successfully: "Bishops and priests of the *Igreja Brasileira*, on repeated occasions, on TV and Radio programs, are accepted by the public as members of the Roman Catholic clergy."[125] The Roman Catholic arguments became fossilized from this point onwards too, and the official position would never change: "[ICAB] is truly a case of mystification which cannot be excused under the pretext of freedom of conscience."[126]

Duarte Costa had died without identifying a successor sufficiently clearly,[127] and this led to a lengthy contest for leadership. More significantly, it led to the balkanization of the movement – every bishop became a Duarte Costa, all of them hydra-like heads of a mass of tiny offshoot groups with hopelessly confusing names. Although Duarte Costa labored to keep a tight authoritarian grip on his organization, his original social and political orientations were abandoned even within his lifetime, presuming that they were ever truly important to him anyway. ICAB became "much more conservative ... ardently anti-Communist ... and [accused] the

Roman Catholics of leftist leanings."[128] ICAB's move to the right was no illusion – a terrifying trend began of fostering friendships with, and endorsing, oppressive regimes. This was something that Duarte Costa had criticized Rome for – indeed it was vaunted as one of the reasons for founding ICAB. They now desperately sought to set up branches in Bolivia under the nationalist regime, and in Paraguay under Stroessner. Luigi Mascolo's leadership would lead to successfully launching a branch in Argentina under the auspices of the horrifying dictatorships of the Seventies. ICAB's Chilean bishop, Arce Moya, would only mull going back to Chile once Pinochet had seized power – though his bid failed. At the same time, "the *Igreja Brasileira* adopted an offensive attitude in relation to the Roman Church,"[129] with a systematic series of articles in a sympathetic newspaper, the *Folha de São Paulo*. ICAB's articles "[accused] the Roman Church of betraying Jesus for Marx, and the Nation for atheistic communism. The accusation that was launched against the Bishop of Maura was now being used by the church he founded, against the Roman Church." [130] It was at the very least a turnaround, an irony, a contradiction – if any ICAB hierarchs also saw it as a betrayal of their canonized founder, they kept silent about it. The Roman Catholic bishops of São Paulo hit back: "Not even the most generous application of the principles of religious freedom would admit a justification of this attitude,"[131] they wrote. "Rather, simple common sense suffices in order to classify it as a genuine abuse of freedom and an uncharitable attack on the religious conscience of our Catholic people."[132] They have always been determined to be the 'bigger men,' though, and typically concluded their condemnations by extending a generous invitation:

> "We would like to appeal with a sincere heart to those leaders of the *'igrejas brasileiras'* and tell them that the doors of the Church will always be open to receive those who, recognizing their error, desire to turn fully to the truth of the Gospel, in the only Church of the Lord Jesus. And the joy of the Church will be immense, in welcoming those who, sincerely converted, request a place in the house of the Father."[133]

Notes

1 An appeal to converts from ICAB, 'Pastoral Letter of the Bishops of the Ecclesiastical Province of São Paulo', CNBB 'Comunicado Mensal' [Monthly Communiqué] No. 243, Dec. 1973, [pp 90-97], p 96

2 Obispo Alejo Pelypenko, *Infiltración Comunista en las Iglesias de América, [Communist Infiltration in the Churches of America]*, Pia Sociedad de San Pablo, Buenos Aires, 1961, p 126. Henceforth 'Pelypenko.'

3 Pelypenko, p 117

4 Cf. Pelypenko, p 140

5 Also spelled Von Röder

6 Pelypenko, p 121

7 Cf. *O Semanário*, Year 3, No. 113, 12th-19th June 1958, p 15 – Fundação Biblioteca Nacional Digital http://memoria.bn.br/DocReader/Hotpage/HotpageBN.aspx?bib=149322&pagfis=1776&url=http://memoria.bn.br/docreader# – [accessed 11th April 2018]

8 Cf. Pelypenko, p 123

9 Cf. *O Semanário*, 12th-19th June 1958, p 15

10 Cf. Pelypenko, p 123

11 Pelypenko, p 121

12 Cf. Pelypenko, p 121

13 Pelypenko, p 115

14 Pelypenko, p 127

15 Pelypenko, p 118

16 Pelypenko, p 126

17 Cf. *O Semanário*, 12th-19th June 1958, p 15

18 Dom Estêvão Bettencourt OSB, in *Pergunte e Responderemos*, Number 55, July 1962, online version at http://www.pr.gonet.biz/revista.php [accessed 05/04/2018]. Henceforth 'Bettencourt.'

19 Bettencourt

20 Bettencourt

21 Cf. Pelypenko, p 136

22 Pelypenko, p 134

23 Pelypenko, p 125

24 Pelypenko, p 126

25 Pelypenko, p 193 and Cf. pp 189-190

26 Bishops of Belo Horizonte, CNBB, *Revista Eclesiástica Brasileira*, No. 18, 1958, p 564 [emphasis added]

27 Cf. Pelypenko, p 131

28 Cf. Pelypenko, p 131

29 Pelypenko, p 131

30 Cf. Pelypenko, pp 132-133

31 Pelypenko, p 133
32 Cf. Pelypenko, p 131
33 Pelypenko, p 117
34 Pelypenko, p 131
35 Pelypenko, p 141
36 Pelypenko, p 144
37 Cf. Pelypenko, p 225
38 Pelypenko, p 144
39 Biographical details in Câmara Municipal de São Paulo, Seção de Protocólo, [City Hall, Protocol Section], case number 5192 of 1968, "Granting of freedom of the city to Dom Luigi Mascolo"
40 Cf. Dom Raimundo Augusto de Oliveira, *Dom Salomão Ferraz e o Ecumenismo [Dom Salomão Ferraz and Ecumenism]*, Feira de Santana, Bahia, undated, p 58. Henceforth 'Oliveira.'
41 Oliveira, p 59
42 Oliveira, p 59
43 Oliveira, p 59
44 Oliveira, pp 60-61
45 Cf. Gary Selin, *Priestly Celibacy*, Catholic University of America Press, Washington, 2006, pp 53-54
46 Oliveira, p 61
47 Cf. Carlos Oviedo Cavada, 'Obispos Irregulares' [Bishops Irregular], Pontifical Catholic University, Chile, 1986 [pp 207-219], p 216 n.46, https://repositorio.uc.cl/handle/11534/16821 [accessed 9th May 2018]
48 Oliveira, p 61
49 Cf. Oliveira, p 62
50 Cf. Oliveira, p 67
51 Cf. Pelypenko, p 190
52 Cf. Pelypenko, p 190 – Pelypenko makes the mistake of assuming that Ferraz was ex-Catholic. "Salomão Ferraz presented … a request to be admitted *once more* into the bosom of the Catholic Church."
53 Pelypenko, p 190
54 Cf. Pelypenko, p 191
55 Cf. Câmara Municipal de São Paulo, Seção de Protocólo, [City Hall, Protocol Section], case No. 3779 1963, "Naming after Dom Jorge Alves de Sousa [sic] of the current planned street between […]"
56 Later 'Apostolic Administrator' of Belém. Died on 6th February 1991.
57 Cf. Raimondo Spiazzi OP, 'Annotazioni', *Monitor Ecclesiasticus* 84, Desclée, Rome, 1959, pp 369-409
58 Cf. Pope John XXIII, 'Virtutes Dignitati Sacerdotum Necessariae: Caput, Cor et Lingua', *Acta Apostolicae Sedis* number 52, 1960, [pp 221-30], p 226, and also Cf. Gary Selin, pp 53-54

59 Cf. Selin, p 54
60 Cf. Raimondo Spiazzi OP, *L'Osservatore Romano*, 10th February 1977, pp 6-7
61 Pelypenko, p 122-3
62 Cf. Pelypenko, p 126
63 Cf. Pelypenko, p 193-194
64 Cf. Bettencourt
65 Cf. *O Globo*, 27th March 1961 (evening edition), p 6. Cf. also Bettencourt
66 Cf. Bettencourt
67 Cf. *New York Times*, 28th March 1961, p 35
68 Cf. *O Globo*, 27th March 1961 (evening edition), p 6
69 Cf. *O Globo*, 27th March 1961 (evening edition), p 6
70 Cf. *O Globo*, 27th March 1961 (evening edition), p 6
71 *New York Times*, 28th March 1961, p 35
72 *New York Times*, 28th March 1961, p 35
73 Câmara Municipal de São Paulo, Seção de Protocólo, [City Hall, Protocol Section] Case 3779, 1963
74 Cf. Bettencourt
75 Câmara Municipal de São Paulo, Seção de Protocólo, [City Hall, Protocol Section] Case 5192, 1968
76 Cf. Câmara Municipal de São Paulo, Seção de Protocólo, [City Hall, Protocol Section] Case 5192, 1968
77 Biographical details can be found in *Luta!* issue -- , October 1949, p 35
78 *Luta!* issue 9, October 1949, p 35
79 Cf. Pelypenko, p 126
80 Pastoral Letter of the Bishops of the Ecclesiastical Province of São Paulo, CNBB, 'Comunicado Mensal' [Monthly Communiqué] number 243, December 1972, [pp 90-97], p 91
81 Bettencourt
82 Pastoral Letter of the Bishops of the Ecclesiastical Province of São Paulo, December 1972, p 92
83 Bettencourt
84 Cf. Pastoral Letter of the Bishops of the Ecclesiastical Province of São Paulo, December 1972, p 95
85 CNBB, Comunicado Mensal No. 252 Sept. 1973, pp 1129-1130 [redacted to avoid repetition].
86 Cf. *New York Times*, 28th March 1961, p 35
87 Cf. *New York Times*, 28th March 1961, p 35
88 Bettencourt
89 Pelypenko, p 116
90 Pastoral Letter of the Bishops of the Ecclesiastical Province of São Paulo, December 1972, p 91

91 Cf. J.O. Beozzo, *Brazilian Council Fathers of Vatican II*, Universidade de São Paulo, São Paulo, 2001

92 Cf. Oliveira, p 71

93 Cf. CNBB, *Report of the Meeting of the Presidency of the CNBB*, 'Comunicado Mensal' [Monthly Communiqué] 252, Sept. 1973, [pp 1129-30], p 1130 -- "[ICAB] uses liturgical, theological, and cate--chetical material from the Roman Church, previous to Vatican II." Also Cf. Aloísio Cardinal Lorsheider, in *Convergência*, CRB Journal, Yr. 25, No. 231, Apr. 1990, [pp 137-142], p 138 "[The ICAB Catechism is] traditional Catholic doctrine, without its more recent developments, above all since Vatican II."

94 CDF, 4th March 1972, CNBB, Comunicado Mensal [Monthly Communique] No. 234, Mar. 1972, p 12

95 Oviedo Cavada, p 216

96 Oviedo Cavada, p 216

97 Cf. Câmara Municipal de São Paulo, Seção de Protocólo, Case 5192, 1968

98 Cf. Câmara Municipal de São Paulo, Seção de Protocólo, Case 5192, 1968

99 Council held 25-27th Feb. 1965, Cf. ICAB document, Preâmbulo Comemorativo dos 65 anos de Organ- -ização Jurídico-Eclesial da Igreja Católica Apostólica Brasileira [Commemorative Preamble for the 65th Anniversary of the Juridical-Ecclesial Foundation of the Brazilian Catholic Apostolic Church] 2010, p 12

100 Cf. ICAB document – Preâmbulo Comemorativo dos 65 anos, 2010, p 12

101 Cf. Wagner Pires da Silva, 'Another Catholicism: The Bishop of Maura and the Brazilian Catholic Apostolic Church', *Revista de História Bilros* (Fortaleza), Vol. 5, No. 8 Jan.-Apr. 2017 [pp 106-125], p 122

102 *New York Times*, 3rd August 1973, p 4

103 *New York Times*, 3rd August 1973, p 4

104 Pires da Silva, p 122

105 Cf. *Luta!* issue 21, April 1955, p 70

106 Pastoral Letter of the Bishops of the Ecclesiastical Province of São Paulo. December 1972, p 95

107 Cf. *Diario da Manha*, Tues. 12th June 1956, p 8: "There were so many people [...] that you could not walk down the street. [When] Dom Carlos, founder of the Church arrived [the] Umbanda groups began to [chant]'Salve o Rei' and to shout 'Saravá' [Umbanda greetings]."

108 Cf. *O Semanário*, 12th-19th June 1958, p 15

109 Pastoral Letter of the Bishops of the Ecclesiastical Province of São Paulo, December 1972, p 91

[110] Pastoral Letter of the Bishops of the Ecclesiastical Province of São Paulo, December 1972, p 91

[111] Pastoral Letter of the Bishops of the Ecclesiastical Province of São Paulo, December 1972, p 93

[112] Born 6th December 1923, ordained priest on 23rd November 1947, died 8th August 2010.

[113] Cf. ICAB document – Preâmbulo Comemorativo dos 65 anos, 2010, p 13

[114] Cf. *New York Times*, 3rd August 1973, p 4

[115] Cf. ICAB document – Preâmbulo Comemorativo, p 13

[116] Cf. ICAB document – Preâmbulo Comemorativo, p 13

[117] *New York Times*, 28th March 1961, p 35

[118] *New York Times*, 28th March 1961, p 35

[119] *New York Times*, 3rd August 1973, p 4

[120] *New York Times*, 3rd August 1973, p 4

[121] Pires da Silva, p 122

[122] Pastoral Letter of the Bishops of the Ecclesiastical Province of São Paulo, December 1972, p 96

[123] Pires da Silva, p 122-123

[124] Pastoral Letter of the Bishops of the Ecclesiastical Province of São Paulo, December 1972, p 92

[125] CNBB, 'Comunicado Mensal' 252, Sept. 1973, [pp 1129-30], p 1130

[126] Pastoral Letter of the Bishops of the Ecclesiastical Province of São Paulo, December 1972, p 91

[127] Cf. *New York Times*, 28th March 1961, p 35

[128] *New York Times*, 3rd August 1973, p 4

[129] Pires da Silva, p 122

[130] Pires da Silva, p 122

[131] Pastoral Letter of the Bishops of the Ecclesiastical Province of São Paulo, December 1972, p 93

[132] Pastoral Letter of the Bishops of the Ecclesiastical Province of São Paulo, December 1972, p 91

[133] Pastoral Letter of the Bishops of the Ecclesiastical Province of São Paulo, December 1972, p 96

VI

"FROM TRADITIONAL TO ESOTERIC AND ULTRACONSERVATIVE TO RADICAL"[1]
— the ICAB phenomenon, its branches and offshoots —

Today it is more accurate to talk about ICAB the phenomenon rather than ICAB the Church. ICAB's tendency to balkanize into independent groups has caused it to blend into a pre-existing subculture. This subculture or phenomenon centers around the pursuit and acquisition of Holy Orders stemming *from* the Roman Catholic Church, *outside* of the Roman Catholic Church. This is then thought to confer upon the individual a legitimate springboard from which to found their own Church – it is in some senses the perpetuation of what Duarte Costa originally did in founding ICAB. With ICAB's profusion of internal schisms, offshoots with elaborate names, and regular output of freelance bishops – "a most dangerous species"[2] – it gave new impetus to this subculture. In its modern form this phenomenon is about 150 years old and is tied up with what might be termed the subculture of *episcopi vagantes* – wandering bishops – or "bishops at large."[3] The phenomenon consists of generally small or very small "micro-churches"[4] which are to varying degrees – and usually debatably – Catholic in character or affinity. Beyond this it is almost impossible to characterize the micro-church phenomenon. Furthermore, this description does not really cover some micro-churches which are more like individual operations rather than groups, nor does it cover groups that are arguably not Catholic at all or do not want to be. The phenomenon is referred to in a great variety of ways – they can be called "splinter denominations,"[5] "splinter churches,"[6] "parallel churches,"[7] or "obscure groupings"[8] and may be considered part of a wider "underground church."[9] Karl Prüter attempted to counter the sinister term of *episcopi vagantes* by replacing it with the far more sympathetic term *Bishops Extraordinary*.[10] Other charitable treatments of the topic refer to "independent episcopacy,"[11] "Independent Catholicism,"[12] the "Independent Sacramental Movement,"[13] and the "Other Catholics."[14] Some authors just write them all off as schismatics.[15] Previously, the main sources of ordination for this subculture of independent micro-churches were the various offshoots of the European Old Catholic movement. Membership of micro-churches can be fairly loose or transient. It may be motivated by predictable objections to official Catholic Church teaching, which Karl Rahner claimed were common to most Catholics.[16] Occasionally very committed or exclusive micro-churches may become fanatical or sect-like.[17] If indeed these phenomena are part of the wider Catholic Church then they constitute an extreme manifestation of the "very deep ruptures"[18] which Pope Benedict XVI lamented.

The variety of groups in this phenomenon can appear very great,[19] but a lot of their diversity manifests itself in superficial elements such as worship style, dress, and paraphernalia, rather than in fundamentals like structure or theology. Similarities across such communities outweigh the differences,[20] not least their common origins. In *The Many Paths of the Independent Sacramental Movement*, John P. Plummer listed some factors common to micro-churches: individual members have often deliberately searched out the community through a process of personal suffering or distress; there may be an appeal for those who feel excluded from the mainstream Church; greater individual commitment and lay involvement is often present and necessary to keep the micro-church going; and there is usually a higher ratio of clergy to laity so it is easier to access ordination.[21] The negative side of this easy access to ordination is well-commented. Aleksei Pelypenko noticed that "'ICAB' ordained anyone priest, with much haste, in order to augment the number of its 'priests'";[22] Estêvão Bettencourt stated that "the intellectual and moral formation of [ICAB's] 'ministers' is very substandard; the candidate may, in some cases, obtain priestly ordination within eight days."[23] Writing about current US-based 'independent catholic churches', not only those originating from ICAB, Julie Byrne called them "hugely diverse, including flavors from traditional to esoteric and ultraconservative to radical."[24] They are surely diverse in 'flavor' but arguably less so in substance. They are most certainly numerous. Consider the example of one US Roman Catholic parish alone: Holy Innocents of Long Beach, California lists in its bulletin *seven* independent catholic churches in its local area,[25] and the Archdiocese of Santa Fe warns against no fewer than *twelve* local "schismatic churches."[26] On inspection, almost all of them descend from ICAB in some way. Considering the names of these independent churches – Holy Trinity, Holy Family, Saint Francis of Assisi, Our Lady of Guadeloupe – they seem united in being oblivious, or perhaps content, about being mistaken for Roman Catholics. This is clearly the un-diverse end of the spectrum where micro-churches in fact aim to accentuate their resemblance to mainstream Catholic churches.

So what about distinguishing fundamental differences? ICAB's offshoot communities and micro-churches can be categorized in a few ways:

1. Big issues

Significant numbers of groups in this phenomenon, including ICAB branches and offshoots, are driven by social and moral issues. They are aspects of broader campaigns concerning sexuality, gender, or ethnicity, for example. They may focus on the promotion and defense of a particular group – such as women's rights or LGBT rights. These groups sometimes revolve around a specific charismatic individual, a 'pioneer' in the particular field – examples of this would include Rómulo Antonio Braschi as a high-profile ordainer of women, and Mark Steven Shirilau as the organizer of the gay-oriented Ecumenical Catholic Church. Many groups function as outlets for those excluded for some reason from the mainstream Catholic priesthood, including former priests and religious who left active ministry to get married. Groups "formed with the goals of providing support for resigned and married priests and their families and working for optional celibacy in the Catholic Church ... have increasingly become structures of organized ministry apart from the official Church, though still identified as Catholic."[27] Other would-be priests of the micro-churches may, fairly or unfairly, have failed in their applications for the mainstream priesthood. Less common motivations include attempts to harmonize non-Christian beliefs with Catholicism, such as reincarnation or UFOs,[28] which may have led to exclusion from a mainstream Church.

2. Politics

Some micro-churches can be identified with strong political stances, as in the case of supporting right-wing dictatorships in Latin America combined with a traditionalist or conservative church outlook. This sometimes sits alongside opposition to liturgical reform and ecumenism – a combination comparable to the Archbishop Lefebvre mindset.[29] The Argentinean branch of ICAB – ICAA – was in fact founded as a puppet of "extreme right-wing Peronism."[30] Other groups may welcome or actually seek the "instrumentalization of religious life by the political powers."[31] Examples such as ICAA encourage the perception of a division between progressive-minded and conservative-minded micro-churches, which generally also conform to progressive and conservative liturgical and ecclesial outlooks.

3. Vatican II

Less commonly, independent micro-churches may be identifiable by a specific position on Vatican II and its vision of the Church –

a divider which is obviously applicable to the broader spectrum of fringe Catholic organizations, not just the micro-churches.[32] Some feel that the full implementation of Vatican II is overdue, that it was betrayed or thwarted by restorationist forces and the Roman Curia.[33] It is important to reiterate that ICAB constituted no more than an accidental precursor to Vatican II – Duarte Costa was not alone in calling for the use of the vernacular in the liturgy. Praise for ICAB's prophetic quality is usually unwarranted, and in fact ICAB sought to undermine the Council; "in the context of ... conciliar renewal, [ICAB] contradicts and prejudices everything that the Council desires."[34] ICAB was not interested in genuine reform. It became "a vast dispensary of ecclesiastical services"[35] just as the Roman Catholic Church began to phase-out that very understanding of the Church's role. ICAB held on to the perception of Catholic tradition as "a heavy gold rock. ... a weighty object mined in the past that is passed unchanged from one generation to the next."[36] Some offshoots may even directly reject everything that Vatican II stands for – in similarity again with the position that "Archbishop Marcel Lefebvre exemplifies."[37] As with the apparently distinct split between progressive and conservative micro-churches, Vatican II tends to divide them into one of two clear factions in spite of common origins. The traditionalists may have "different dynamics, [but] they are closely related to their liberal cousins, and there is more cross-fertilization than either side generally cares to admit." [38] The divisions and splits are not necessarily watertight – even the generally conservative ICAB mother church occasionally reveals that it harbors progressive and open-minded tendencies.[39]

4. Weathervanes

Offshoot micro-church groups are often celebrated for presaging imminent changes in the mainstream Church. They may inadvertently act as a kind of weathervane or barometer to show

how wider swathes of silent Catholics are feeling about "urgent contemporary questions."[40] This seems to have always been the case to some extent with breakaway Catholic groups – 100 years ago when Polish immigrants in the US felt underserved and marginalized they started their own parishes. This became the Polish National Catholic Church. After a few decades the Vatican 'caught up' and recognized the need for special pastoral care for specific immigrant, language, and ethnic groups. The advent of 'proven' married men – *viri probati* – being ordained priests will without doubt be the next big innovation in the Catholic Church, and it will of course come about in Brazil first.[41] However, the image of ICAB and the micro-churches as ecclesiastical fortune-tellers should not be exaggerated. The arguments for married priests and liturgical reform did not start with ICAB. Nor did ICAB ever explore other areas of reform which the mainstream Church over time has begun to address, such as the roles of women and laypeople in positions of responsibility.

To attempt a complete catalogue of all ICAB's offshoots would be a mammoth task even for the most painstaking and tenacious researcher, and I would still not wish it on that researcher. There have been so many offshoots, and so many have left nothing published in any form. What can be attempted in one chapter is to describe those ICAB offshoots which distinguish themselves as being either a) enduring and / or current; b) famous or notorious – they made the news; c) well-documented through their own publications, outsiders, or scholars; or d) significant in size, in impact, or remarkable for some other reason. Some offshoot micro-churches may tick more than one of these boxes and writing about them becomes a lot easier. The opposite also occurs – there can be little to say about a group that does not tick any of these boxes, as history may only record a name and a location. This chapter will look at ICAB's international branches, its offshoots around the world, and the current state of ICAB itself, in that order.

It is worth distinguishing between an Offshoot and a Branch, the latter being a community or group outside of Brazil that ICAB has expressly recognized as part of its international family. 'Branch' does not necessarily mean subordination – they could also be called sister- or partner-churches – though ICAB obviously enjoys a certain seniority in the family. An attempt was made to organize this family of branches into an international communion – the World Council of Catholic Apostolic Churches, or WCCAC – but enthusiasm seems not to have lasted. WCCAC claimed eighteen national church members in July 2007,[42] though several of these were ejected or left soon afterwards. The then-US branch under *Arch*bishops Queen and Gubala is now known as the Old Catholic Church of the United States and claims to have a 'Worldwide Patriarchate' of its own. Ten years on hardly any of the original eighteen branches appear to be recognized by ICAB. If ICAB branches seem difficult to keep within the fold, it is a far greater challenge to just keep track of the offshoots. Offshoots are those micro-churches or groups which have either broken links with ICAB or whose relationship with the mother church was never intended to be lasting. Some offshoots result from the more-or-less individual initiative of bishops who may or may not have broken ties to ICAB at the time. During his long leadership of ICAB Castillo Mendez was apparently not scrupulous about whom he consecrated. Bishop candidates did not have to belong to ICAB or one of its branches. Age and education were no barriers. It is widely inferred that such recipients of Holy Orders were usually happy to contribute financially to the ICAB cause – as in almost any Church, perhaps, something had to go into the coffers. Cardinal Aloísio Lorscheider simply called it simony.[43]

ICAB's Worldwide Branches

It is perhaps fitting that Castillo Mendez, who empowered many – and any – offshoot or branch with his consecrations, had himself led the first external branch of the ICAB family, the Venezuelan Catholic Apostolic Church. As we know, ICAV was short-lived

(1947 to 1950) though there currently appears to be an attempt to revive it, according to scant information offered on one or two websites. Castillo Mendez also wanted to launch a Colombian branch at the same time. A new Colombian branch began in 2005 – *Iglesia Católica Apostólica Nacional Colombiana* – under Guillermo Pacheco Bornacelli, but they were soon expelled from WCCAC. Estêvão (Stefano, Esteban, or Stephen) Corradi (1912-1979) was one of the first of many to be ordained priest[44] and then consecrated bishop[45] by Castillo Mendez back in ICAV days. Corradi in turn soon consecrated Albert A. Steer who was already an irregular 'Old Catholic' bishop, and who then attempted to found a Panamanian branch – *Iglesia Católica Apostólica Panamense*.[46] Using the name Stephen Meyer Corradi Scarella, Corradi moved to the USA, where he continued to be involved in the short-lived micro-church phenomenon. He eventually consecrated at least three bishops, between them spawning a hierarchy of around 150 North American bishops. This dynasty of bishops includes the following notables who have all made news in various ways: George Stallings of the Imani Temple in Washington DC and Peter Paul Brennan, who were both later re-consecrated by Archbishop Milingo; Forest Ernest Barber, who took ICAB to the Philippines (see below) and also consecrated Peter Paul Brennan; Emilio Federico Rodriguez y Durand (aka Fairfield) who also consecrated Peter Paul Brennan; Bertil Persson; Joseph Grenier of the Celtic Christian Church; author John P. Plummer, an expert on Independent Catholicism; James Alan Wilkowski of the Evangelical Catholic Church (see below); and Mark Steven Shirilau of the Ecumenical Catholic Church (see below). Corradi lost contact with his comrades in Brazil and began associations with various US-based Old Catholic groups. By 1970 he was calling his denomination the Diocese of the Old Catholic Church of America, which in 1973 became the Holy Catholic Apostolic Church. After his death this was first renamed the Western Orthodox Church in America and then the Catholic Apostolic Church in North America (CACINA) Patriarchate of Brazil, formerly a recognized branch of ICAB.

ICAB's next two attempts at branches produced meager fruit. Duarte Costa consecrated his sixth bishop specifically in order to found an overseas branch. Pedro Luis Hernandez was consecrated on 29th June 1955 for a new Bolivian National Church, hoping to take advantage of a moment of nationalist fervor, but he died of a heart attack shortly afterwards. Later that year Duarte Costa planned a branch in Chile and duly consecrated a 29-year-old called Orlando Arce Moya. Arce Moya's defection to ICAB would not last very long, and he was later taken back into the Catholic Church – as a layman. He spent some time living with a Salesian community in Germany as a lay helper before petitioning unsuccessfully to return to Chile as a Roman Catholic bishop in the 1970's. In 1966 the intended Paraguayan branch under Antonio Ramon Talavera Goiburu, a former Roman Catholic priest who had married and started a family, also failed. A new attempt at a Paraguayan branch – *Iglesia Católica Apostólica Nacional de la República del Paraguay* – was launched in 2010 under Bishop Rafael Ruiz. Argentina remains the ICAB overseas branch with the most success, durability, and closeness to the mother church.

1962 saw the first serious attempt to establish a branch in Argentina, under Guillermo Campos Insiarte, but it was in 1971 that the *Iglesia Católica Apostólica Argentina* – Argentinean Catholic Apostolic Church – was founded. Like previous branches of ICAB, ICAA benefited from a political 'moment' characterized by social unrest, nationalism, right-wing extremism and anticlericalism. [47] ICAA fitted in with the schemes of an influential government 'advisor' called José López Rega. He was nicknamed *El Brujo* – the Sorcerer or the Witchdoctor – for his love of the occult and the esoteric. ICAA became one of the Witchdoctor's pet projects.[48] President Juan Perón recklessly appointed López Rega as Minister of Social Welfare in order to appease and contain the dangerous right-wing of his party, but López Rega's powers became extremely wide-ranging. He controlled 30% of the national budget and commanded death squads to eliminate opponents at his and his master's bidding. He is regarded as Argentina's Rasputin, especially since the First Lady (and President-to-be) Isabel de Perón fell completely under López Rega's spell. When Perón's much-anticipated third term (18 years after his first) and third marriage were cut short by his death aged 78, his widow, as Vice-President, stepped in and became the world's first woman President. Ill-suited for the role, *Isabelita* handed effective control to the Witchdoctor and his sinister right-wing clique. López Rega's usefulness under Juan Perón had been to keep the extreme right wing of Peronism in check, but after Perón's demise there was no-one to keep the Witchdoctor himself in check. It was in this atmosphere that the *Iglesia Católica Apostólica Argentina* (ICAA) achieved the highly prized recognition of the government's *Registro Nacional de Cultos* – the National Register of Religions – a distinction which opened many doors and acknowledged ICAA as one of the authorized religions of the State.

Like much of the continent itself, ICAB had by that time shifted politically towards the right.[49] Accordingly, in 1972 ICAB gladly stepped in to endorse ICAA as its sister church. Dom Luigi Mascolo personally consecrated ICAA's leader Leonardo Morizio Dominguez as head bishop, only three steps away from Duarte Costa in the ICAB family tree of Apostolic Succession. Perhaps ICAA's crowning achievement came at Christmas 1974 when its patron, minister López Rega, publicly snubbed the Roman Catholic Church – the official religion – in favor of ICAA. The Witchdoctor allowed ICAA to lead the festive celebrations at the site of the new 'Altar of the Fatherland' in Buenos Aires, provoking the official indignation of the Roman Catholic Church.[50] In that same period López Rega and his right-wingers did more than just snub the Catholic Church: dozens of 'progressive' priests and religious were persecuted, arrested, and interrogated, and the most prominent of them, Father Carlos Mujica, was gunned down by the Witchdoctor's death squad. But ICAA was riding high and safe for the moment. The subsequent military coup of 1976 was even more anti-progressive – *many* more priests, religious, catechists, activists, and at least one bishop would be murdered by the *dictadura*. But the leaders of the

1976 coup considered themselves devoutly Roman Catholic, in contrast to Perón, who was anti-Catholic and effectively indifferent to religion. With the Witchdoctor fleeing the country, there was no more 'special relationship' for ICAA after 1976.

ICAA, like ICAB, became a magnet for interesting characters. Pedro Ruiz Badanelli (1899-1985) was to become a kind of elder statesman of ICAA. In keeping with the ICAB tradition of making a nonsense of 'nationalizing the clergy' Ruiz Badanelli was from Andalusia, Spain.[51] He had enjoyed a high profile at various times; he had authored serious books; he had been pally with Perón and Spanish royalty; it had been rumored that *he* planned to be consecrated bishop by Duarte Costa as part of Perón's plan to launch an *Iglesia Nacional Peronista* or *Iglesia Justicialista Argentina*[52] – Ruiz Badanelli denied this in his 1960 book *Perón: La Iglesia, y Un Cura* – 'Perón: the Church, and a Priest.'[53] Even so, he was won over to the ICAA cause and consecrated bishop by Morizio Dominguez in 1973. Morizio Dominguez later consecrated his eventual successor José Eugenio Tenca Rusconi (c. 1930-2003) in 1980. Though its glory days were short-lived, ICAA survived, even after its protector López Rega fell from grace. As ICAA dwindled, officials saw no further justification for it to be enshrined in the National Register of Religions – if there had ever been a justification – and it was removed. Subsequent attempts at reinstatement have fallen flat. ICAA was originally a puppet of "extreme right-wing Peronism"[54] and an example of the "instrumentalization of religious life by the political powers."[55] ICAA has never complained about being instrumentalized, however – in recent decades the current hierarchy have explored outlandish possibilities such as linking-up with the Chinese Patriotic Catholic Association or helping to establish a National Church in Hugo Chavez's Venezuela.[56]

Almost as long as it has existed, ICAA has fallen victim to the balkanization effect – internal schisms, splinters and defections – which had become a key feature of ICAB as well. In ICAA's early days it was almost simultaneously called the American Catholic Apostolic Orthodox Church, with a free exchange of personnel between the two – the alternative Primate being Jacobo Antonio Lozano Sánchez. ICAA also subsumed the former attempt at a national church,[57] and this continued, in name only. As time progressed, the number of ICAA splinter groups soared; Congregation of Mary Mystic Rose; Liberal Apostolic Church of Christ; Charismatic Catholic Movement; Congregation of Worker Priest Missionaries; Congregation of Saint Joseph the Worker; Dissident Augustinian Congregation; Dissident Apostolic Christian Priests; Missionary Church of Evangelization – Order of the Holy Spirit, etc. etc. – all with frequent exchanges of members and the indispensable internal feuds. The last splinter church on the list, the Missionary Church of Evangelization, Order of the Holy Spirit (*Iglesia Misionera de Evangelización – Católica Apostólica Nacional - Orden del Espíritu Santo* – or IME) is perhaps worthy of a special mention. Founded in the 1970's by Bruno Tinivelli Fangelli, it boasts the novelty of preserving a miraculous bleeding communion wafer, possibly inspired by a similar independent church in Mexico City. Other more recent ICAA absurdities included a scandalous roadside 'Requiem' Mass to the accompaniment of *cuarteto* music. This took place at the location of a fatal collision, which killed a *cuarteto* music idol, the singer Rodrigo 'El Potro' Bueno, in 2000.[58] "Thousands of people prayed. Among them, furtive sellers peddled candles, posters, key rings, flowers and headbands. The ceremony concluded with a massive Communion."[59] In another characteristic departure from ICAA's traditionalist right-wing repertoire, the governing bishop also officiated at a same-sex marriage.[60]

8th November 1988 saw the arrival of ICAB in the Philippines – *Igreja Católica Apostólica Brasileira nas Filipinas* (ICABF) – courtesy of Forest Ernest Barber who was consecrated bishop by Castillo Mendez. Barber seems to have been ordained around fifteen times in total, bishop and priest, for fifteen different micro-churches, according to various sources. He also seems to have consecrated a dozen or so bishops himself. It is difficult to establish the current situation of ICABF. Its presence was significant enough by 2012 to warrant a note from the Nuncio's office to the Roman

Catholic Bishops' Conference, pointing out that "schismatic communities" in the Philippines are "not recognized in anyway [sic] by the Catholic Church."[61] The warning stated that ICAB went under at least two names in the Philippines – the Roman [sic] Catholic Society of Pope Leo XIII (RCSPLXIII) and "a certain Sacred Cruces Franciscanum (Sacred Cross Franciscans), an offshoot of the ICAB … present in at least three dioceses."[62] Convention dictates that no Roman Catholic society would ever use 'Roman Catholic' in its title; therefore any genuine Roman Catholic organization would instantly recognize RCSPLXIII as some sort of parody. RCSPLXIII was apparently the initiative of a British bishop expelled from ICAB. However, the prize for best title may go to the 'Sacred Cruces Franciscanum." This macaronic attempt at Latin speaks volumes in spite of being totally meaningless – it manages to combine three different languages in a name of just three words. The excommunications of all involved were duly affirmed. Since November 2015 ICAB has had a branch in Bolivia, 59 years after the first attempt. The Roman Catholic Bishops Conference energetically condemns this "group made up of priests dismissed from the priesthood or suspended by their respective bishops,"[63] which includes an ICAB-consecrated bishop called Richard Lipacho. "The sacraments they supposedly celebrate and offer are schismatic acts which damage the unity of Christ's Church,"[64] the Secretary General of the Bishops' Conference said. ICAB's branches receive short shrift wherever they appear, including at the Vatican itself.

"The strange case of 'His Eminence' Bell"[65] in 2012 brought an inordinate and undignified amount of publicity to the UK branch of ICAB. Its bishops made sure that they were repeatedly photographed while attending Mass in Saint Peter's Square, for which they had contrived to acquire invitations. Then in 2012 the Roman Catholic bishop of Fiesole in Tuscany caught 'His Eminence' Bell in the act of ordaining two deacons at a former convent in San Giovanni Val d'Arno. Although then known as David Bell, Archbishop of London no less, he was previously and is currently known as James Atkinson-Wake, "His Eminence, Archbishop of Birmingham & Dudley."[66] As *La Stampa* pointed out, "the title 'Eminence' [is] reserved for cardinals."[67] The Tuscany ordinations took place at the invitation of a newly founded religious community that had secured the use of the former convent – the community was immediately stripped of its diocesan authorization and suppressed. Bishop Meini confirmed that "a schismatic act" had been committed "and that both [the ordaining bishop] and the two ordained priests … incurred excommunication."[68] James Atkinson-Wake – aka Bell – fired back with "an immediate, sour and tough response"[69] and *La Stampa* reported that Bell "prepared a 'curse' against Bishop Meini, asking God to 'forgive his mistakes' … Bell [also] put down on paper his conviction that Messini [sic] was a bad bishop 'who wears the miter of Satan.'"[70] ICAB had already parted company with its UK branch at this stage, in part perhaps over the 'traditionalist' UK branch's ordinations of women. ICAB definitively disowned Bell in 2013.[71]

Another high-profile ICAB branch was launched in Guatemala in 2007. Like the UK branch ratified the previous year, Guatemala would be out of the ICAB communion a few years later. Monsignor Eduardo Aguirre Oestmann – who received that title from Pope St. John Paul II in 1985 – was excommunicated by the Vatican in 2006 after refusing to dissolve a "controversial [and] schismatic group"[72] which he had founded. No fewer than eight ICAB bishops flew in to consecrate him bishop at a massively well-attended ceremony. Aguirre Oestmann's community is now part of the official Syriac Orthodox Church of Antioch. Yet another highly visible and energetic branch is ICAB's mission in Long Beach, California – *Misión Católica del Divino Nazareno*. Its leader, Rodrigo Romano Pereira, was consecrated bishop in 2013. The local Roman Catholic parish lists *Divino Nazareno* as one of at least seven 'rival' catholic churches in its area.[73]

It is clear that ICAB has had difficulty in maintaining the unity and continuity of its worldwide communion of branches. It is possible to identify some of the reasons for this: the priorities of each branch do not always seem to be in harmony; they have clearly produced some strong characters with visions of their own; and it becomes difficult at times to see what the point of having an international communion is supposed to be. In ICAB's defense, perhaps, it cannot be easy to hold breakaway groups in a communion, however loose a communion it may be – it is almost a direct contradiction in terms.

ICAB's Worldwide Offshoots

ICAB's first offshoots, begrudgingly recognized by Duarte Costa, were Ferraz's Free Catholic Church (ICL) and Order of Saint Andrew, which in reality predated ICAB. After Ferraz was received into the Roman Catholic Church, the ICL and the OSA found themselves asking 'What now?' The Order's members were for the most part married priests ordained by Ferraz. At his suggestion they took a Catholic oath of allegiance in the hope that this would ease their acceptance into the Roman Catholic Church – Ferraz hoped to plead their case in person to the Pope. When this came to nothing, the Order strapped in for the long haul. Robbed of Ferraz, the Free Catholic Church continued under Bishop Manoel Ceia Laranjeira, whom Ferraz had consecrated bishop in 1951. Under Laranjeira the ICL would adopt a new name for a new era – the Independent Catholic Apostolic Church in Brazil *(Igreja Católica Apostólica Independente no Brasil)* – ICAIB. It is not clear whether it was the *intention* to cause confusion with ICAB, but whatever the case there was now an 'other ICAB'; ICAIB. Dom Manoel would go on to consecrate a number of bishops. Of these, Benedito Pereira Lima, who subsequently consecrated José Machado, became responsible for a number of offshoots including the Charismatic Catholic Church[74] and the Traditional Anglican Province of Brazil.[75] Laranjeira also consecrated Lapercio Eudes Moreira and Felismar Manoel, who remained with the core ICAIB Church. In 1969 Laranjeira consecrated a 27 year-old Sicilian,

Vittorio Giovanni Maria Busa, who would go on to become one of the prolific consecrators of the micro-church phenomenon. Busa helped to spread ICAB and ICAIB offshoots around Italy and the rest of Europe, and candidates for ordination were not always scrupulously selected. One of Busa's protégés, Bishop Vittorio Maria Francescone, seems to have built up an astonishing résumé in the criminal underworld around Naples and Salerno.[76] In this century ICAIB suffered internal conflict and saw the 'old guard' break off under Felismar Manoel. This faction has become a 'continuing' Church, renamed the Independent Catholic Apostolic Church '*Solomonite* Tradition' – ICAI-TS – (*Igreja Católica Apostólica Independente – Tradição Salomonita*) in reference and homage to Bishop Salomão Barbosa Ferraz.

The last bishop to be consecrated by Manoel Ceia Laranjeira was Roberto Garrido Padin in 1989, when Laranjeira was 86 years old. Padin had been ordained priest within ICAB by Luigi Mascolo. Padin made the news in 2002 – mistakenly identified as an ICAB, rather than an ICAIB, bishop – as the consecrator of Rómulo Antonio Braschi, who performed the 'Danube Seven' ordinations. The Danube Seven are a group of seven German and Austrian Catholic women who petitioned to be ordained as priests in 2002 and gave rise to the Roman Catholic Womenpriests [sic] (RCWP) movement. The ceremony took place on a pleasure barge on the Danube – among other reasons to make the exact jurisdictional location of the event difficult to pinpoint. The bishop who agreed to officiate, and who had hoped to involve other bishops, was Rómulo Antonio Braschi Basualdo. Braschi was born in Buenos Aires at Christmas 1941 and was ordained as a diocesan priest on 15th August 1966. As Argentina regressed through a series of increasingly draconian dictatorships, Braschi aligned himself to the progressive clergy and associated with Bishop Jerónimo Podestá. Braschi was detained during the anti-progressive repressions of the early 1970's and subsequently drifted away from the Church. He later married, settled in Germany, and eventually returned to ministering. With his wife he founded small faith communities to which he later gave the somewhat cumbersome name 'Catholic Apostolic Charismatic Church of Jesus the King.' He was consecrated bishop by Roberto Garrido Padin in 1998. The Vatican's response to the Danube Seven's ordinations was predictably swift and uncompromising – the women were given the customary time to repent, and then excommunicated. The *Osservatore Romano* reported the Congregation for the Doctrine of the Faith's position that the women's ordinations were invalid – specifically due to their being women, not because the ordinations were unauthorized – but refrained from commenting on the sacramental status of Braschi, who was referred to as Bishop.[77] The Decree of Excommunication specifically targeted the seven women but was preceded by a Premise which aimed "to dispel any doubts about the canonical status of Bishop Romulo Antonio Braschi," stating that "the Congregation for the Doctrine of the Faith confirms that, as a schismatic, he has already incurred an excommunication reserved to the Apostolic See."[78]

Braschi's community and RCWP are not the only members of the ICAB family tree to venture into women's ordination (there was the case of the former UK branch) but they are by far the most high-profile. The worldwide movement campaigning for women's ordination has been divided over whether the 'riverboat ordination' route is justified and appropriate, a prophetic sign of protest, or actually detrimental to the cause. One of the pioneers of theology in support of women's ordination, John Wijngaards, said, "in a way they [the Danube Seven] have a point, but on the other hand … they put themselves in mortal danger of really drifting away from the Catholic community."[79] The growing RCWP movement has been determined to maintain links to the wider Church and not be cut off. Further ordinations of the Danube Seven and their own consecrations as bishops have reportedly been carried out clandestinely by mainstream Roman Catholic bishops who secretly support the movement. Open support from Roman Catholic clergy, however, is dealt with resolutely – in 2012 Father Roy Bourgeois was excommunicated, dismissed, and defrocked – the "three biggies, all at once"[80] – for his active support of RCWP. Bourgeois was ejected from Maryknoll, the Catholic Foreign Missions Society of America, after 45 years of service. RCWP, in turn, has created a spiritual refuge within its ranks for dismissed or laicized priests. This includes those ordained–then–married Roman Catholic men "whose mission long ago expanded from readiness to resume traditional ministry as an individual [priest] to a fuller awareness and support of an expanded priesthood."[81] This may make RCWP one of the few meaningful pathways for both men and women aiming not just to perpetuate the current 'clericalist' model of priesthood in an independent form, but to radically address the conceptions and culture underpinning priesthood. Women's ordination supporters affirm that the aim is "not simply to include women in the present model of patriarchal clericalism, but to transform the Church into a more democratic, participatory community in which the clergy [male and female] would be the animators of the ministry of the people, rather than rule over them as a superior caste."[82] This strand of offshoot micro-church is therefore possibly unique, not for ordaining women but for looking toward a fuller and fundamental rethink of what it means to be priests and church.

Other ICAB offshoots are vehemently opposed to any rethink of priesthood and church, shunning women's ordination, LGBT issues, and the progressive agenda in general. Such hardliners include the Charismatic Evangelical Church, whose top brass were group-consecrated by the compliant Castillo Mendez in 1997. On the fringes of strictly Catholic traditionalism sits the Priestly Society of Christ the King[83] (SSCR) in California, founded as an independent Latin Mass organization in 1994. The SSCR is connected to ICAB through Castillo Mendez's consecrations. Way back in 1982 Castillo Mendez consecrated Antônio José da Costa Raposo for a conservative Portuguese branch of ICAB. Today this appears to have evolved into an Orthodox-style micro-church – *Igreja Católica Ortodoxa Hispânica* – claiming to be "of Genuinely Orthodox Faith and of Western (Latin) Catholic Tradition and Rite."[84] Examined from any angle this is palpable gibberish. The 'Hispanic Orthodox' placed themselves under the "Canonical Recognition and Universal Ecclesiastical Patronage of His Holiness Viktor Ivan I [The First] Busa"[85] – none other than Vittorio Giovanni Busa of Sicily. Unlike their fellow offshoots aiming to progressively reform the Church, some micro-churches seem to want to regress back through the centuries instead. Another 'His Holiness' in the ICAB offshoot genealogy is to be found in Kansas at his 'Vatican in Exile'[86] – the only exiled hill in the world, presumably.

Pope Michael was elected Pope by six people, including his parents and himself. They carefully followed pre-Vatican II electoral procedures after the Council's reforms had left the Catholic Church without a 'valid' Pope, in their view. Pope Michael, born David Bawden, is considered a current example of an anti-Pope or claimant to the office of Pope. Pope Michael is also the subject and title of a fascinating 2010 documentary by Adam Fairholm. Bawden offers a highly visible example of *conclavism*, a rare strain of *sedevacantism*, which is itself a variant of extreme Catholic Traditionalism. Sedevacantists maintain that the Papal Office is vacant, generally through the heresy and / or apostasy of recent Popes (arguably rendering their election null and void); conclavists hold that a Papal Election – a conclave – must be held (on the conclavists' own initiative) to resolve this problem. Bawden was thus elected to the Papacy in 1990, though he had not been ordained. 21 years later, clearly not one to rush things, he was finally ordained and took his place in the ICAB Apostolic Succession, though in a rather long and little-documented branch of it.[87] Nevertheless, thanks to ICAB the ultra-conservative Pope Michael now shares the same episcopal lineage as Roman Catholic Womenpriests and some of the world's most progressive Catholics.

In 2013 in the Archdiocese of Agrigento on the southern coast of Sicily, a former Catholic seminarian in his thirties resurfaced in the town of Licata as an Archbishop, operating from a garage-conversion chapel. He was also a former drag queen – under the stage name Lorella Sukkiarini – and president of the local branch of Arcigay, the national Italian LGBTI Association. The new Archbishop – Agostino de Caro – was a member of the Ecumenical Catholic Church, another incarnation of the ICAB succession in the USA founded in 1987. The ECC traces its roots through several other small ICAB offshoots. Its lineage of bishops sits within the vast dynasty of Castillo Mendez, and also within the descendants of Milton Cunha, one of the last bishops to be consecrated by Duarte Costa. The ECC grew out of the Californian founder's experiences in two larger churches: the Metropolitan Community Church (MCC) – an LGBTQ-focused church – and the Episcopal Church. For founder Mark Steven Shirilau, the latter church was not fully inclusive to people in same-sex unions due to its understanding of marriage, while he also found the MCC's lack of a full sacramental, episcopal dimension unsatisfying.[88] An authentic 'gap' was therefore identified and the ECC was born. It is striking and perhaps to the detriment of the Ecumenical Catholic Church that its name conveys nothing of its purpose, orientation, and character. Furthermore, the use of the term 'Catholic Church' only ever seems to generate confusion and consternation. Cardinal Montenegro, the Archbishop of Agrigento, circulated a letter in response to the appearance of the ECC in Licata, declaring Bishop de Caro's ordinations invalid and illegitimate.[89] The usual back-and-forth of warnings to the faithful, quoting of Canons, and threats of excommunication ensued. The situation in Sicily had barely started to cool when over on the east coast of mainland Italy a similar clash got under way between Gianni di Marco, another bishop of the ECC, and the local Roman Catholic Bishop Michele Seccia (currently Archbishop of Lecce). This case in Alba Adriatica witnessed the usual accusations of confusing the Catholic faithful, ambiguous titles and parish names, and suspicions of ECC clergy going door-to-door offering blessings. After various excommunications and expulsions Di Marco is no longer part of the ECC[90] and has founded the Ecumenical *Apostolic* Church instead, subtitled the Episcopal Prelature of Europe. Its members continue to appear in the news from time to time for being confused with

Roman Catholic clergy. Agostino de Caro has also now quit the Ecumenical Catholic Church (ECC) for the larger Ecumenical Catholic Church of Christ (ECCC) – they are not the same thing: the ECCC, unlike the ECC, is not an offshoot of ICAB.

Also in 2013, in Bend, Oregon, Father James Radloff of Baker diocese was removed by his Bishop from priestly duties for reasons up to now not made public. The dispute – *National Catholic Reporter* calls it the Bend Controversy[91] – escalated to the point where Father Radloff joined the 'ECC' and started his own parish. But this was not the Ecumenical Catholic Church, it was the *Evangelical* Catholic Church. The Evangelical Catholic Church does share some heritage with the Ecumenical Catholic Church. In addition, the ECC presiding bishop's credentials descend from an offshoot launched by an ICAB priest called Dylmar Correia Balduino da Costa. Balduino da Costa was consecrated bishop by Luigi Mascolo on 5th June 1969. He strayed from ICAB and founded the Catholic Apostolic Church of *Jerusalem,* though it does not appear that he ever relocated to the Holy Land. Balduino da Costa did however consecrate more bishops inside Brazil – Jorge dos Santos Costa, then aged only 22[92] and currently identifying as an Anglican bishop[93] – and José Elias Jacomo dos Santos, who founded the *Reunited* Catholic Apostolic Church – they were clearly in need of some reuniting by that stage. Father Radloff's reception into the Evangelical Catholic Church in 2014 prompted 78 enquiries from other dismissed and former priests, keen to explore their own options with the ECC. NCR also reported that the ECC had received about 50 enquiries from women with theology degrees interested in ordination with the ECC, after reading about Father Radloff and the Bend Controversy.

The offshoots described here constitute some of the more organized, substantial, well-documented, and noteworthy examples. They have all made the news but they vary in orientation, 'flavor' and church-view. There are, and have been, countless other offshoots not mentioned here – the Free Ibero-American Catholic Apostolic Church; the Neo-Luciferian Church; the Belorussian

Slavic Orthodox Catholic Apostolic Church of the Slavic Byzantine Rite in the Americas and the World. This latter is just another example of a small micro-church from Brazil, in spite of the absurd name. It describes itself as "an *inseparable* part of the Church of Christ"[94] and seems to have been founded by Vittorio Giovanni Busa of Sicily – the Sicilian Belorussian Patriarch of Brazil. Even putting aside the farcical end of the spectrum, there are some characteristics of the micro-churches which appear time and time again: bishops receiving multiple consecrations; extravagant names and titles; name changes and high turnover; internal schisms with new offshoots appearing; and of course, conflict with the local Roman Catholic Church. This is not intended to be an attack on the offshoot micro-church subculture. There can be no doubt, and it must be stressed, that serious and worthwhile attempts to form genuine faith communities are included among the apparently less well-adjusted groups. But the common characteristics may allow us to really get to grips with the ICAB phenomenon. The ICAB movement broke away from the Vatican, but removing the 'Head' did not automatically render the body of bishops collegial. They have never constituted a real college of bishops – or a real international communion – but rather a vast number of individual kingpins. Duarte Costa had kept his bishops in line with his personal authority – they were all effectively his priests, not bishops. Papacy, for all its possible flaws, acts as a safeguard against the whims of individual bishops – there is no-one to effectively rein in an ICAB offshoot bishop or hold him to account. Attempts to assert authority, for example by senior bishops like Castillo Mendez, just prompted new internal schisms. ICAB does not have doctrinal or legal institutions or advisory bodies to which bishops are expected to show due deference; nor does ICAB recognize external, neutral institutions or bodies which might have a moderating or restraining influence. The ICAB founding principle, which permeates throughout the movement, is deeply rooted – if you are not happy with the way things are, you can just quit and start up again on your own. The world of the ICAB offshoots is simply the perpetuation of Duarte Costa's original 1945 schism, played out again and again in new contexts and for new audiences.

ICAB today

In spite of everything the ICAB 'mother church' kept going. Luis Fernando Castillo Mendez finally cemented his grip on ICAB at the eighth National Council, 5th to 6th July 1982, when he was elected President of the Bishops' Conference.[95] Six years later he was proclaimed, in addition to President, "Patriarch of ICAB" no less.[96] This period also saw the Canonization of Manoel Carlos Amorim Correia, founder of the original ICAB of Itapira in 1913.[97] The next big step was for the National Council to move ICAB's HQ to Brasilia, Castillo Mendez's patch, though everyone recognized that this was the *de facto* situation already.[98] Castillo Mendez did a good job of stabilizing and conservatizing ICAB, but the Roman Catholic Church always remained firm in its positions:

"1 – Since there is no guarantee of the validity of the sacraments received in the *'igreja brasileira'* they are to be re-conferred *'sub conditione.'*

"2 – Let it be known among our faithful that it is gravely illicit to attend or take part in religious events of the *'igreja brasileira'* or to contact their ministers.

"3 – Those who consciously attend the worship of such 'churches' or adhere to them cannot be accepted as Godparents at Baptisms or Confirmations."[99]

In spite of all this, ICAB today is the renegade Catholic Church that has found a kind of place in Brazilian society. The Roman Catholic Church sometimes voices its outrage – ICAB *still* uses similar vestments, symbols, and language, which may confuse the innocent faithful – but modern Brazilians are not easily shocked. Talking to young Brazilians in Rio de Janeiro and São Paulo, they are vaguely aware of the *Igreja Brasileira*, they have seen signs or announcements of it somewhere, but are unable to pinpoint anything distinctive or special about it. One student in Rio de Janeiro told me that she had been to an ICAB wedding – the same as other weddings she had been to, she said, except that it was outdoors, and slightly more fun. Official Roman Catholic movements in Brazil offer radical and exciting options for committed young people, from ultra-conservative to super-progressive, but mainstream Catholicism leaves the majority of young Brazilians wholly unmoved. ICAB long ago chose to sit parallel to mainstream Catholicism, not to challenge it. As long as ICAB offers its same old product line it is likely to continue to be a welcome last resort for those such as the divorced and remarried who cannot access the services they want from the Roman Catholic Church. If Brazilians' attachment to Roman Catholicism continues to weaken, but their attachment to the traditional rituals of baptism and marriage remain, then ICAB's popularity is likely to continue to steadily rise.

The results of Brazil's decennial religious census begin alphabetically with the Catholic Church – appropriately enough as it is also the majority religion. Brazil is home to over 150 million Catholics, predicted to rise to an astonishing 215 million in 2050[100] in spite of the onslaught of Pentecostalism, Evangelicalism, and Umbanda. The census lists both the *Igreja Católica Apostólica Romana* and the *Igreja Católica Apostólica Brasileira*[101] – both are recognised by the State. They could hardly be more different in size, though, with one representing 64.6% of the population, the other a mere 0.29% – 560,781 people (in 2010). This figure does not count people who may have declared a *dual* affiliation, those who may be *occasional* dual affiliates (these two groups are listed separately) or non-respondents. In 2006 Patriarch Castillo Mendez, who passed away in 2009, ventured an estimate of 15 million ICAB members, tempered by a Roman Catholic estimate of 3 million.[102] In the densely populated industrial conurbation known as Grande ABC[103] in São Paulo State, ICAB showed growth of 95.8% between the 2000 and 2010 censuses. This far outdoes even the

Evangelicals' growth of 35.6%, and goes alongside an actual drop in Roman Catholic allegiance of 9.4%.[104] In terms of ICAB clergy there is always bound to be some fluctuation, but numbers seem to have plateaued over the last decade at 50-something bishops and around 300 priests – six priests to every bishop.[105] But with ICAB's adherents growing by a steady 12% nationally,[106] it will be truly astonishing if theologians and commentators continue to be able to ignore ICAB. The results of the 2020 Census will be eagerly anticipated.

ICAB continues to be a haven for priests who, for a range of motives, part company with the Roman Catholic Church. One of the most common reasons may still be marriage, but it is not the only factor. In 2003 a Roman Catholic priest, Father Roosevelt de Sá Medeiros, was excommunicated for presumed involvement in drug dealing – a boy carrying cocaine and marijuana had been found in his bedroom and arrested by police. Father Roosevelt was also arrested and held for 15 days before being released without charge. In the meantime, the local bishop had not delayed in arranging Father Roosevelt's excommunication. "I gave my life to the Church and, in the end, I got booted out,"[107] he said. Father Roosevelt de Sá Medeiros soon made the switch to ICAB, was elected bishop, and duly consecrated. "If I had come across to ICAB when I was younger, I would have got married as well, but I have ended up all alone,"[108] he added. 2014 saw ICAB make international news when it suspended one of its bishops – Dom Fernando Pugliese – for officiating at a same-sex marriage.[109] Dom Fernando Pugliese then began giving interviews defending his belief in UFOs and the extraterrestrial origin of Jesus. Around the same time Dom Raúl Clementino Smania resurfaced – the by-now retired army nurse, aged 88, who had been branded a traitor by ICAB in the 1950's. Smania had started his own offshoot – the Holy Catholic Apostolic Church – but still stuck to a classic ICAB-style open-door policy at his wedding chapel – "The only thing I do not accept is bigamy. [Other than that] God does not discriminate. And what I do is just a bridge between the couple and God."[110] It is not difficult to understand how ICAB continues to have an appeal.

What next?

The original dynamism of *"abençoada rebeldia"*[111] – blessed rebelliousness – has long gone out of ICAB. As Brazilian scholar Wagner Pires da Silva wrote, it seems that "the Brazilian Catholic [Apostolic] Church is a shadow of what Dom Carlos Duarte da Costa pictured when he founded it in the 1940's."[112] The biggest internal enemy of the ICAB and micro-church movement is perhaps its tendency to balkanize or atomize into smaller sects. As Frédéric Luz wrote:

> "It is without doubt one of the greatest paradoxes of our century, to have provided the spectacle, on the one hand, of the 'big churches' all leaning, through a globalizing ecumenism, towards organizational unification, and on the other hand small independent communities that multiply turgidly."[113]

It seems that once a group threatens to destabilize the Church it becomes cursed to never, enjoy stability itself. They are "fluid and unstable in character due to their rebellious spirit and lack of uniform structure,"[114] as Kathleen Kautzer wrote about US micro-churches. Independent Catholicism has always seemed condemned to be a fissiparous reality.[115] The absence of recognized forms of hierarchical authority appears to result in the repetitive negative behavior mentioned in these pages. Occasionally a micro-church bypasses the tendency to split by improving cooperation with other groups and by encouraging internal diversity – a striking example of internal diversity being the Womenpriests who accept male members.[116] But the secret to being accepted and recognized by society and the authorities generally eludes the micro-churches. Since the early ICAB days the quest to "direct [the Church] onto the track of legality"[117] has confounded dissident priests such as Michael Von Roeder Michels; Pelypenko had disillusioned him saying "Your wish is in reality a dream which can never be realized."[118] Rumors of bishops and priests being accepted back into the Roman Catholic Church with full honors frequently tantalize micro-church hopefuls who are eager for recognition, but in reality the Vatican's position is utterly unswerving.

In defense of these aspects of the phenomenon, it could be said that some micro-churches simply consist of looser associations and a less rigid structure, allowing them to maximize their creativity and flexibility – what may look like a fractious collection of sub-groups may in fact be a more efficient working model. They would not be alone in envisaging flexible models for the future Church:

> "Maybe we are facing a new and different kind of epoch in the Church's history, where Christianity will again be characterized more by the mustard seed, where it will exist in small, *seemingly insignificant groups* that nonetheless live an intensive struggle against evil and bring the good into the world."[119]

For Catholic micro-churches to flourish they must secure valid Holy Orders. Ultra-traditionalists have even had to appeal to bishops from progressive lineages to procure ordinations for them,[120] with "more cross-fertilization than either side generally cares to admit."[121] Some offshoots, in similarity to the ICAB mother-church, seem to reject everything 'Roman' apart from the titles, vestments, hats, paraphernalia, rituals, rites, and jewellery. This can lead to accusations of merely 'playing church,'[122] but simply dismissing Catholic micro-churches as cranks carries risks of its own. Avery Dulles warned Catholics against pushing 'floating groups' further into schism because these offshoots are signs and symptoms of deeper unease – "a true crisis of identity"[123] happening at the grass-roots. Reaching out to the ICAB movement, though, has not been straightforward, as Cardinal Lorscheider wrote:

> "True ecumenical work with ICAB is not easy. This does not preclude prudent relations and a personal dialogue with individuals who are sincere and of good faith ... The difficulty arises, generally, from their questionable attitudes and low cultural level."[124]

Vatican II, however, insisted that the authentic Church may be found even among lowly, hopeless, and uncomfortable realities, "though they may often be small and poor ... Christ is present through whose power and influence the One, Holy, Catholic and Apostolic Church is constituted."[125] The Church of the future will continue to face the task of discerning, understanding, and identifying where and what the authentic Church of Christ actually is. As Avery Dulles predicted, dealing with the phenomenon he called the "underground church"[126] is a dimension of that task which should not be ignored.

Notes

[1] Julie Byrne, 'Catholic But Not Roman Catholic', *American Catholic Studies* Vol. 125, No. 3, Fall 2014, [pp 16-19], p 17
[2] Peter Hebblethwaite, *The Runaway Church*, Collins Fount, Glasgow, 1978, p 246
[3] Peter F. Anson, *Bishops At Large*, Faber and Faber, London, 1964
[4] John P. Plummer, *The Many Paths Of The Independent Sacramental Movement*, Apocryphile Press, Berkeley, CA, 2006, p 86
[5] David V. Barrett, *Sects, 'Cults' and Alternative Religions*, Blandford (Cassell), London, 1998, p 121
[6] Peter F. Anson, *Bishops At Large*, Faber and Faber, London, 1964, p.25
[7] *"Les Églises Parallèles"* is a 1991 work by Fr. Bernard Vignot, an Old Catholic priest, published by Cerf–fides, Paris. Frédéric Luz used the term in the subtitle of his 1995 book, published in Paris by Claire Vigne.
[8] Giles Hibbert OP, *Apostolic Succession – magic, power and priesthood*, Belfriars, London, 2002, p 2
[9] Avery Dulles, *The Resilient Church*, Gill and Macmillan, Dublin, 1978, p 15 – *The Underground Church* is also the title of a study by Kathleen Kautzer, published by Haymarket Books, Chicago, 2013
[10] Karl Prüter, *Bishops Extraordinary*, Saint Willibrord Press, Highlandville MO, 1985
[11] David V. Barrett, *Sects, 'Cults' and Alternative Religions*, p 122
[12] John P. Plummer and John R. Mabry, *Who Are The Independent Catholics?*, Apocryphile Press, Berkeley CA, 2006
[13] John P. Plummer, *The Many Paths Of The Independent Sacramental Movement*, 2006

14 Julie Byrne, *The Other Catholics: Remaking America's Largest Religion,* Columbia University Press, New York, 2016

15 Cf. John L. Allen Jr., *The Future Church,* Image, New York, 2009, p 91

16 Karl Rahner, *Theological Investigations XVII,* Darton, Longman and Todd, London, 1981, pp 197-198

17 Cf. Kathleen Kautzer, *The Underground Church,* 2013, p 15

18 Joseph Ratzinger, *Salt of the Earth,* Ignatius Press, San Francisco, 1997, p 243 – "In the Catholic Church herself there are, in fact, very deep ruptures, so much so that one sometimes really has the feeling that two Churches are living side by side in one Church." (pp 242-243)

19 Cf. Julie Byrne, 'Catholic But Not Roman Catholic,' p 17

20 Cf. John P. Plummer, *The Many Paths of the Independent Sacramental Movement,* pp 1-2

21 Cf. John P. Plummer, *The Many Paths of the Independent Sacramental Movement,* pp 66ff

22 Cf. Obispo Alejo Pelypenko, *Infiltración Comunista en las Iglesias de América,* Pia Sociedad de San Pablo, Buenos Aires, 1961, p 193

23 Cf. Dom Estêvão Bettencourt OSB, in *Pergunte e Responderemos,* Number 55, July 1962, online version at http://www.pr.gonet.biz/revista. php [accessed 05/04/2018]

24 Julie Byrne, 'Catholic But Not Roman Catholic', p 17

25 Holy Innocents, Long Beach CA, 'Warning! Not all 'Catholic Churches' are Catholic', parish bulletin, 24th Sept. 2017 – https://www.lbcatholic. com/documents/2017/9/09.24.17.pdf [accessed 21st April 2018]

26 Archdiocese of Santa Fe (USA), 'Local Schismatic Churches', undated – http://www.archdiocesesantafe.org/HomeFiles/LocalSchismatic Churches.pdf [accessed 19th April 2018]

27 Bernard J. Cooke, 'Progressive Approaches to Ministry', in Mary-Jo Weaver and R.Scott Appleby (eds), *What's Left? Liberal American Catholics,* Indiana University Press, Bloomington, 1999 [pp 135-146] p 142

28 Cf. *El Tiempo,* 29th April 2014 – http://blogs.eltiempo.com/alternativa-extraterrestre/2014/04/29/el-vaticano-sabe-de-extraterrestre/

29 Cf. Yves Congar OP, *Challenge to the Church,* Collins Liturgical Publications, London, 1977

30 Humberto Cucchetti, 'Algunas lecturas sobre la relación iglesia/ peronismo (1943-1955)' [Some readings on the Church/Peronism relationship (1943-1955)], *Revista Confluencia,* Yr. 1 No. 1, 2003, Mendoza, p 14

31 Humberto Cucchetti, p 16

32 Cf. Joseph A. Komonchak, 'Interpreting the Council – Catholic Attitudes toward Vatican II', in Mary Jo Weaver and R. Scott Appleby

(eds), *Being Right – Conservative Catholics in America*, Indiana University Press, Bloomington IN, 1995, [pp.17-36] see pp 19-20

33   Cf. Ormond Rush, *Still Interpreting Vatican II*, Paulist Press, New York/ Mahwah NJ, 2004, p 58

34   Pastoral Letter of the Bishops of the Ecclesiastical Province of São Paulo on the "Igreja Brasileira" in CNBB – Conferência Nacional dos Bispos do Brasil [National Conference of Bishops of Brazil], 'Comunicado Mensal' [Monthly Communiqué] number 243, December 1972, [pp 90-97], p 91

35   Pires da Silva, pp 122-123

36   Terrence W. Tilley, *Inventing Catholic Tradition*, Orbis Books, Maryknoll, NY, 2000, p 25

37   Ormond Rush, p 58

38   John P. Plummer, *The Many Paths of the Independent Sacramental Movement*, pp 1-2

39   Cf. Guia Mundo em Foco, *Óvnis - Eles estão entre nós [UFOs – they are among us]*, Sixth Edition, On Line Editora, undated, p 78, and Cf. Rose Lopes, *Dimensões Dos Aliens [Dimensions of the Aliens]*, Club de Autores, 2015, p 61 and Cf. *O Globo,* 27th January 2015 – 'Bispo é suspenso da Igreja por realizar casamento gay em Maceió' – http://g1.globo.com/ al/alagoas/noticia/2015/01/bispo-e-suspenso-da-igreja-por-realizar-casamento-gay-em-maceio.html [accessed 22nd April 2018]

40   Ormond Rush, p 36

41   Cf. *The Catholic Herald,* 9th March 2018 – 'Married priests likely to be on 2019 synod agenda' – http://www.catholicherald.co.uk/ commentandblogs/2018/03/09/analysis-married-priests-likely-to-be-on-2019-synod-agenda/ [accessed 22nd April 2018]

42   Cf. Phyllis Zagano, *Women & Catholicism – Gender, Communion, and Authority,* Palgrave Macmillan, New York, 2011, pp 59-60

43   Cf. Aloísio Cardinal Lorscheider, '"Igreja Brasileira," Esclarecimento e Procedimento', in *Convergência* (Journal of the Conference of Religious of Brazil – CRB), Yr. 25, No. 231, Apr. 1990, [pp 137-142], p 141

44   Cf. *Luta!* issue 7, August 1948, p 21

45   Cf. *Luta!* issue 8, July 1949, p 16

46   Cf. Bettencourt

47   Cf. Humberto Cucchetti, p 11

48   Cf. Humberto Cucchetti, p 14

49   Cf. *New York Times,* 3rd Aug. 1973, p 4 – ICAB "adopted a much more conservative line after Duarte Costa's death … it is ardently anti-Communist and accuses the Roman Catholics of leftist leanings."

50   Cf. Gabriel Seisdedos, *Hasta los Oidos De Dios,* Ediciones San Pablo, Buenos Aires, 1999, p 117

51 Cf. José C. Garcia Rodriguez, *Pedro Badanelli – La Sotana Española de Perón*, Akrón, Astorga, 2008
52 Cf. Pedro Badanelli, *Perón: la iglesia y un cura*, Tartessos, Buenos Aires, 1960, p 99, Cf. Cucchetti, p 11
53 Pedro Badanelli, p 99
54 Cucchetti, p 14
55 Cucchetti, p 16
56 Luis Bergonzi – conversation with the author, November 2005, at the ICAA Sanctuary, Alejandro Korn.
57 *Congregación Cristiana Católica Apostólica; Sacerdotes Obreros para la Argentina* [Catholic Apostolic Christian Congregation; Worker Priests for Argentina] founded around 1962.
58 Cf. *La Nación*, 25th July 2000, 'Thousands of people pray to pay homage to Rodrigo' – https://www.lanacion.com.ar/26145-miles-de-personas-rezaron-para-rendir-homenaje-a-rodrigo [accessed 22nd April 2018]
59 *La Nación*, 25th July 2000, 'Thousands of people pray to pay homage to Rodrigo' –
60 Cf. Alberto Miguel Dib, Fundación S.P.E.S. (Servicio Para el Esclarecimiento en Sectas [Service for Clarification on Sects]), http://es.catholic.net/op/articulos/683/cat/847/movimientos-de-origen-y-contenidos-catolicos-catolicos-disidentes.html [accessed 22nd April 2018]
61 CBCP (Catholic Bishops Conference of the Philippines) News, 5th Nov. 2012, 'Vatican warns CBCP against schismatic group in PH' – http://www.cbcpnews.com/cbcpnews/?p=7355 [accessed 23rd April 2018]
62 CBCP (Catholic Bishops Conference of the Philippines) News, 5th November 2012
63 *El Universal* (Ecuador), 24th Aug. 2017, 'En Bolivia advierten a fieles sobre 'sacerdotes'' – https://www.eluniverso.com/noticias/2017/08/24/nota/6345268/bolivia-advierten-fieles-sobre-sacerdotes [accessed 23rd April 2018]
64 *El Universal* (Ecuador), 24th August 2017, 'En Bolivia advierten a fieles sobre 'sacerdotes''
65 *La Stampa – Vatican Insider*, 1st August 2012, updated 31st March 2014, 'The strange case of "His Eminence" Bell' – http://www.lastampa.it/2012/08/01/vaticaninsider/eng/inquiries-and-interviews/the-strange-case-of-his-eminence-bell-XNfFjSKhSQwjPdRUdbd5qL/pagina.html [accessed 23rd April 2018]
66 Cf. Catholic Church of [sic] England & Wales [not to be confused with the Catholic Church in England and Wales] http://www.catholicchurchofenglandandwales.info/superior-general [accessed 23rd April 2018]

67 *La Stampa – Vatican Insider,* 1st August 2012, updated 31st March 2014

68 *La Stampa – Vatican Insider,* 1st August 2012, updated 31st March 2014

69 *La Stampa – Vatican Insider,* 1st August 2012, updated 31st March 2014

70 *La Stampa – Vatican Insider,* 1st August 2012, updated 31st March 2014

71 Cf. Bishop Manoel José da Rocha Neto, Administrative Secretary, 'Declaração Acerca do Arcebispo David Bell' [Declaration Regarding Archbishop David Bell], 12th July 2013 [accessed 20th May 2018] http://noticiasicab.blogspot.com.br/2013/07/declaracao-acerca-do-arcebispo-david.html?m=1

72 *Aciprensa,* 18th October 2006, 'Sacerdote que fundó secta en Guatemala quedó excomulgado' [Priest who founded sect in Guatemala is excommunicated] – https://www.aciprensa.com/noticias/sacerdote-que-fundo-secta-en-guatemala-quedo-excomulgado [accessed 25th April 2018]

73 Holy Innocents Catholic Church, Long Beach, Califormia, '¡Cuidado! No todas las 'Iglesias Católicas' lo son' [Warning! Not all 'Catholic Churches' are Catholic], parish bulletin, 24th September 2017 – https://www.lbcatholic.com/documents/2017/9/09.24.17.pdf [accessed 21st April 2018]

74 Igreja Carismática Católica https://sites.google.com/site/ccchurchbrasil/para-os-pobres-e/patristica---ditos/didaque/didaque-comentada-/celebracao-da-vida/lista-dos-padres-do-desert/o-novo-patriarca-da-ccchurch/concilio-mundial-ccc/secessao-vetero-catolica/sucessao-apostolica-vaticana [9th May 2018]

75 Anglicanos Tradicionais – http://anglicanotradicional.blogspot.com/2010/01/ [accessed 23rd April 2018]

76 Cf. *La Repubblica,* 7th Aug. 1987 – Francescone, absconding while under house arrest for his offenses, was arrested as part of "the most significant offensive against the organized racket in Southern Italy in recent years." – http://ricerca.repubblica.it/repubblica/archivio/repubblica/1987/08/07/manette-al-fuggiasco-travestito-da-vescovo.html [accessed 23rd April 2018]

77 Cf. *L'Osservatore Romano,* (English Edition), Number 32/33, 7th-14th August 2002, p 12

78 Congregation for the Doctrine of the Faith, *Decree of Excommunication,* 5th August 2002 – http://www.vatican.va/roman_curia/congregations/cfaith/documents/rc_con_cfaith_doc_20020805_decreto-scomunica_en.html [accessed 23rd May 2018]

79 John Wijngaards, in conversation with the author, 28th October 2014

80 *National Catholic Reporter,* 'Roy Bourgeois: They finally got him', 20th November 2012 – https://www.ncronline.org/blogs/ncr-today/roy-bourgeois-they-finally-got-him [accessed 24th April 2018]

81   Carol Ann Breyer, 'Common Collars: A Study of Collaboration Between Roman Catholic Married Priests and Roman Catholic Women Priests', *CORPUS Reports,* Vol. 37, No. 5, Sept. / Oct. 2011, p 23

82   Rosemary Radford Ruether, 'Women-Church', in Mary-Jo Weaver and R.Scott Appleby (eds), *What's Left? Liberal American Catholics,* Indiana University Press, Bloomington, Indiana, 1999, [pp 46-64], p 48

83   Not to be confused with the Institute of Christ the King Sovereign Priest, a traditionalist Latin Mass society canonically erected within the Roman Catholic Church.

84   ICOH – http://www.igrejaortodoxahispanica.com/Def_Principal.html [accessed 24th April 2018]

85   ICOH – http://www.igrejaortodoxahispanica.com/Def_Principal.html [accessed 24th April 2018]

86   Vatican in Exile – www.vaticaninexile.com, [accessed 25th April 2018]

87   Pope Michael was consecrated on 10th December 2011 by Robert Biarnesen; Biarnesan was consecrated exactly one month previously on 10th November 2011 by Alexander Justice; Justice was consecrated on 20th January 2003 by John Parnell; Parnell was consecrated on 5th May 2002 by Juergen Bless; Bless was consecrated on 4th January 1986 by Paul C.G.W. Schultz; Schultz was consecrated on 18th May 1975 by Emilio Federico Rodriguez y Durand (aka Fairfield) who was consecrated by Stefano Corradi in 1954.

88   Cf. Archbishop Mark Shirilau, *History and Overview of the Ecumenical Catholic Church: The First Ten Years: 1985-95,* Healing Spirit Press, Villa Grande CA, 1995, pp 21ff

89   Cf. *Today* (Italy), 1st July 2013, *'Da presidente Arcigay a prete; l'arcivescovo: "Rischia la scomunica" [From president of Arcigay to priest; the archbishop: "He risks excommunication"]* http://www.today.it/citta/presidente-arcigay-prete-agrigento.html

90   Cf. Center for Studies on New Religions, Italy – http://www.cesnur.com/la-chiesa-autocefala-ortodossa-ucraina-e-la-chiesa-cattolica-ecumenica/ [accessed 24th April 2018]

91   Cf. *NCR,* https://www.ncronline.org/feature-series/bend-controversy/stories [accessed 24th April 2018]

92   This beats Castillo Mendez's record for the title of World's Youngest Bishop when he was aged 25.

93   Cf. http://dioceseanglocatolicasantacruz.blogspot.com/p/blog-page_15.html [accessed 9th May 2018]

94   The Belorussian Slavic Orthodox Catholic Apostolic Church of the Slavic Byzantine Rite in the Americas – http://www.panaghia.org.br/ -- [emphasis added] [accessed 25th April 2018]

95 Cf. ICAB document – Preâmbulo Comemorativo dos 65 anos de Organização Jurídico-Eclesial [Commemorative Preamble for the 65th Anniversary of the Juridical-Ecclesial Foundation], p 14

96 Cf. ICAB document – Preâmbulo Comemorativo, p 15

97 Cf. ICAB document – Preâmbulo Comemorativo, p 15

98 Cf. ICAB document – Preâmbulo Comemorativo, p 15

99 Pastoral Letter of the Bishops of the Ecclesiastical Province of São Paulo, December 1972, p 95

100 Cf. John L. Allen Jr, *The Future Church*, Image, New York, 2009, p 18

101 IBGE (Instituto Brasileiro de Geografia e Estatística) website at: ftp:// ftp.ibge.gov.br/Censos/Censo_Demografico_2010/Caracteristicas_ Gerais_Religiao_Deficiencia/tab1_4.pdf [accessed 19 December 2014]

102 Cf. *Diário de Natal*, 9th April 2006, p 14

103 The original cities making up Grande ABC were Santo André, São Bernardo, and São Caetano. It is a major center of manufacturing, especially cars, and also known as a hotbed of left-wing politics.

104 Cf. *Diário do Grande ABC*, 10th March 2013, 'Eles são católicos mas ignoram o papa' [They are catholics but they ignore the pope] by Fábio Munhoz, http://www.dgabc.com.br/Noticia/91241/eles-sao-catolicos- mas-ignoram-o-papa [accessed 19 December 2014]

105 Cf. *O Globo – G1*, 'Ordenado primeiro bispo da Igreja Católica Apostólica Brasileira na Guatemala' [First bishop for Guatemala ordained by the Brazilian Catholic Apostolic Church], 27th October 2007 – http:// g1.globo.com/Noticias/Mundo/0,,MUL160878-5602,00-ORDENA DO+PRIMEIRO+BISPO+DA+IGREJA+CATOLICA+APOSTO LICA+BRASILEIRA+NA+GUATEMA.html [accessed 20th May 2018]

106 Cf. *'Diário do Grande ABC'*, 10th March 2013, 'Eles são católicos mas ignoram o papa'

107 Father Roosevelt de Sá Medeiros, quoted in *ISTOÉ*, Number 2283, 16th August 2013, 'A vida dos padres excomungados' [The lives of excommunicated priests] – https://istoe.com.br/319468_A+VIDA+ DOS+PADRES+EXCOMUNGADOS/ [accessed 25th April 2018]

108 Father Roosevelt de Sá Medeiros, quoted in *ISTOÉ*, Number 2283, 16th August 2013

109 Cf. *O Globo*, 27th January 2015, 'Bispo é suspenso da Igreja por realizar casamento gay em Maceió' – http://g1.globo.com/al/alagoas/ noticia/2015/01/bispo-e-suspenso-da-igreja-por-realizar-casamento- gay-em-maceio.html [accessed 25th April 2018]

110 Dom Raúl Smania, *Igreja de um bispo só [The Church with just one bishop]*, Gauchazh news, 18th August 2013 – https://gauchazh.clicrbs. com.br/geral/noticia/2013/08/igreja-de-um-bispo-so-a-historia-

do-homem-que-criou-uma-igreja-e-agora-luta-para-que-ela-se-perpetue-4237532.html

111   From the title of G.A. de Freitas, *Igreja Brasileira: Abençoada Rebeldia*, CET-ICAB, São Paulo, 1987

112   Wagner Pires da Silva, 'Another Catholicism: The Bishop of Maura and the Brazilian Catholic Apostolic Church', *Revista de História Bilros* (Fortaleza), Vol. 5, No. 8, Jan-Apr. 2017 [pp 106-125] p 123

113   Frédéric Luz, *Le Soufre et L'Encens [Sulphur and Incense]*, 1995, p 15

114   Kathleen Kautzer, *The Underground Church*, 2013, p 14

115   Cf. Peter F. Anson, *Bishops At Large*, Faber & Faber, London, 1964, p 29, "the sects about which I have written have been connected either directly or indirectly with previous rents in the garment of the Bride of Christ." Cf. H.R.T. Brandreth, *Episcopi Vagantes and the Anglican Church*, SPCK, London, 1961, pp 4-5

116   Cf. Carol Ann Breyer, 'Common Collars', 2011, p 23

117   Pelypenko, p 119

118   Pelypenko, p 118

119   Joseph Ratzinger, *Salt of the Earth*, Ignatius Press, San Francisco, 1997, p 16 [emphasis added]

120   Cf. 'The Consecration of Pope Michael', 18th Aug. 2012, [accessed 24 December 2014] http://popemichael.vaticaninexile.com/Files/The%20Consecration%20of%20Pope%20Michael.pdf,

121   John P. Plummer, *The Many Paths of the Independent Sacramental Movement*, p 2

122   Cf. John P. Plummer, *The Many Paths of the Independent Sacramental Movement*, p 67

123   Avery Dulles, *The Resilient Church*, Gill and Macmillan, Dublin, 1978, p 15

124   Aloísio Cardinal Lorscheider, in *Convergência* (CRB), Yr. 25, No. 231, Apr. 1990 [pp 137-142] p 142

125   *Lumen Gentium* 26

126   Avery Dulles, *The Resilient Church*, Gill and Macmillan, Dublin, 1978, p 15

VII

"WHERE AND WHAT IS THE CHURCH?"[1]
— Theological critique of the
ICAB phenomenon —

These days the idea of a person starting their own Church is neither scandalous nor shocking. The grip of the institutional Churches has been replaced with a religious freedom that makes it both possible and acceptable for a person to found their own religion if they feel the need to. But for the individual Christian the objective is not just to have something satisfying or fun to belong to – the Church "is not a club we join because we like what it offers or find the people congenial"[2] – rather, the objective is to actually encounter Christ, in the Church which Christians believe he founded. Seekers are therefore faced with the question, "is this Church or that, which calls itself the Church of Christ, really Christ's Church?"[3] ICAB's self-understanding affirms that it is the Church in just the same way and as much as – if not more than – the Roman Catholic Church or any other Church. ICAB displays many features of Catholicism – not least, having priests, bishops, and sacraments – and declares itself to be a legitimate manifestation of that Church brought into being by Jesus Christ. So how can this claim be tested?

> "In view of the many false developments, of fanaticism and heresy, even the possibility of a pseudo-Church … [this question] constantly confronts us and demands an answer: where and what is the Church? … Not only the universal Church, but the local Church too … has to ask itself, must ask itself, what it is that makes it legitimate."[4]

The ICAB phenomenon serves as a reminder that the Church must face this demand for evidence of its own authenticity, as it

187

is the right and duty of the individual Christian to know the true Church. By what shall we know the true Church? By what must we test its authenticity and, if it claims to possess it, its Catholicity? A theological discussion of the ICAB phenomenon presents a challenge in that it has no distinct theology of its own, as observers both inside and outside of the movement have always pointed out. The existence of ICAB and its branches and offshoots, however, clearly touches on several theological themes, and raises pertinent questions for the whole Church:

a) *Does Catholic Church necessarily mean* Roman *Catholic Church?*
b) *Is the Papacy relevant?*
c) *Can the Church be both inclusive and Catholic?*
d) *"Internal ecumenism"[5] or "unacceptable diversity"[6] – what are the Church's limits?*
e) *Lex suprema salus animarum?*
f) *What about the validity of Sacraments and understanding of Priesthood?*

Credo in unam, sanctam, catholicam, et apostolicam Ecclesiam. The creedal marks of the Church are traditionally believed to "summarize the whole essence of Christ's teaching and testimony,"[7] but it is not clear "whether the creed is asserting a fact about the Church as it actually exists, an ideal of what it ought to be, or a promise about what it eventually will be."[8] Relying on Creeds may risk highlighting outward conformity alone, while the Church "can only be recognised for what it is through faith."[9] Faith is even more important than the initiative, innovation, and courage that have always been key features of the pioneering, militant Church. "The basic foundation of the Church" wrote Johann Adam Möhler "is the *living* Christ, the God who became human, not the search as to whom he might be."[10] Even the question of locating and identifying the authentic Church only has value in partnership with the question of discovering and nourishing faith. God's grace, after all, works always and everywhere, by definition; it is not held captive inside the Church. In Catholic theology God's grace is inclusive of people and exclusive of other faiths; whether you are Christian or not, the theology goes, there is no way to salvation except through Christ.[11] This is the dilemma and the challenge of interreligious dialogue. The 'inclusive' approach holds "that all non-Christian religious truth belongs ultimately to Christ."[12] This approach "avoids confrontation, but seeks to discern ways by which the non-Christian faiths may be integrated creatively into Christian theological reflection."[13] So even the inclusive approach is both inclusive and exclusive at the same time. This approach can be extended to recognizing God's grace also moving among 'separated groups' and even in cases of wilful and stubborn separation – schism. The decision to separate oneself from the communion of the Church may be an error, but the choices an individual makes in relation to the Church must surely risk error because they must be made freely. Christians' freedom stems from their faith, so even the individual making an unwise choice in their Church life may still hold on to an unchanging faith – which is sure because they are exercising freedom; "The freedom of the Christian is living faith within, which cannot be changed since Christ is the same today and forever."[14] But the people of God, in their freedom, have also developed 'markers' to identify and delineate the Church and membership of it, in order to steer clear of error.

a) Does Catholic Church necessarily mean Roman Catholic Church?

Karl Adam wrote that "communion with Peter and the Roman church has been regarded from the earliest times as a fundamental necessity of the Catholic conscience."[15] Clement, Ignatius, and Cyprian all recognised the pre-eminence of the church in Rome as "an authoritative and decisive influence on the development of doctrine, morals and worship."[16] What this has meant in practice has obviously been the subject of development. What is the Vatican for Catholics today – Head Office, HQ, a thing to visit, or is it truly their moral and spiritual fountainhead?

Catholics may experience only a tenuous connection to Rome. Paul Lakeland wrote that "most Catholics look to Rome for *some* kinds of leadership, [but] most if not all Catholics are primarily nourished in their faith life by the local community, not by the diocese or the national or world Church."[17] Catholics may have a sense of being in a 'world Church' but the real and immediate task of being a Catholic *in* the world is on their doorstep; reaching out to the suffering, the excluded, the lonely, the marginalized, the non-Catholic, and the non-believing.

Identifying as Catholic is unlikely to be driven by a tangible personal relationship with Rome at its center and is more likely to begin with some personal concern, experience or need – even something as undramatic as curiosity, doubt, residual childhood faith, or a nagging sense of obligation. It stands to reason that feeling in some real sense 'Roman' struggles to find its place in the list of priorities – unless Roman Catholic means no more than the sound of rosary beads rattling in one's pocket. Catholic identity often seems to hang on "a fragile thread"[18] and the word Catholic "is claimed and changed by various self-described Catholics – including Roman Catholics."[19] Locally specific ways of being Catholic have always exercised a powerful influence, too, even if modern ways of being Catholic have tended to relegate the geographical dimension.[20] Diversity is the future as well as the past of Catholicism. The idea of the 'world Church' doing everything exactly the same in all places and for all ages is an illusion. In our time the Church's move "from monolithic to pluriform unity"[21] is not only irreversible but is also a recognition of reality. Pining for the old certainties under a godlike Pope is not likely to be satisfied – most of the Vatican II Popes have been *pro*-Vatican II Popes, and even after "35 years of traditionalist appointments to the Electoral College, the 120 Cardinal Electors of 2013 chose one of the most progressive amongst them, having almost elected him at the previous conclave of 2005."[22] The Catholic understanding of 'Rome' is likely to continue to develop as part of a global-and-local rather than a global-and-centralized outlook.

The ICAB dispute can be seen in terms of the wider debate on the relationship between the universal and local church[23] and what this says about the sources of Catholic experience and Catholic identity in a particular place. Within a couple of generations, the Church in Brazil passed from the *padroado real* to religious freedom, and then into a period of rigorous Romanization. Under royal patronage the Church was effectively State power itself, but all appointments were at least Brazilian. In the First Republic period, when all religions gained equal legal footing, Protestant missionaries began to arrive. Then, waves of immigration – Armenian, Syrian, Russian, German, Polish, etc. – brought their quotas of pastors, priests, and rabbis. Brazil became extraordinarily diverse. In response the Catholic Church 'Romanized.' Senior appointments, now emanating from the Vatican, were increasingly Italian, and missionary orders, also predominantly Italian, flooded the country. From 1913 ICAB (in its earlier incarnation) constituted the extreme end of the resistance to Romanization, supported by anticlericals, nationalists, and Freemasons. Duarte Costa relaunched ICAB in 1945 and envisaged it as the true Church in its truly local, Brazilian expression. The *ICAR* on the other hand – the *Igreja Católica Apostólica* Romana – was to be rejected as a European and mainly Italian import, foisted upon Brazil and not authentically the Brazilian Church. It was an imposition, an illegitimate overseas extension of the Roman diocese, which should occupy itself with the church in Rome. ICAB, like some of its offshoots, is firmly rooted in a particular place and a local experience of Catholicism, so that they are arguably a legitimate expression of that place's way of being Catholic.

The ICAB phenomenon poses the question of whether, and in what sense, there is a need to be *Roman* Catholic. Even for the ICAB movement the answer may not be a foregone conclusion – it may be possible to recognize Rome's pre-eminence and a special role for the Pope, while rejecting the requirement of administrative and ideological submission to the Vatican apparatus. When we add together all the adherents and sympathizers of non-Roman – that is,

Independent – Catholic churches and communities it seems that a significant number of Catholics not only question and condemn the Vatican's supposed monopoly on being Catholic, but actively reject it. That monopoly, in fact, has long been broken. It is the Roman Church, ICAB has argued, that does not want or even tolerate true unity and rejects diversity – not in principle, of course, but because diversity is practically incompatible with rigid and total conformity. Rome masquerades as superior, ICAB suggests, as demonstrated in the false addition of non-Biblical and non-Apostolic tags such as Eminence, Archbishop, Metropolitan, and Cardinal, which ICAB rejects, as it does with the honorific 'Monsignor.'[24]

Difference and individuality, according to Johann Adam Möhler, do not have to be suppressed for the sake of unity.[25] The whole Church, in fact, only exists through the "free development and unhindered movement"[26] of individuals. At the same time, the Christian is never really free from the historical and political reality of which the local church is also a product. The whole Church works within structures it has inherited, which were not necessarily designed for the task at hand. This is achieved within the context of a generalized crisis of confidence in institutions – governments, corporations, NGOs – which have so often earned people's distrust. People have "grown disillusioned with conventional religious institutions"[27] and even Catholics do not refrain from seeking non-Catholic solutions. This has long coincided with increased missionary zeal by non-Catholic religions,[28] and this is especially true of Brazil. Many Catholics experience "a pervasive sense that the Church has failed them."[29] But as long as the struggle to maintain unity in the Church is on the agenda, traditional sources of unity will continue to be valued as well as debated. Duarte Costa had served the Roman Catholic Church for 34 years without experiencing an aversion in principle to papal primacy. He then objected to the Papacy as he saw it in a particular moment in time – we cannot know for certain how he would have reacted to the Papacy as it is exercised today. Was Duarte Costa short-sighted? He railed against a model of the Church which he assumed could never change, but he ignored his own history lessons. He also kidded himself that his own new Church would somehow be immune to fossilization, stagnation, and error.

b) Is the Papacy relevant?

The Brazilian Roman Catholic bishops warned that "Rebelling against Peter – that is, the Pope – is to founder in the faith." [30] Walter Kasper wrote that "acceptance of the primacy of the Bishop of Rome is a very hallmark of Catholic identity"[31] but he admitted that the actual function of primacy is still debatable: "The ... relation between primacy and collegiality, the relation between the universal and the local church, the interpretation of the direct jurisdiction of the pope in all local churches, ... and other issues raise theological and practical questions which remain open."[32] The Papacy is a role that never has been defined once and for all time, except in rather broad theological terms. Papacy as absolute sovereignty clearly offers one historical attempt at a definition[33] just as future interpretations and developments will offer something else. The history of the development of the Papacy can be viewed critically as "a first period of healthy, organic development ... *centrum unitatis* ... and a second period of cancerous, metastatic growth."[34] In 1945, when Duarte Costa rebuffed his excommunication, quoting Tertullian, Vatican II had not yet reaffirmed the ancient autonomy of local churches[35] and that the bishop does not *derive* his authority from the pope: "[bishops are not] to be regarded as vicars of the Roman Pontiff; for they exercise the power which they possess in their own right."[36] As Kasper pointed out, these relationships are works in progress. The nature and role of the Papacy is neither set in stone and nor is it taboo any longer; John R. Quinn wrote in 1999 that "For the first time it is the Pope himself who raises and legitimizes the question of reform and change in the papal office in the Church. Pope John Paul II calls for a widespread discussion of how this reform could be brought about and what shape it could take."[37] To rebel against a never-changing Church or a never-changing Papacy, as Duarte Costa did, is to rebel against a myth.

The Second Vatican Council (*Lumen Gentium* 14) reaffirmed hierarchy – along with faith and sacraments – as a fundamental 'mark' and focus of the Church's unity.[38] The Brazilian Roman Catholic hierarchy denied condemning ICAB "out of sectarian instincts,"[39] but were unequivocal in stating that ICAB "cannot present itself as the legitimate Catholic Church of Christ [because] it is separated from the visible center of unity of the Church of Christ, who is the Pope! [sic]"[40] Avery Dulles wrote that "the Church may be *expected* to assume a 'sectarian' stance precisely in order to make a distinctively Catholic contribution."[41] Precisely because the Papacy is able to adapt to the times, Klaus Schatz argued, it has often been the focus of contention – "the problem of *continuity* or *rupture* arises whenever the primacy, in response to new historical challenges, takes on a new historical form."[42] The core problem of ICAB with regard to the papal primacy is that it rejected it in principle in its historicity, not just how it has been historically exercised. Even so, ICAB's own appointments of General Supervisor, Dean of Bishops, President of the Episcopal Conference, Patriarch etc. point to the need for someone in a presiding role as a point of reference, a focus and symbol of unity. The need for someone with precisely such a uniting task is felt by many Christians. The concept of a ministry with *Petrine* characteristics and primacy continues to enjoy support among Catholics and non-Catholics alike – there has never been a significant movement in favor of abolishing the Papacy, which would be anti-historical. Many institutions of the Church "have had their times of failure and of self-aggrandizement, and we do not therefore conclude that they must be discarded,"[43] Michael Ramsey wrote. Some Protestant theologians argue that even Martin Luther did not reject the Papacy in principle, contrary to popular belief,[44] and "the issue of papal primacy [remained] for the Lutheran Reformers … an 'open question.'"[45] Anglicans, facing increased conflict within their Communion,[46] recognize the need to address "ministry at the global level"[47] and they have not abandoned the topic of Primacy and Petrine ministry.[48] "All primacy is ... a Petrine ministry"[49] aimed at balancing "unity and diversity, a diverse unity and a united diversity."[50] For Catholics, doing ecumenism need not mean trying to hide the Papacy under the carpet or knock sharp corners off it, and it is not necessarily the biggest obstacle to Christian unity – the issues of sacraments, ordination, ministry, and gender arguably constitute bigger stumbling blocks.

In comparison to some churches, ICAB and its offshoots may only have a handful of differences with Rome, but if they reject the idea of Primacy or a *Petrine* role in the World Church – in practice as well as historically – then dialogue is impossible. And if there is no openness to dialogue then ICAB looks more sectarian than Catholic. The state of separation of *individual* 'separated brethren' may not be certain, however. The status in Canon Law of some offshoot groups may be ambiguous, and it may be too sweeping to brand them all individually as schismatics without assessing the details. Yves Congar, writing about the SSPX case, called for "internal ecumenism,"[51] which "should be less difficult than the other kind of ecumenism since we have many more points of reference in common. Indeed, we have (nearly) everything in common!"[52] Something similar could be said about ICAB. The splintery ICAB movement, furthermore, could badly use "a focus (and locus) of unity"[53] as the Papacy has been described. What else – and this is no rhetorical question – could do the job of "symbolizing the unity of the Church"[54] for them if not a gifted individual with a vocation for that task? The danger of rejecting the Petrine principle is the danger of rejecting continuity with the historic Catholic communion – unity with the past of the Church as well as the present. Duarte Costa's contemporary critics were not sure precisely upon what basis he rejected papal primacy. Father Dubois pointed out the inconsistency in Duarte Costa's argument that the Pope is just a bishop as he is, a man as he is, with no right to excommunicate a fellow bishop – "A sublime argument! Father Carlos Duarte accepted his nomination [as bishop, in 1924] in spite of it coming from a man just like Father Carlos Duarte and like all the others."[55] If he recognized the right of the Pope to appoint him bishop, he should have recognized the right of the Pope to depose him. He did not become a pastor of souls on his own, or by the 'will of the people.'

c) Can the Church be both inclusive and Catholic?

Johann Adam Möhler used the image of a choir to explain the interdependent relationship between unity and diversity in the Church.[56] A choir is composed of people of different ages, genders, talents, pitches. Harmony could never be achieved by them all making the same sounds, nor would it be quite the same if even one voice were missing. While sin equals division and disunity, virtue is in unity and union – "just as each individual in the whole is grounded in God, God can be known by the individual only in the whole."[57] The Catholic Church really does hold together enormous diversity, though differing factions may appear to have very little in common. Richard McBrien wrote that "it has become increasingly evident that there are sometimes sharper divisions *within* the Catholic Church than there are between some Catholics and some Protestants."[58] Karl Rahner pointed out that divergence of belief between different denominations of Christians is mirrored by at least equal divergence of belief between the individual Christian and the official teaching of their Church. The extent of divergence may vary, he said, and may not be directly or consciously contradictory. It is a general difference of perception as to what faith involves on a day-to-day basis.[59] The possibility of Christian unity is therefore a multi-faceted problem and has nothing to do with "presenting a template to the Christian [and] inviting acceptance as the mark of possessing 'the Faith.'"[60] The experience of Christians in all traditions, Rahner observed, includes dissent. This points to the tantalizing possibility that Christians may be closer to each other in what they actually believe and practise than denominational templates suggest.

The Church, however it is identified and demarcated, is ultimately made up of flawed people – "the converted [who] are always in the process of conversion."[61] The Church did not descend fully formed on a cloud, nor is it inevitable. It requires the daily, free decision of people to keep it going[62] – *ecclesia semper reformanda est* – it is a constantly re-*form*ing Church. Nor is the nature of the Church inevitable either, even if some fundamental characteristics can be identified.[63] Constantly re-forming the Church is a free decision because the "freedom of the Christian is living faith within, which cannot be changed since Christ is the same today and forever."[64] The tendency to bemoan 'the state of the Church,' meaning the sum of its various dissidences, flaws, and inadequacies, risks failing to grasp the historical reality of the Church. Even the Apostles "did not get along with one another particularly well, they squabbled at times and remained a pretty fractious bunch throughout [Jesus's] public ministry, but these personal idiosyncrasies are dwarfed in importance by the common work they did of leading the young Church they built on Jesus' foundations."[65] The unity of the Church has never been measured by the extent of agreement or good fellowship between its members. It may be necessary to give up the idea that disunity means everyone disagreeing with each other, and that unity equates to uniformity of positions, rather than the recognition of shared purpose and the actual real presence of Jesus Christ.

d) *"Internal ecumenism"*[66] *or "unacceptable diversity"*[67] *– what are the Church's limits?*

The Catholic Church may be much less homogeneous than is generally presumed and this need not be seen as a great tragedy or paradox. To talk of a common Catholicity relies more on shared theology – sacraments, mediation – than common praxis in the day-to-day.[68] Catholic theology is incarnational, consisting of outward manifestation of inner mystery.[69] Idealizing formal – outward – convergence and even pretending that there is one type

197

of Catholicism "places a premium on the human dimension"[70] and is a move away from mystery. As a result, 'joint worship' events even among Roman Catholics of different cultures or rites always seem impossible to achieve with solemnity and decorum; they end up looking "like religious consumerism or syncretism."[71] It does not follow from diversity that anything goes; there is "acceptable and unacceptable diversity."[72] But diversity itself is an inescapable fact, Möhler argued, because even the passing of time changes the way religion presents itself: "religion begets various views of the world according to various periods, cultures, races, peoples, families, individuals, indeed according to various stages of development."[73] Diversity is not just tolerable or inevitable but desirable: "religion can make itself known completely *only* in an infinity of such variations."[74] But how could acceptable diversity be encouraged with those who insist on standing apart?

For all that was permissive about Vatican II there was no watershed on allowing open access to the Eucharist. This is because of "the intrinsic connection between eucharistic [sic] communion and ecclesial communion. The one signifies *and calls for* the other."[75] The Eucharist is a sign of unity, but not an open invitation to join in. Full ecclesial communion between Churches would mean that "they not only share the same faith with regard to the sacraments of Holy Orders and Eucharist, but also recognize one another's Eucharist as fully valid."[76] The Roman Catholic Church has no such confidence in the Holy Orders and Eucharist of the ICAB movement, incidentally, even while admitting that there may be individual cases of validity. Does this mean that it is the Roman Catholic Church that is sectarian? It means that formal or outward unity is not the only goal – essential communion of faith is what unites the Church. The Church may indeed "assume a *'sectarian'* stance"[77] in its actual practice because the faith – the core – of the Church is only understood "by looking at the actual practice of Christian believers."[78] Getting to the heart of the Church's practice circumvents the temptation "to trot out a series of definitions from the Nicene Creed or the *Catechism of the Catholic Church*"[79] in an attempt to explain the faith. The challenge of distinguishing which elements of Church practice are products of history, designed to accomplish a particular goal, and which elements are fundamental, still remains.[80] The Eucharist and Scripture are regarded as fundamentals "because although one could imagine a community of faith that has neither ... it would not be *this* particular community of faith."[81] Beyond the essentials, Christianity must obviously accept degrees of difference and even separation – a kind of internal 'great schism'[82] – because the illusion of agreement on everything is no realistic or desirable target.

Duarte Costa's ecumenism was certainly well in advance of the Second Vatican Council, which gave the biggest push to the inclusivist approach.[83] The post-Vatican II Catholic Church would have less difficulty in theory with Duarte Costa's attitude since the Church "rejects nothing of what is true and holy in [other] religions."[84] Furthermore, the Council itself was silent on what form this attitude was supposed to take in practice.[85] Duarte Costa's attitude towards other religions was extremely relaxed. Roman Catholic bishops were shocked that "where they have not yet constructed churches of their own, ministers of the *'igreja brasileira'* operate out of Umbanda and Candomblé premises, where they even go so far as to 'administer sacraments'!" [86] It is fair to conclude that ICAB has always operated a very open Eucharistic table in these and other situations. This level of 'unacceptable diversity' underlines "the difficulty of true ecumenical progress with the *'Igreja Brasileira'*"[87] – and there is no indication that ICAB would want it any other way.

e) Lex suprema salus animarum?

Micro-churches of the ICAB tradition sometimes appeal to Canon 1752 of the Code of Canon Law by way of justification. It is the last of the canons, and makes *reference* – this point is crucial – to the *'lex suprema'* or supreme law of the Church, which is the salvation of souls. Karl Rahner mentioned the *lex suprema* in the context of justifications for the ordination of married men and women[88] and it has been frequently used in their defense since then. The *lex suprema* does not appear in the Code as a stand-alone law, however; it is tagged onto the guidance for the transfer of a pastor, and the whole canon reads as follows:

> "Canon 1752 — In cases of transfer the prescripts of can. 1747 are to be applied, canonical equity is to be observed, and the salvation of souls, which must always be the supreme law of the Church, is to be kept before one's eyes."

While this law is indeed, as Thomas J. Paprocki wrote, "meant to apply to all areas of canonical jurisprudence" and "helps make the law approachable" for the uninitiated, it must not "lose its effectiveness ... by becoming too easily invoked in any and every situation."[89] The danger of such a general maxim, however important, is obvious: it "could be cited for conflicting sides of the same argument. ... Each could argue his position based on his concern for the supreme law of the Church."[90] To reach agreement in such a situation would require reference to other canons, providing those appealing to Canon 1752 are not under the illusion that its invocation renders the rest of the Code of Canon Law irrelevant. There is no suggestion whatsoever that Canon 1752 is intended to take precedence over all the other canons. Canon 1752 *refers* to the 'supreme law' – it is not 'the supreme canon' that trumps all the others. The supreme law *is to be kept before one's eyes* in harmony with the rest of the canons; and "that is only one reason why the Code of Canon Law contains one thousand seven hundred and fifty-two canons instead of just this one supreme law!"[91] The whole of the law – and every canon – in fact must be directed towards the salvation of souls, as an expression of the whole collective effort of the Church. The most common delicts in the world of ICAB and its offshoots would be Canon 1364 for Schism, which carries an automatic excommunication, and Canon 1382, unauthorized episcopal consecration, which also carries an automatic major excommunication. A typical defense appealing to Canon 1752 would be that the ordaining bishop is providing priests, and therefore access to the sacraments, for one section of the Church which has somehow been excluded or isolated. This may betray a superficial or immature understanding of what the salvation of souls is, equating salvation with frequent access to the sacraments by any means. Furthermore, it promotes a conception of the priest as intermediary, savior, and dispenser of sacraments; salvation depends on having access to *him* rather than being in communion with the Church, which is a distortion of the Catholic understanding.

Any group perceiving itself as 'saving the Church' or 'revitalizing the Church' or 'returning the Church to its origins' risks aligning itself, according to Möhler, with the attitude of the ancient heretics for whom "the preservation of Christian doctrine must be viewed as a human work because they believed that *they* were to call upon human beings to discover it again."[92] Möhler explained this as a fundamental lack of faith in the "Holy Spirit who continually preserves the Church, [which is] formed and enlivened by that Spirit"[93] and not by human saviors. The heretic believes in human saviors coming to the rescue, not God. Enlightened groups of Church-savers tend to break away from the mainstream as though "Christianity and Christ could be grasped most certainly in a separatistic and egotistic manner aside from any Church community."[94] This is echoed in Richard McBrien's observation that the opposite of Catholic is *Sectarian* rather than Protestant, as is often thought.[95] For heretics, the faith is constantly slipping from our grasp, and it is always a good time for drastic action. All of this unfortunately rings very true of the ICAB movement, longing to purge Catholicism of all its flaws. A more mature appreciation of the Church accepts that it exists in a state of tension rather than idyllic peace, and that tensions "can be fruitful and are, in fact, a sign of life. When tensions stop, there is death,"[96] Walter Kasper wrote. ICAB and its micro-churches tend to dispense with tension and go directly to blaming the eternal enemy, Rome.

In the years after Vatican II, as Wagner Pires da Silva noted, the Roman Catholic Church in Brazil wanted to "put a check on popular

Brazilian Catholicism."[97] ICAB stepped into that breach, churning out sacraments "and sacramentalization"[98] as though the sheer accumulation of rituals and blessings mathematically added up to greater and greater 'salvation.' They aimed for the lowest common denominator "with the emphasis on baptisms, confirmations, and weddings."[99] The Roman Catholic bishops condemned ICAB for "the falsification of the idea of religion."[100] ICAB aspired to "the ritual-based image of the ordained ministry"[101] like the ancient heretics, who venerated the rituals themselves "in which no spirit dwelt."[102] ICAB, the bishops said, stood in opposition to an "authentic ecclesial renewal" and the reception of sacraments in a "conscientious, active, and fruitful way, [consistent] with the teaching of Vatican II."[103] The CNBB decided that it was important to "remain alert to new developments ... that may arise from the *Igreja Brasileira* and independent groups"[104] so that the Roman Catholic Church itself could avoid reproducing "all these negative aspects"[105] themselves.

f) *What about the validity of Sacraments and understanding of Priesthood?*

ICAB's faithful had "certain reservations"[106] about the validity of ICAB sacraments, Pelypenko reported. The Roman Catholic bishops of São Paulo stated that "the faithful themselves demonstrate that they are perplexed and anxious, and frequently question us over the validity of [ICAB's] sacramental acts."[107] The Roman Catholic Church made its position clear as early as 1947 stating that "the Church has not recognized, does not recognize, and will not recognize the ordinations conferred by the Bishop of Maura, meaning, therefore, that those who are [thus] ordained will be considered as laymen."[108] This statement cautiously stops short of declaring the ordinations invalid. The Roman Catholic bishops of Belo Horizonte were among the first to publish their doubts about the actual validity of ICAB's sacraments.[109] The Vatican later confirmed that in the case of Holy Orders, perhaps the most contentious of the sacraments, "re-ordination would be necessary including in the case of a 'bishop' of this 'church' ... If the Holy See demands conditional re-ordination it is because it has grave doubts over the validity of the 'priestly orders' of the 'ministers' of the 'igreja brasileira,' and consequently over the validity of the ministry that they exercise."[110] Pelypenko concluded that ICAB's ordinations were invalid because they were so contrary to the will of God's Church that the ministers could not possibly have the intention to do what the Church does.[111]

But what are 'valid' and 'invalid' when referring to sacraments? They are deceptively commonplace words and their everyday uses do not correspond to their theological uses. 'Valid' may mean official or based in fact, as in the case of a passport or ticket that it is current and recognized. These meanings are only coincidentally similar to theological sacramental validity. The sacraments are understood as efficacious signs of God's grace enacted through the Church; in practical terms they are also rites of passage and the conferral of sacred roles. They act as milestones of a person's faith life – Baptism, Confirmation, Marriage, the Anointing of the Sick. Two of the sacraments, Holy Communion (or Eucharist) and Reconciliation (or Confession) are particular in that they are meant to be repeated throughout life – repeating any of the other five sacraments is considered sacrilege. The validity of these sacraments, in simple terms, means that they are administered effectively and actually transmit God's graces. Can a Catholic really know that it comes from God? There is a sort of guarantee. For Catholic theology, the validity of the sacraments is assured because the minister has, in turn, been made a minister *validly* – he has validly received the sacrament of Holy Orders.

This chain must be demonstrably unbroken – a bishop ordains priests, some of whom are later consecrated bishop, and they go on to ordain more priests, who in turn provide the sacraments to the people. This 'genealogy' of ministers traces back through a vast family tree of bishops who succeeded bishops, in theory leading back to one or other of the Apostles – it is therefore referred to as the Apostolic Succession. In practice, records of this 'family tree' are only usually thorough back to the sixteenth or seventeenth century. Once Apostolic Succession is established there are then only three criteria for the conferral of a valid sacrament: the correct *Matter* – the things, actions, and people used in the ceremony; the correct *Intention* – which should be in line with what the Church does when conferring the sacrament, for example intending to make a new priest; and the correct *Form* – the essential *words* of the rite. In order to challenge the validity of a sacrament, or for there to be a doubt over the validity, one of these three criteria would have to be 'defective.' Other flaws may be considered wrong or sacrilegious, such as the repeated or multiple reception of Holy Order, or conferring some sacraments outside of Mass, or even the minister being a heretic, apostate, or schismatic, without necessarily affecting the validity.

Whenever Duarte Costa ordained someone "he made a point of declaring publicly, before the ceremony, that he intended to do what the Roman Catholic Apostolic Church desires to do in its ordinations and consecrations and to follow the Roman Rite to the letter."[112] Duarte Costa defended ICAB's early ordinations when responding to what he erroneously called "A Papal Decree";[113] he said that "with scrupulous exactitude, the Roman Pontifical was used, and above all the Credo was recited ... so that nothing may be alleged regarding the intention of the Church."[114] This was before Duarte Costa was legally forced to reform ICAB's liturgy to differentiate it from the Roman Catholic Church. Once the liturgical books – the Pontifical – had been translated and altered, the ICAB rite was no longer the Roman Rite. This is important because the ordaining minister is traditionally *presumed* to have the correct sacramental *Intention* as long as the correct sacramental *Form* – the Roman Pontifical – has been employed. Canon Law never presumes to know what is going on inside a person. Consequently it is extremely difficult to make a pronouncement about a minister's sacramental intention. Logically, the use of the *Form* prescribed by the Church is the most clear and obvious indicator that the ordaining bishop also has the correct *Intention* prescribed by the Church. The Roman Catholic bishops of Belo Horizonte, writing in 1958, were correct in that validity could not be presumed in the case of ICAB sacraments; "They do *like* the Church does, but they do not do *what* the Church does,"[115] they wrote. But Canon Law is generous and reasonable where it might be expected to be unforgiving and strict – it is also often simple when it might be expected to be complex. 'What the Church does' in an ordination is make a new priest. If ICAB's ordaining minister understands in general terms what a priest is, then they can intend to make one. Whether or not they really appreciate the complexity of the theology of the priesthood, or have the ability to train said priest, or hope to make some money out of ordaining said priest, are irrelevant where validity is concerned. Pelypenko eventually backed down and surmised that ICAB orders were probably "null" – valueless – rather than theologically invalid.[116] The Vatican usually errs on the side of caution – it "does not recognize, and will not recognize [ICAB's] ordinations."[117] In practice this places technical, theological validity in second place to recognition – licitness, or liceity.

Conferring the sacrament of Holy Orders is not designed to spring from the individual initiative of the minister, but to be a response to the call of the Christian community.[118] The Council of Chalcedon (451) condemned any consecrations that were not grounded in such a call, and 'freelance' consecrations were always regarded as null and void. [119] "The distinction between clerics and laity" in the early Church, Möhler wrote, "was seen as nothing other than a distinction of gifts,"[120] and the cleric's gifts did not set him apart as autonomous or autocephalous. The schismatic cleric must not forget that 'his' power was in origin delegated power, which should be rooted in a community. The more persistently and arbitrarily a schismatic bishop exercises his power to ordain, for example, the more he deviates from the will and tradition of the Church, his mandate. It may become impossible to presume that his intention is the same as the Church's –

ordaining priests must simply mean something different to him. This is demonstrated in the case of Archbishop Milingo, who was excommunicated in 2006 after consecrating four married men as bishops. He was laicized in 2009 and the Vatican stated that any further ordinations by Milingo the layman would be *invalid* as well as unrecognized.[121] Even though it is open to being abused, Apostolic Succession is hailed in Western Catholicism as a guarantee of continuity and stability, while Eastern Orthodoxy takes the opposite view – the validity of Holy Orders stems from the stability of the Church which gives its mandate.[122] "This view insists that valid orders depend upon the Church's life, and that authorization by the whole Church is an integral part of their validity."[123] In practice though, the Roman Catholic Church enforces the same policy as the Orthodox. Rome "does not recognize, and will not recognize"[124] ICAB's ordinations, utterly regardless of whether or not they are technically valid.

Theological validity has no currency without the Church's endorsement, as Canon VI of the Council of Chalcedon asserted. At one point a senior ICAB member sought in vain to establish links with the Orthodox Churches in order to legitimize their sacramental actions,[125] but as Pelypenko explained, bishops ordained by a suspended bishop are not bishops for the Orthodox – nor bishops ordained by only one bishop.[126] He also pointed out upon meeting Von Roeder Michels' wife and six daughters that even Orthodox bishops cannot be married.[127] Rome did recognize one exception when it accepted Salomão Barbosa Ferraz into its ranks as a bishop. The Vatican showed signs of regretting this unprecedented decision. In terms of sacramental validity too, it was a unique case. It was the first consecration, only a month after the foundation of ICAB. Duarte Costa was not yet excommunicated to the higher degree of *vitandus*. He used the correct Roman Pontifical in Latin – this was before the revision and translation of the liturgy. But the biggest mitigating factor was Ferraz himself – a non-Catholic who was a friend of the Catholic Church. He had not directly wounded the Church and had not committed Schism – as a non-Catholic he was not subject to Canon Law. The Church neither condemned not endorsed his consecration at the time, so it could therefore retroactively give it its mandate.

The story of Ferraz tends to give hope to those involved in the ICAB phenomenon.[128] Having – being – valid bishops is of supreme importance to Catholic micro-churches.[129] From this well they "draw all the legitimacy of their existence."[130] But the disproportionate proliferation of bishops and priests risks pushing the whole micro-church phenomenon into the realm of the absurd, and raises doubts about their very understanding of priesthood. They often seem to affirm the exclusive, clericalist conception of priesthood which they frequently criticize as being too 'Roman', particularly when it means being exclusively male, celibate, and aloof.[131] It remains rare for ICAB branches or offshoots to call for a "thorough overhaul"[132] of priesthood and ministry, as Michael Richards phrased it. Progressive Catholic groups of all types seem unable to reconcile "these two demands for ordination *and* Church renewal"[133] wrote Rosemary Radford Ruether of the women-priests. Securing ordination can therefore present problems of continuity and credibility. Ultra-traditionalists – such as Pope Michael – have stooped to accepting Holy Orders from progressive branches of ICAB.[134] Meanwhile, some progressive branches seem to have rejected everything Roman apart from vestments, titles, and pomp. Back in 1964 Peter Anson decried the micro-churches of the day; though claiming to "revive primitive Christianity"[135] they mimicked "later developments of ecclesiastical polity, ritual and ceremonial."[136]

> "In almost every instance they have taken over the late medieval or post-Tridentine conception of prelacy – lock, stock and barrel. This, of course, has involved wearing vestments and other regalia in the Baroque, Gothic Revival, or Oriental fashions."[137]

The micro-church phenomenon has not changed in these superficial respects. Most of its exponents hold fast to the conception of prelacy described here. ICAB itself became "a vast dispensary of ecclesiastical services for those who could not procure them from the Roman Church."[138] There are no demonstrable grounds for presuming the validity of the sacraments which ICAB 'dispenses.' Since they created their own liturgy, ICAB has had a different, non-Roman Catholic rite, which cannot just be presumed to be valid. ICAB's liturgy has been reformed again and again since then, and bishops are free to introduce their own local touches and alterations. The correct sacramental *Intention* cannot be presumed on the basis of ICAB ministers using the prescribed *Form*, therefore, because they do not. Even if, upon close examination, the schismatic rite were to appear valid, the absence of unified practice among ICAB bishops means that consistent use of that rite cannot be presumed. The grounds for doubt far outweigh the grounds for presuming validity, not just the fact of ICAB being a 'dispensary of ecclesiastical services':

> "It is not their simony that raises doubt over the validity ... but the combination of factors – the formation of their ministers, questionable moral conduct, doctrinal fluctuation, the manifest desire to trick people, in addition, that is, to their financial motives." [139]

Technical validity – often impossible to establish or refute with certainty – becomes of secondary importance when it comes to ICAB's doubtful sacraments, which are discarded as "null and void acts, which do not transmit nor can they transmit Grace, because they are cut off from Jesus and from the Church."[140]

Conclusions

"If we analyze the Theology of Christ's Church the doubts [about ICAB], far from dissipating, become even more accentuated,"[141] the bishops of São Paulo wrote. ICAB was founded upon the rejection of the Papacy[142] and for the Roman Catholic Church the "legitimate hierarchy" and the "communion of bishops" exist "by the express will of Christ, as a 'sacramental form' of him."[143] ICAB, furthermore, has no faithful of its own:

"Their 'ministers' operate among people who are already committed to the [Roman] Catholic Church and already have legitimate pastors ... The people they manage to draw into their temples are people who do not realize the error they are being drawn into, nor are they contemplating abandoning the Church of their baptism!"[144]

For its part the Roman Catholic Church dismisses the suggestion that ICAB is even a Church *stricto sensu*. "Neither in terms of faithful ... because they have none, nor as a hierarchy, does the so-called *'igreja brasileira'* really exist as a church and much less as the Church of Christ."[145] ICAB does not even offer authentic religion but rather "the misrepresentation of the idea of religion. With the emphasis ... on blessings and devotions, with a clear cultivation of the sense of the magical."[146] Nevertheless, the Roman Catholic bishops drew potential positives from the experience of dealing with ICAB "notwithstanding all these negative aspects."[147] There could clearly be some useful lessons to learn, specifically about ways not to be a Church: "We must always remain alert to new developments and different attitudes that may arise from the *Igreja Brasileira* and independent groups, which may in turn impact on our own."[148] This has in fact been the case. The Roman Catholic bishops of São Paulo were prompted by the ICAB phenomenon into improving the instruction – catechesis – of their faithful, with particular attention to demystifying the supernatural dimension of the Faith "which, misdirected, leads to superstition, religious syncretism, ritual formalism, [and] devotionism of a folkloric hue."[149] This dimension of Catholicism, played-down since Vatican II but favored by ICAB, "obscures the deeper sense of Man's relationship with God."[150]

Whether ICAB can correctly be called a Church or not is obviously a multi-layered question. ICAB has been on a long journey to establish its identity, as any 'emergent' group of

Christians would understandably be.[151] Emergent Christian groups experience difficulty reconciling the boundaries necessary to define the group and projecting an attitude of positive inclusivity.[152] Not all small groups have been unsuccessful. The Catholic Worker movement is one example of a group with both a firm (Roman) Catholic identity and an essential practice of inclusivity in what it does on a daily basis.[153] The Catholic Worker overcomes the dilemma of community identity versus inclusivity by dealing personally and face-to-face with "people ... different from them in the real world, rather than merely theorizing about them in an abstract way."[154] Ultimately, all discussion of Catholic identity and inclusivity takes place in the context of what Pope Benedict XVI called "very deep ruptures [in the Catholic Church itself], so much so that one sometimes has the feeling that two Churches are living side by side in one Church."[155] Real schism, as we have seen throughout the ICAB story, is neither confined to the Middle Ages nor always unmistakably announced with bells and incense. Constant measures to avoid schism are called for and, as Pope Benedict put it, "much is already done if no further inner ruptures occur."[156] There are not only lessons to learn from the ICAB phenomenon but also an agenda of concrete action to draw up, resulting in and from the practical and "moral *necessity* of dialogue with those within and outside the church."[157]

In our age of pluralism the apparent stand-off between unity and diversity and between Catholic and sectarian worldviews is not just a Church issue. It seems that "the world is in need of people who can feel several loyalties, several affinities, several identities."[158] The whole question of delineating membership and belonging may be moot for the modern world citizen: "Being a loyal, docile member of a single tribal group does not offer salvation any longer, if it ever did."[159] What hope does Catholicism have in this scenario? Karl Rahner appeared to appeal for compromise – "the sole hope of the future," he wrote, "is a vision of the Church as a family of 'Churches forming a unity of Churches."[160]

"We have to do what we can so that out of the many Churches the one Church of Christ may develop ... but we must not permit this to mean the simple abolition of the diversity of the Churches as communion in the one Church."[161]

The Roman Catholic Church can no doubt find ways of adapting and coping – it has never known anything else.[162]

Notes

1   Hans Küng, *The Church*, Search Press, London, 1978, p 263
2   Paul Lakeland, *Church – Living Communion*, Liturgical Press, Collegeville MN, 2009, p 8
3   Hans Küng, *The Church*, p 264
4   Hans Küng, *The Church*, p 264
5   Yves Congar OP, *Challenge to the Church – The Case of Archbishop Lefebvre*, Collins Liturgical Publications, London, 1977, p 72
6   Avery Dulles, *The Catholicity of the Church*, Clarendon Press, Oxford, 1987, p 77
7   Johannes L. Witte SJ, 'One, Holy, Catholic, and Apostolic,' in Herbert Vorgrimler (ed), *One, Holy, Catholic and Apostolic*, Sheed and Ward, London, 1968, p 6
8   Avery Dulles SJ, *The Catholicity of the Church*, p 13
9   Hans Küng, *The Church*, p 264
10 Johann Adam Möhler, *Unity in the Church or the Principle of Catholicism*, Catholic University of America Press, Washington DC, 1996, p 130
11 Cf. Paul Lakeland, *Church – Living Communion*, pp 38-42
12 Alan Race, *Christians and Religious Pluralism*, Orbis, Maryknoll NY, 1983, p 38
13 Alan Race, p 38
14 Johann Adam Möhler, p 130
15 Karl Adam, *The Spirit of Catholicism*, Sheed & Ward, London, 1934, p 106
16 Karl Adam, p 107
17 Paul Lakeland, *Church – Living Communion*, p 49 [emphasis added]
18 Paul Lakeland, *Church – Living Communion*, p 4
19 Julie Byrne, 'Catholic But Not Roman Catholic,' *American Catholic Studies* Vol. 125, No. 3, Fall 2014, [pp 16-19], p 17
20 Cf. Paul Lakeland, *Church – Living Communion*, p 51
21 Avery Dulles SJ, *The Catholicity of the Church*, p 77

22 Ray Lyons, 'We are the orthodox Catholics today', in RENEW, March 2018, p 3

23 Cf. Kilian McDonnell, 'The Ratzinger / Kasper Debate,' *Theological Studies*, No. 63, 2002, pp 227-50

24 Cf. Gerard O'Connell, 'Pope abolishes honorary title of Monsignor for Diocesan Priests' *La Stampa,* http://vaticaninsider.lastampa.it/en/the-vatican/detail/articolo/ 31027/ [accessed 9th May 2018]

25 Cf. Johann Adam Möhler, p 174

26 Johann Adam Möhler, p 166

27 Gerardo Marti and Gladys Ganiel, *The Deconstructed Church*, OUP, Oxford, 2014, p 40

28 Cf. Avery Dulles, *The Resilient Church,* Gill and Macmillan, Dublin, 1978, pp 11-12

29 Paul Collins, *Papal Power,* Fount / Harper Collins, London, 1997, p x

30 Pastoral Letter of the Bishops of the Ecclesiastical Province of São Paulo on the "Igreja Brasileira" in CNBB 'Comunicado Mensal' [Monthly Communiqué] No. 243, Dec. 1972 [pp 90-97] p 92

31 Walter Kasper, *That They May All Be One,* Burns and Oates (Continuum) London, 2004, p 136

32 Walter Kasper, *That They May All Be One,* p 142

33 Cf. Walter Kasper, *That They May All Be One,* p 145

34 Klaus Schatz SJ, 'Historical Considerations Concerning the Problem of the Papacy', James F. Puglisi (ed), *Petrine Ministry and the Unity of the Church,* Liturgical (M. Glazier) 1999, Collegeville, [pp. 1-13], p 2

35 Walter Kasper, *That They May All Be One,* p 144

36 *Lumen Gentium* 27

37 John R. Quinn, *The Reform of the Papacy,* Crossroad/Herder & Herder, New York, 1999, p 14

38 Cf. Paul Lakeland, *Church – Living Communion,* p 14

39 Pastoral Letter of the Bishops of the Ecclesiastical Province of São Paulo, December 1972, p 92

40 Pastoral Letter of the Bishops of the Ecclesiastical Province of São Paulo, December 1972, p 92

41 Avery Dulles, *The Catholicity of the Church,* p 66 [emphasis added]

42 Klaus Schatz SJ, 'Historical Considerations Concerning the Problem of the Papacy', p 2

43 Arthur M. Ramsey, *The Gospel and the Catholic Church,* Longmans, Green & Co., London, 1936, p 233

44 Harding Meyer, '"Suprema auctoritas ideo ab omne errore immunis": The Lutheran Approach to Primacy', in Puglisi (ed), 1999, [pp 15-34], p 18

45 Harding Meyer, 'Suprema auctoritas ideo ab omne errore immunis', p 20

46   John Hind, 'Primacy and Unity': An Anglican Contribution to a Patient and Fraternal Dialogue', in Puglisi (ed), 1999, [pp 35-57], p 50
47   John Hind, 'Primacy and Unity,' p 49
48   Cf. John Hind, 'Primacy and Unity,' pp 36-37
49   John Hind, 'Primacy and Unity,' p 52
50   John Hind, 'Primacy and Unity,' p 52
51   Yves Congar OP, *Challenge to The Church*, p 72
52   Yves Congar OP, *Challenge to The Church*, p 72
53   John Hind, 'Primacy and Unity' p 52
54   Arthur Michael Ramsey, pp 64-5
55   Padre Dubois, p 83
56   Cf. Johann Adam Möhler, p 194
57   Johann Adam Möhler, p 153
58   Richard P. McBrien, *Catholicism*, Geoffrey Chapman, London, 1994, p 9
59   Karl Rahner, *Theological Investigations XVII*, Darton, Longman and Todd, London, 1981, pp 197-198
60   Paul Lakeland, *Church – Living Communion*, p 6
61   Paul Lakeland, *Church – Living Communion*, p 25
62   Cf. Hans Küng, *The Church*, p 263
63   Cf. Hans Küng, *The Church*, p 263
64   Johann Adam Möhler, p 130
65   Paul Lakeland, *Church – Living Communion*, p 8
66   Yves Congar OP, *Challenge to The Church*, p 72
67   Avery Dulles, *The Catholicity of the Church*, p 77
68   Cf. Richard P. McBrien, *Catholicism*, p 9
69   Avery Dulles, *The Catholicity of the Church*, p 32
70   Thomas F. Best, 'Ecclesiology and Ecumenism,' in Gerard Mannion and Lewis S. Mudge, (eds), *The Routledge Companion to the Christian Church*, Routledge, Abingdon, 2008, [pp. 402-420]: p. 405
71   Gerardo Marti and Gladys Ganiel, p 39
72   Avery Dulles, *The Catholicity of the Church*, p 77
73   Johann Adam Möhler, p 196 [emphasis added]
74   Johann Adam Möhler, p 196 [emphasis added]
75   Francis A. Sullivan SJ, *From Apostles to Bishops – The Development of the Episcopacy in the Early Church*, The Newman Press, New York / Mahwah NJ, 2001, p 2 [emphasis added]
76   Francis A. Sullivan SJ, *From Apostles to Bishops*, pp 2-3
77   Avery Dulles, *The Catholicity of the Church*, p 66 [emphasis added]
78   Paul Lakeland, *Church – Living Communion*, p 6
79   Paul Lakeland, *Church – Living Communion*, p 6
80   Cf. John E. Thiel, *Senses of Tradition*, Oxford University Press, Oxford, 2000, pp 84ff

81   Paul Lakeland, *Church – Living Communion*, p 11
82   Avery Dulles SJ, *The Catholicity of the Church*, p 77
83   Cf. Alan Race, p 39
84   Austin Flannery OP (Ed), *Vatican Council II, The Conciliar and Post-Conciliar Documents*, Dominican Publications, St Saviour's, Dublin, 1975, p 739
85   Cf. Alan Race, p 45
86   Pastoral Letter of the Bishops of the Ecclesiastical Province of São Paulo, December 1972, p 95
87   CNBB, 'A Igreja Brasileira,' *Comunicado Mensal*, No. 252, Sept. 1973, [pp 1129-30], p 1130
88   Karl Rahner, *The Shape of the Church to Come*, SPCK, London, 1974, p 111
89   Thomas J. Paprocki, 'Part V: … (cc. 1732-1752)', in John P. Beal et al (eds), *New Commentary on the Code of Canon Law*, Paulist Press, New York / Mahwah NJ, 2000, [pp. 1818-47], p 1847
90   Thomas J. Paprocki, p 1847
91   Thomas J. Paprocki, p 1847
92   Johann Adam Möhler, pp 124-125
93   Johann Adam Möhler, p 125
94   Johann Adam Möhler, p 124
95   Richard P. McBrien, *Catholicism*, p 3
96   Cardinal Walter Kasper, 'The whole truth is only found together,' in *The Tablet*, 6th July 2002, p 4
97   Wagner Pires da Silva, 'Another Catholicism: The Bishop of Maura and the Brazilian Catholic Apostolic Church,' *Revista de História Bilros* (Fortaleza), Vol. 5, No. 8, Jan.-Apr. 2017 [pp 106-125] p 122
98   Wagner Pires da Silva, p 122
99   Wagner Pires da Silva, p 122
100   CNBB, 'A Igreja Brasileira,' September 1973, p 1130
101   Michael Richards, *A People of Priests*, Darton, Longman and Todd, London, 1995, p 113
102   Johann Adam Möhler, pp 141-142
103   CNBB, 'A Igreja Brasileira,' September 1973, p 1130
104   CNBB, 'A Igreja Brasileira,' September 1973, p 1130
105   CNBB, 'A Igreja Brasileira,' September 1973, p 1130
106   Obispo Alejo Pelypenko, *Infiltración Comunista en las Iglesias de América*, Pia Sociedad de San Pablo, Buenos Aires, 1961, p 191
107   Pastoral Letter of the Bishops of the Ecclesiastical Province of São Paulo, December 1972, pp 93-94
108   *Luta!* issue 2, November 1947, p 32

109 CNBB, *Revista Eclesiástica Brasileira*, number 18, 1958, p 564 [emphasis added]

110 Pastoral Letter of the Bishops of the Ecclesiastical Province of São Paulo, December 1972, p 94

111 Cf. Pelypenko, p 172

112 Aloísio Cardinal Lorscheider, ' "Igreja Brasileira," clarification and procedure', in *Convergência – Journal of the Conference of Religious of Brazil (CRB)*, Number 231, April 1990, [pp 137-142], p 139

113 *Luta!* issue 2, November 1947, p 32

114 *Luta!* issue 2, November 1947, p 32

115 CNBB, *Revista Eclesiástica Brasileira*, number 18, 1958, p 564 [emphasis added]

116 Cf. Pelypenko, p 173

117 *Luta!* issue 2, November 1947, p 32

118 Cf. Richard P. McBrien, *Ministry*, Harper & Row, San Francisco, 1988, pp 37-38 and pp 45-46

119 Cf. Richard P. McBrien, *Ministry*, pp 45-46

120 Johann Adam Möhler, p 225

121 Cf. Frances D'Emilio, 'Vatican dismisses defiant archbishop from clergy', AP, 18th Dec. 2009, http://www.boston.com/news/world/africa/articles/2009/12/18/vatican_defrocks_defiant_african_archbishop/?camp=pm Cf. John L. Allen Jr., 'The last act in the Milingo story?' NCR 17th December 2009, http://ncronline.org/blogs/ncr-today/last-act-milingo-story [both accessed 9th May 2018].

122 Cf. Arthur Michael Ramsey, p 218

123 Arthur Michael Ramsey, p 219

124 *Luta!* issue 2, November 1947, p 32

125 Pelypenko, p 115

126 Pelypenko, p 118

127 Pelypenko, p 121

128 N.b. The legend of Orlando Arce Moya being received back by the Vatican is entirely untrue.

129 Cf. Michael W. Cuneo, *The Smoke of Satan*, Johns Hopkins University Press, Baltimore MD, 1999, pp 98-102 – "There are fewer things more valuable than being able to lay claim to a bishop. In addition to wanting to perpetuate themselves, such groups ... are strongly committed to a theory of apostolic succession. They want to be seen as standing in sacred, unbroken continuity with the primitive church, a living link with the apostolic past; and for this, a duly consecrated bishop of one's own is an absolute necessity." – p 98

130 Frédéric Luz, *Le Soufre et L'Encens, [Sulphur and Incense]* Claire Vigne, Paris, 1995, p 25

131 Cf. Herbert Haag, *Clergy and Laity,* Burns & Oates, Tunbridge Wells, 1998

132 Michael Richards, *A People of Priests,* Darton, Longman & Todd, London, 1995, p 115

133 Rosemary Radford Ruether, 'Women-Church,' Mary-Jo Weaver and R. Scott Appleby (eds), *What's Left? Liberal American Catholics,* Indiana University Press, Bloomington 1999 [pp 46-64] p 48 [emphasis added]

134 Cf. John P. Plummer, *The Many Paths of the Independent Sacramental Movement,* Apocryphile Press, Berkeley CA, 2005, p 2

135 Peter F. Anson, *Bishops At Large,* Faber and Faber, London, 1964, p 27

136 Peter F. Anson, p 27

137 Peter F. Anson, p 27

138 Wagner Pires da Silva, p 123

139 Aloísio Cardinal Lorscheider, '"Igreja Brasileira," Esclarecimento e Procedimento,' 1990, p 141

140 Pastoral Letter of the Bishops of the Ecclesiastical Province of São Paulo, December 1972, p 96

141 Pastoral Letter of the Bishops of the Ecclesiastical Province of São Paulo, December 1972, p 94

142 Pastoral Letter of the Bishops of the Ecclesiastical Province of São Paulo, December 1972, p 94

143 Pastoral Letter of the Bishops of the Ecclesiastical Province of São Paulo, December 1972, p 94

144 Pastoral Letter of the Bishops of the Ecclesiastical Province of São Paulo, December 1972, p 94

145 Pastoral Letter of the Bishops of the Ecclesiastical Province of São Paulo, December 1972, p 94

146 CNBB, 'A Igreja Brasileira,' September 1973, p 1130

147 CNBB, 'A Igreja Brasileira,' September 1973, p 1130

148 CNBB, 'A Igreja Brasileira,' September 1973, p 1130

149 Pastoral Letter of the Bishops of the Ecclesiastical Province of São Paulo, December 1972, p 96

150 CNBB, 'A Igreja Brasileira,' September 1973, p 1130

151 Cf. Gerardo Marti and Gladys Ganiel, p 141

152 Gerardo Marti and Gladys Ganiel, pp 140-1

153 Gerardo Marti and Gladys Ganiel, p 141

154 Gerardo Marti and Gladys Ganiel, p 141

155 Joseph Cardinal Ratzinger, *Salt of the Earth – Christianity and the Catholic Church at the End of the Millenium,* Ignatius Press, San Francisco, 1997, pp 242-243

156 Joseph Ratzinger, *Salt of the Earth,* p 243

157   Gerard Mannion, *Ecclesiology and Postmodernity – Questions for the Church in Our Time,* Liturgical Press, Collegeville MN, 2007, p 39

158   Naomi R. Goldenberg, *Resurrecting the Body,* Crossroad, New York, 1990, p 65

159   Naomi R. Goldenberg, p 65

160   Karl Rahner, *Theological Investigations XVII,* Darton, Longman and Todd, London, 1981, p 196

161   Karl Rahner, *Theological Investigations XVII,* p 196

162   Cf. Bernard Hoose, 'Should the Church Change?', in Gerard Mannion (ed), *Church and Religious 'Other',* T&T Clark, London, 2008, [pp 221-231] p 221

VIII

"A FREE DECISION OF FAITH"[1]
— Theological defense of the
ICAB phenomenon —

The Roman Catholic Church might be expected to have only harsh words for ICAB today just as it did in 1945. However, while it is clear that the ICAB movement has endured through the decades, the theology of those who originally condemned ICAB may not have stood the test of time. Modern theology is a lot more accommodating and understanding of the ICAB phenomenon. This chapter examines some objections to the foundation and existence of ICAB, its branches and offshoots, and explores what theology, ecclesiology, and Church history have to say about them, in a spirit of mounting the case for the defense of ICAB. This chapter is not directly concerned with Canon Law – it takes for granted that in 1945 the Church's (then) laws were accurately applied, and for that matter that 1945-vintage theology has had its say as well. This chapter discusses modern theology's responses to some commonplace objections:

a) *Surely, you cannot just decide to set up your own 'branch' of the Church?*

b) *Surely, all branches of the Church must be part of recognized canonical structures – dioceses, societies, orders, etc.?*

c) *Where does the authority come from to set up ICAB?*

d) *What about a bishop's authority – did Duarte Costa not ignore the rightful authority and jurisdiction of the local bishop?*

e) *If you claim Apostolicity, does that not mean communion with an Apostolic See?*

f) *If you claim Apostolicity, how can you question the role of the Pope?*

a) Surely, you cannot just decide to set up your own 'branch' of the Church?

After Vatican II the Catholic Church found itself in uncharted territory. Scholars attempted to interpret the signs of the times and speculate on what the Church of the future would be like. With today's advanced methods of data collection, research and analysis, making predictions about the future Church is much more accessible and scientific, but in any case it has always involved observing trends and seeing what Catholics were actually doing in practice. A new breed of theologians engaging in this game of prediction included Hans Küng, Karl Rahner, and Joseph Ratzinger, who all predicted significant changes in the shape of the future Church. They painted a picture of a future Church revitalized by spontaneous, grass-roots, fringe, emerging communities – there is no shortage of adjectives to describe them of course – or "self-contained social groups."[2] These groups would be driven by the issues and concerns of the faithful themselves, including conflict with Church teaching or a sense of having been marginalized. It would be like a return to the Church's roots; such communities would be "small and will have to start afresh more or less from the beginning"[3] rather than fitting into established canonical structures. The theologians were actually warning the Church that it would have to address this emerging ecclesiology, but neither a uniform nor sympathetic approach for dealing with the phenomenon was ever developed.

Many of the communities and micro-churches emerging from the ICAB phenomenon would fit the description of the 'self-contained groups' outlined above, especially those motivated by specific social and ethical issues. The theologians' predictions were not prompted by the emergence of the ICAB movement specifically, but rather by the (at that time) more visible 'base ecclesial communities' (CEB) of Latin America. That phenomenon is in turn not unrelated to the ICAB one; ICAB had already been exploring and experimenting with new ecclesial models, while the Catholic Church looked on oblivious to modern urban poverty. It is fair to point out that the theologians began 'predicting' these small self-contained communities once they were already starting to appear. Then, the ICAB movement also began to produce offshoot communities which increasingly matched the criteria described by the theologians. Catholic theology is not at all closed to this kind of "search for interpersonal community,"[4] but surely, one might ask, theology does not sanction breaking the rules, changing disciplines, ignoring the local parish system? In fact the theologians foresaw 'home-Masses,' 'floating parishes,' and "liturgical practices contrary to the official rubrics"[5] as inevitable rather than expressly undesirable. Karl Rahner saw the future Church as "built from below by basic communities as a result of free initiative and association"[6] rather than by permission from above. No talk here of bishops, jurisdictions, canonical structures, Canon Law, or consulting the Nuncio.

Future Pope Benedict XVI, Joseph Ratzinger, keenly anticipated the emergence of new understandings of priesthood, saying in 1969 that the future Church will undoubtedly "discover new forms of ministry and will ordain to the priesthood approved Christians who pursue some profession."[7] It will be by necessity "a more spiritual Church,"[8] he said, "no longer ... the dominant social power to the extent that she was until recently; but she will enjoy a fresh blossoming and be seen as man's home."[9] The emergence of this future model of the Church was seen as positive, except that the Church must urgently be made ready for it. "We should make every effort not to hold up, but to promote this development and direct it onto the right lines,"[10] wrote Karl Rahner. But the Church hierarchy's old guard – already shaken to the core by Vatican II – would never come close to giving ground to fringe groups, married priests, women priests, working priests, or liturgical experimentation. Some commentators expected the stand-off to result in a wide-scale progressive-conservative schism.[11]

So no courageous and innovative approach to the small spontaneous communities ever came forward. What actually transpired was that fringe groups were either kept on the fringes, or pushed from the fringes into obscurity – thus the 'emerging church' became the "underground church."[12] There can be no doubt that these theologians correctly identified impulses and trends, concerns and issues, which have at least in part found expression as branches and offshoots of the ICAB movement, with all its innumerable flaws. If the ICAB movement and similar phenomena are not what they were predicting, then what were they predicting? After all, the theologians predicted the coming of the future Church, not the coming of the perfect Church. It may be shocking or unpalatable, but the ICAB phenomenon is an authentic feature of the logical and theological evolution of the Catholic Church.

b) *Surely, all branches of the Church must be part of recognized ca-nonical structures – dioceses, societies, orders, etc.?*

During the course of the last 50 years, the Catholic Church has repeatedly recognized that its organizational and administrative structures do not always suit particular needs and situations. As society has continually changed, the Church's system of strictly demarcated territorial jurisdictions – dioceses and parishes – has at times proved to be a hindrance to providing effective pastoral care. The Church has frequently responded intelligently – it has demonstrated the ability to create new organizational structures to work outside of and alongside the traditional ones, and across administrative boundaries if necessary. The Church can also amend and apply Canon Law creatively in order to address issues it deems worthy. This has long been the case with certain immigrant and / or minority-language groups for example. Logically, such groups, though perhaps well-represented nationally or regionally, may only constitute a small number in each individual Church jurisdiction – they may live in areas which straddle several parish or diocesan boundaries. In response the provision of pastoral care – chaplaincies, minority-language Masses, and social services for example – can be organized in such a way that it crosses jurisdictional lines. Several parishes and / or dioceses can work together, and canonical structures can take second place to pastoral need.[13] But the Church has had to learn this the hard way – inadequate pastoral care to specific immigrant and ethnic groups in the US has led to several other (non–ICAB-related) significant and enduring schisms, such as the Polish National Catholic Church (PNCC) starting in 1897, the Old Roman Catholic [sic] Church from the 1910's onwards, and the African-American Catholic Congregation (Imani Temple) founded in 1989.

The Catholic Church does therefore demonstrate the ability to address situations that challenge its recognized canonical structures. This is also true in response to emergent Catholic communities who otherwise wavered on the fringes of the official Church. The 'Personal Prelature,' a recent invention, straddles and overlaps jurisdictions and even crosses international boundaries. Personal Prelature is the canonical status famously granted to Opus Dei. Though encouraged to nurture good relations with diocesan bishops, as its name implies, a Personal Prelature has its own prelate, or bishop. Its vague purpose is "to accomplish particular pastoral or missionary works for various regions or for different social groups"[14] – one searches in vain for a clearer definition. Cynics see the Personal Prelature model as a hall pass to operate as and where they wish. The 'Personal Ordinariates' for former Anglicans are territorially limited, but they cover vast areas, such as the whole of North America. These Ordinariates follow on from the previous 'pastoral provision' for former Episcopalians in the USA. Crucially, as with the Personal Prelature, this is a canonical innovation in response to a pastoral need identified by the faithful themselves. When Archbishop Lefebvre's 1988 consecrations split the traditionalist Priestly Society of St. Pius X (SSPX) from the Catholic Church, the Vatican responded *within days* by founding its own rival version, the Priestly Fraternity of St. Peter. The Church had not objected in principle to Lefebvre's plan to consecrate bishops – they had been in negotiations to officially authorize a 'flying bishop' for the SSPX. Elsewhere in the traditionalist movement there was talk of launching a 'Latin Mass Ordinariate.'[15]

It is clear that innovations in the Church's organizational structures have been prompted 'from below' by unofficial and fringe groups. One of ICAB's most contentious features is the setting up of competing, parallel dioceses, but the Vatican itself does not refrain from setting up 'rival' or parallel organizational structures, even within exactly the same area as an existing canonical entity. When the SSPX's counterpart in Brazil – the Society of St John Vianney – reconciled with the Vatican, Pope St. John Paul II announced a unique new canonical structure to accommodate them – a 'Personal Apostolic Administration.' This sounds like a conflation of pre-existing terms and it effectively is; a 'Personal Prelature' being a bishop-led group without boundaries, like Opus Dei, and an 'Apostolic Administration' being a kind of diocese – mix the two together and you get, well, a 'Personal Apostolic Administration." Its jurisdiction "covers exclusively the Diocese of Campos, in Brazil" and it is "immediately subject to the Holy See."[16] A parallel diocese and a rival altar – it would be textbook schism except that they answer directly to the Pope. Also in Brazil and also under the Pope's direct rule, the first 'International Private Association of the Faithful of Pontifical Right' of the new millennium, the Heralds of the Gospel, is another strictly orthodox, traditionalist, and socially conservative group. It recruits from the younger generations even though the founder and long-time leader, João Scognamiglio Clá Dias, was born in 1939. He was ordained along with the first cohort of 'Heralds' priests in 2004, aged 64. Clá Dias was heavily involved in the ultra-conservative Catholic organization 'Tradition, Family, and Property' (TFP) along with Bishop Antônio de Castro Mayer of Campos – Lefebvre's fellow consecrator at the 1988 consecrations.

Our changing world demands that the Vatican exercise all its available flexibility and creativity in order to hold the Catholic Church together, but it is abundantly clear that the Vatican has expended more energy to accommodate conservative and traditionalist groups (including Anglican traditionalists) than it has with analogous liberal or progressive groups. The SSPX revolt prompted an immediate, concrete canonical response; Canon Law was quickly amended, an SSPX-style canonical structure was launched, and the Pope personally declared the Latin Mass suddenly available for all Catholics. The traditionalists of Campos, Brazil, as well as Opus Dei, each enjoy totally unique canonical structures in order to guarantee them maximum freedom – under the direct authority of the Pope. There *is* flexibility, therefore, and the priority to hold the Church together is strong, but the ICAB movement would be ill-advised to sit and wait while the Vatican conjures up an innovative new canonical structure to accommodate it. Parts of the ICAB movement take issue with things so fundamental to the structures and governance of the Catholic Church that they would not want to be incorporated into the existing framework anyway. Others, like the ICAB mother church itself, are actually founded on making a show of prophetic protest, and reaching a compromise would mean the end of their *raison d'être*.[17] The Catholic Church for its part only very cautiously moves the canonical goalposts, though not necessarily slowly, but nearly always only for conservative and traditionalist groups.

Canonical structures are not everything. Johann Adam Möhler warned against being too attached to the Church's organizational structures, as these can be mistaken for permanent and venerable features of the Church. Even the Church itself must not be revered as an institution "founded for the preservation and perpetuation of the Christian faith. Rather, she is much more an offspring of this faith, an action of love living in believers through the Holy Spirit."[18] Nor should the Church be raised to an object of faith or worship.[19] While acknowledging these dangers, the post-Vatican II Church still lacks ecclesiological vision,[20] and there has never been the coherent overarching response to emerging Catholic communities which theologians called for. Any forthcoming ecclesiological vision would have to somehow harness "in creative and conflictual tension differing elements, standpoints, and ways of ecclesial being"[21] which exist even within the mainstream and not just on the Church's fringes. Will the Catholic Church ever reach out to the 'underground church' as it has with traditionalist groups? Would at least opening a dialogue not be the minimum that charity demands, or would the Church then be forced to say, with Father Faber, "Our charity is untruthful because it is not severe; and it is unpersuasive, because it is not truthful ... Where there is no hatred of heresy, there is no holiness."[22] But leaving aside any heretics and schismatics, there are now generations of Catholics who have been born and grown up within the ICAB movement – they did not 'break' with any Church, and the crime of schism is not passed on genetically. Others, probably more numerous, were baptized in other Churches (or not at all) and have come to the Catholic faith through the ICAB movement, not through Rome. These faithful are simply Catholics, a non-Roman variety. Continuing to deny their presence in the Church is not an act of truth or holiness; it is merely beating them with the same worn-out stick of 1945.

c) Where does the authority come from to set up ICAB?

The question of the sources of authority is one of the most divisive and problematic issues between Christian denominations and in theology generally.[23] Church authority arguably starts with Baptism. The experience of Baptism, common to practically all Christians, confers a kind of authority or mandate in simple terms, as it opens the door to full membership of the Church. There are no degrees of Baptism nor are there 'ranks' within it. Receiving the rank of Cardinal or Metropolitan pales into insignificance compared to Baptism. Baptism is not just an 'initial' or minor sacrament, and in tandem with faith it carries all the rights and responsibilities of the Church member. No special authorization is needed for Christians to gather, pray, and responsibly discuss faith or other issues that concern them, which could of course include social or political concerns. The Christian may, and really should, gather together and speak to others about their faith, witness their faith, and try to bring others to the faith in God through Jesus Christ. Within this hypothetical gathering of Christians it is natural and legitimate that roles should develop, as within any social group. According to Karl Rahner this quick outline constitutes the essence of the Church, fully true to its nature and in no way subversive of it. Rahner predicted that the Church of the future would spring from "a free decision of faith and the formation of congregations on the part of individuals in the midst of a secular society."[24] He did not mention denomination in this context – he did not mention the Catholic Church.

According to Rahner the big institutional conception is not a *source* of authority since "faith is always a *freely* and *personally* activated decision."[25] The spontaneous, emerging, grass-roots groups he envisaged are not the authentic future Church *in spite* of being a loose initiative by individuals, but because of it; for "it cannot be contrary to the Church's nature to be more clearly visible than formerly as a social reality."[26] In other words, all manifestations of the Church are good, and any manifestations of the Church are better than none. The members of the Christian gathering described above "have just as much right as a territorial parish to be recognized as a basic element of the ... whole Church,"[27] Rahner wrote. But it truly becomes "a local Church ... when it can really sustain the essential, basic functions of the Church (organized proclamation of the gospel, administration of the sacraments, Christian charity and so on)"[28] with the priorities being the gospel and the Eucharist.[29] To this end the congregation have the right, wrote Rahner, to put forward a candidate for ordination, "even if he is married,"[30] Rahner stressed. And he saw "no reason in principle"[31] why a woman could not be ordained, quoting *salus animarum suprema lex* – the salvation of souls is the supreme law of the Church.[32] Rahner's predicted 'shape of the Church to come' very clearly mirrors tendencies and characteristics of groups within the ICAB movement, but for the official Catholic Church this is all pure fantasy. The Church's official positions are still light years from this vision, even taking into account real progress in attitudes to ministry, women, the laity, and the urgent matter of married priests. While support for these and similar reforms has spread exponentially among Catholics, who are themselves ever more vocal and pro-active, the 'big institution' is notoriously immobile. It is impossible to imagine even very uncontroversial communities such as L'Arche, Focolare, or Les Foyers de Charité even putting forward their own qualified, male, unmarried candidates for ordination and having them accepted.

For the 'real' Catholic Church the ordained minister is still "simply and solely the appointed representative of the episcopal great Church and cannot be conceived otherwise."[33] Rahner's theology goes a long way towards vindicating the ICAB movement, but the big institution never bends. It stands somewhat in contrast to the early Christians who, believing that the end was nigh, prioritized witnessing the gospel rather than establishing a disciplined hierarchical organization to stand unchanging throughout the ages.[34] They did not attempt to make their various practices – poverty, common ownership, abstaining from marriage – binding on everyone else. The individual Christian did not try to "raise *their* practice to a general law."[35] The holy mission of the Church ensured, however, that while it is surely made up of sinners, it came to understand itself over the centuries as *societas perfecta* – meaning complete rather than morally perfect.[36] Over time this was distorted and enshrined as the image of the Church as 'perfect society,' Paul Lakeland argued, for which "Evangelization is not so much proclaiming the Gospel as it is drawing converts into the Church, the community of the saved. Moreover, faith itself rapidly becomes a matter of assent to a series of propositions that operate as a sort of constitution for the Church."[37]

The dominant understanding of the Church is still distinctly top-down, beginning at the top with all that is revealed, supernatural, and doctrinal.[38] This conception of the Church tends to place it above critical historical analysis, as it tends to attribute to God that which we see of the Church. In other words the Church as it stands is presumed to be the way God willed it to be, and God's continued direct involvement in the Church is taken as thorough approval of it.[39] Innovation or spontaneity from below are bound to look not just audacious but like going directly against God's will. The Church and its structures as presently constituted are posited as effectively divine and unchallengeable, they trump everything. This "self-understanding of the church, takes on a special authority in its own right. It elevates itself above challenge and criticism."[40] The Church puts forward a model of absolute authority – in reality it is not the exercise of authority at all but the exercise of command – which automatically precludes, outlaws, stigmatizes and quashes any challenge. Can it really be seriously argued then, that it is the ordinary baptized Christians of the ICAB movement who have exceeded or usurped authority?

d)   *What about a bishop's authority – did Duarte Costa not ignore the rightful authority and jurisdiction of the local bishop?*

ICAB appears to be a textbook demonstration of "the refusal of submission to the Supreme Pontiff or of communion with the members of the Church subject to him"[41] – schism according to the Code of Canon Law. Communion with the local bishop is the fundamental sign of communion with the Church and submission to the Pope. But understandings of the nature of communion have changed – even understandings of what a bishop is have changed. Is there an objective reason, transcending these changing understandings, which precludes envisaging some sort of repaired communion for the ICAB movement? Communion, of course, does not mean uniformity – it exists between churches of different rite, language, and discipline. In every Catholic country there are various rites of married priests, for example, serving harmoniously alongside the other rites; there is diversity precisely because of communion, not in spite of it. But the equating of communion with the Church to communion with the bishop is an enduring obstacle; it is also problematic because the current conception of a bishop has been the product of such uneven development.

The Church of the first centuries was a movement composed of diverse, autonomous, somewhat insular local groups, John E. Lynch explained: "Though there was a vivid awareness of the Church universal, unity was expressed in faith rather than in organization or discipline."[42] The community invariably elected its own leader, but endorsement by the leaders or bishops of neighboring Christian communities – consecration – was considered a necessary sign of unity with the wider Church.[43] Who was the bishop for the early Church? He was "the personified love of the congregation"[44] and "a servant of all."[45] As mentioned, the bishop was elected by the community, from within the community, "not raised above the others, since he was understood as one with the congregation ... the pure product of its love."[46] This holistic vision of the congregation was shared by the Apostles, who "did not send their Epistles to the bishops of congregations, but to the congregations directly."[47] This model of bishop and community was not isolated to the very early Church, however, and "was certainly the practice of the church over much of its first millennium."[48] It is a stark contrast to the situation in today's Church, in which a new bishop is "imposed upon"[49] a diocese "because he is well connected in Rome"[50] or "because of his close identification with powerful ecclesiastical figures that he has assiduously cultivated over the years."[51] Needless to say there has been, over the centuries, a radical transformation in the conception of what a bishop is. Today's Church still bears the imprint of the Middle Ages and feudalism, when the ruling class co-opted the senior clergy to be a branch of itself, and the Church created a false division between priestly 'power' and community participation – thus repudiating the early Councils of the Church.

There is currently no shortage of calls for another radical transformation of the conception of a bishop, or simply for more faithfully putting Vatican II into practice. It would begin with giving back to the congregation – "and hence to the laity – a decisive voice in the selection of its own bishop – the selection of the local bishop should ordinarily be made by the local church."[52] Indeed, if "the bishop is to exhibit the love of all in a living image, all must be active in his selection."[53] Once democratically elected, bishops should, it is argued, be expected to commit themselves to their diocese for good, thus reaffirming "the ancient canonical prohibition that forbids a bishop's leaving one see to obtain another."[54] The early Church aimed to eliminate this "endless source of clerical ambition, rivalry, and self-promotion,"[55] which later became part and parcel of the modern careerist bishop's agenda. The Tridentine Church dismissed the early Councils' emphatic affirmations "of the union that should exist between the bishop and the people of his diocese"[56] while still paying lip service to the image of the bishop as "a residential pastor who presides in a stable manner over the church in a city and its environs."[57] But lip service is unlikely to suffice for much longer, as modern Catholics increasingly do not give automatic deference to bishops. "Whether they like it or not church leaders are frequently forced to consult the laity as they seek to exercise authority."[58] Future leadership is much more likely to be participative, and authority likely to exist by consensus or not at all. According to Michael J. Buckley, Catholics expressly reject the current disconnect between leadership and laity: "if the present system for the selection of bishops is not redressed, all other attempts at serious reform will founder, and greater and greater numbers of Catholics will move toward alienation, disinterest, and affective schism."[59]

Is it any wonder that Duarte Costa talked about a return to the early Church? Determined to practice what he preached, he declared his goal to "democratize the Church"[60] and claimed to be Bishop of Rio de Janeiro by 'popular acclamation." As this idea was gradually rolled out within ICAB it also became a feature of some ICAB branches and offshoots. In 1945 talk of democratization in the Church was at best laughable and at worst scandalous, but elements of democracy have become reality for the Catholic Church; "authority in the church is now usually exercised in relation to those who voluntarily choose to accept its authority. ... Authority is more likely to be negotiated rather than simply accepted."[61] The topic of increased democracy in the Church is now far from scandalous; it is almost mainstream debate. Few would deny to Duarte Costa the distinction of having been the most vociferous and dramatic advocate of episcopal reform in his particular time and place. There is certainly no similarly critical figure on record, especially from within the ranks of the Roman Catholic episcopate itself.

Communion with the Catholic Church equals communion with the local bishop, but this invites a demand for clarification as to who the bishop really is – solely an appointed representative of the ecclesiastical old-boys' club, or the local community's true choice of leader? Does the bishop "exhibit the love of all [the congregation] in a living image"[62] or is he biding his time until a more attractive posting becomes available? To what extent is such a bishop himself in real communion with the local Church? The real point of communion, it seems, is not unity with the local Church so much as submission to centralized power. The theory goes that the bishop is the Successor of the Apostles, but this is another example of the Church paying lip service to a pretty empty theory: "the apostles were missionaries and founders of churches; there is no evidence, nor is it at all likely, that any one of them ever took up permanent residence in a particular church as its bishop."[63] The notion that the Apostles were bishops, wrote Francis A. Sullivan, is problematic: "On the one hand, it is no doubt true that the mandate Christ gave to the apostles included the threefold office of teaching, ruling and sanctifying, which Vatican II described as conferred by episcopal consecration [*Lumen Gentium* 21]. However, the correctness of describing the apostles as 'bishops' is another question."[64] The late Medieval, Tridentine, feudal model of bishop which the Church has inherited is not fit for purpose, and it does not invite serious, dignified recognition as a symbol of communion with the Church. The modern bishop, light years from being an Apostle, is an agent of remote top-down power, which inspires only "alienation, disinterest, and affective schism"[65] in today's Catholics. The idea of the bishop as currently endorsed by the Catholic Church clearly does not trace its origins to the early Christians, and this makes a mockery of Apostolicity. More than ever before, theologians take issue with it, and Duarte Costa's voice would not be alone today.

e)   If you claim Apostolicity, does that not mean communion with an Apostolic See?

One, Holy, Catholic, and Apostolic – the four 'marks' of the Church that Pope St. John XXIII maintained "truthfully summarized the whole essence of Christ's teaching and testimony."[66] These marks of the Church are identifiable through faith[67] rather than forensics, and Catholic theology since Vatican II recognizes that they are also to be found in other Christian communities.[68] Apostolicity is perhaps the slightly more elusive and least evocative of the marks of the Church; "it is not entirely clear what claim we are making about the church when we say it is apostolic,"[69] John Burkhard wrote, pointing out that it was the last of the marks of the Church to be included in the creed.[70] In practice, maintaining concrete links to the original Apostolic Sees has been a tenuous business for the Church; the first few hundred years of Catholicism in Brazil are an example, when the Church was cut off and independent in every practical sense. Over time this narrow interpretation of Apostolicity has been relativized in favor of other aspects of the Apostolic inheritance. Apostolic in its simplest sense implies a continuity with the Church of the first century; that the beliefs and practices, while they can hardly be expected to be the same, can yet somehow be seen as sitting within the same tradition.

Realistically of course, today's Catholics would be utterly lost and mystified if they were to wander into a first-century church. Everything, from the logistics and conventions of meeting and worshipping, the language, climate and dress, to the social norms, pressures and concerns of the day, even the body language, sights and smells, would all combine to make the experience of the early Church profoundly alien for modern Christians. Apostolicity would have it, however, not that the Church is the same, but that there is an essential continuum which can be identified. The other things – language, clothes, administration, logistics – may be regarded as accidental and subject to change. This continuum, a general historical Apostolicity across time, can be distinguished from another aspect that we might describe as an ethos of active Apostolicity. This is living out the spirit or 'way' of the Apostle.[71] The first, historical type of Apostolicity relates to the interior workings and governance of the Church – elements less likely to be of immediate interest to outsiders – while the ethos of Apostolicity is a missionary outlook, the way of relating to the world in the day-to-day. John Thiel suggested that Apostolicity can best be appreciated by observing what the faithful actually do – it is those attitudes and values that "endure in the hearts and actions of the faithful."[72] Paul Lakeland wrote that this helps to put ordained ministry into its proper context; "Apostolicity … is a mark of the Church primarily carried by laypeople, since it is the laity who shoulder by far the greater part of the task of being the loving presence of God in the world."[73] Accentuating the daily Apostolic spirit and attitude brings out the real role of the numerically overwhelming laity, and places it at the forefront of the Church.

Being Apostolic therefore emerges from the haziness of the Creed to become real day-to-day mission – practice, in harmony with what is preached. The Creed itself illustrates the two aspects of Apostolicity, being a summary of theoretical beliefs with an underlying ethos of action. The Creed "looks back to certain events in history wherein God has acted and … looks forward to God's own consummation of these acts."[74] The truths of the Creed are grounded in actions and events both computed and yet to be realized, reminiscent of Karl Barth's phrase that "[truth] is not what we say about God, but what He does and will do and has done."[75] It is also true that Apostolicity is a historically traceable connection reaching across two thousand years, but in the character of spiritual inheritance rather than an inventory or checklist. Apostolicity is bound to be largely intangible.[76] Even though the Creeds are not checklists for validating the true Church this does not mean it is impossible to identify fundamentals and also non-fundamentals: "If we could travel back in time ... We would not always find the Church if we went looking for features of our present-day Church such as celibate clergy or permanent deacons or diocesan finance councils or cardinals or Gothic cathedrals."[77] The threefold ministry of bishops, presbyters, and deacons – sometimes held up as the mark *par excellence* of being Catholic and Apostolic – has itself had a complex development and took a long time to emerge. Apostolic Succession should ideally serve to demonstrate both types of Apostolicity; continuity of belief, in that a successor is elected to continue to embody the beliefs and practices of the Apostles, combined with the practical aspects of the daily Apostolic mission – sacrifice and service. Apostolic Succession, highly prized and maintained by ICAB and its descendant groups, is one important expression of Apostolicity, even though it is not the sum total of it.

Apostolicity "does not mean that everyone has always at all times been utterly faithful to the apostolic tradition but, rather, that the community as a whole over the long haul has remained discernably in continuity with the apostolic faith."[78] The biggest bone of contention between the Vatican and the ICAB movement would be submission to the universal jurisdiction of the Pope; but since neither institution, the Vatican nor ICAB, are products of Apostolic times, Apostolicity does not actually have much to say about the quarrel. Neither institution has 'always at all times been utterly faithful to the apostolic tradition." Both of them display signs of the Apostolic inheritance, but they are also both quite recent developments as they stand. The Papacy, which could be expected to have the last word, does not live outside of history either; like ICAB and the Vatican it is an institution which strives to live out its faith in continuity with the Apostolic inheritance. Apostolicity is fundamentally aspirational. The presence of Apostolic continuity could be doubted if one party were to fall short of *desiring* that One, Holy, Catholic, Apostolic Church professed in the Creed. The question could arise as to whether that Church or institution were doing enough to fulfil its professed commitment to work for that aspired-to Church. Here too it is the spirit of Apostolicity that counts, not the letter.

f) If you claim Apostolicity, how can you question the role of the Pope?

Questioning and debating the role of the Pope are fundamental to a responsible understanding of Catholicism and do not have to be done disrespectfully. The most contentious issues around the role of the Pope are the result of the Papacy's chequered historical development rather than its scriptural, theological, or spiritual foundations. The Papacy as we know it grew out of a "perceived need for central authority"[79] in the Church. This recognition of central authority developed into a theory of *universal* authority, which was not rooted in the early Church. "There is nothing in the first thousand years of the history of the church to suggest that the primacy of the Roman See should entitle or require its occupant to determine who is to be the bishop of every see in the church"[80] for example. But Church history is a history of conflict, "much of it over the relative degree of weight which was to be attached to the authority of the different bishops."[81] Rome was the center of the Empire, and its eventual predominance in the Church owed much to its relationship to civil power. It was the beginning of the Church-State symbiosis which would become the norm everywhere, and the early Church became unrecognizable after it was made the official religion of the Empire.

It is difficult to say whether, or in what form, Christianity would have developed or even survived without the advent of Christendom — arguably the ultimate necessary evil. Whether the emphasis should be on 'necessary' or 'evil,' the fact is that "those days are, for the most part, gone, and ... the church would profit immensely from retrieving something of the freedom and self-direction of the local churches of the first millennium."[82] In that first millennium, "meetings of neighboring churches were held, to be sure, but they were convened to discuss common problems rather than to enact binding decisions. Whatever accommodation occurred was the result of self-adjustment rather than the imposition of standards from outside."[83] Papal infallibility has dominated and clouded the wider discussion of *Church* infallibility. The First Vatican Council underlined "the largely juridical understanding [of infallibility] as the definition and legitimate use of extraordinary papal power."[84] The Second Vatican Council expanded this "otherwise limited horizon by speaking of the infallibility of the whole Church … as the unerring faith of the people of God."[85] But we would hardly say that this constitutes a general rebellion against the Pope.

It is perhaps ironic that in recent decades, which have seen the Papacy held up for debate and discussion more than ever before, people have truly loved the Popes. From Pius XII, the first 'Televisual Pope' through to Francis, the first 'Selfie Pope,' recent Popes have demonstrated – in very different ways – extraordinary gifts in communicating and generating *simpatia*. But bones of contention remain. Are we forced to choose between adulation and vilification, and if so by what? What has been so divisive as to split the Church this way – infallibility, universal jurisdiction, the Curia, Vatican I, Vatican II?

> "It is not the authority of the pope which is in doubt among faithful sons of the Church, but the 'system' which holds him prisoner … What is wanted is to liberate everyone, even the Holy Father himself, from the system – which has been the subject of complaint for several centuries, and yet we have not succeeded in really loosening its grip or re-shaping it."[86]

Some features of this papal 'system' obviously once served a purpose but may need reforming or indeed abolishing – Curial careerism, bureaucrat bishops-of-nowhere, pompous titles, pointless sinecures in the Vatican, the bloated diplomatic corps. These are the things that Duarte Costa had a problem with, not the Pope himself. He criticized the overwhelming 'Italianness' of the College of Cardinals which laughably represented the universal Church; in the Conclave that elected Pius XII, 33 out of the 62 Cardinals were

Italian, including of course the winner. But within just two decades (1945-1965) the composition of the College of Cardinals would be utterly transformed, permanently and irrevocably. The whole world and the whole Church would be transformed permanently and irrevocably. The fortress-like institution that Duarte Costa railed against has arguably gone; the Papacy, constantly re-examined since the 1960's and understood in new lights, is no longer untouchable or above criticism, whether by progressives or conservatives.

Some of Duarte Costa's most outrageous comments and criticisms of the 1940's are now mainstream if not totally comfortable theological observations. Many of his objections would be meaningless if made today, given that Vatican II's clarifications on the Papacy, infallibility, governance, collegiality, the *sensus fidelium*, and worship have laid a lot of his grievances to rest. Many of Duarte Costa's remaining objections have finally made it onto the list of items for review, such as the ordination – in Brazil, especially – of married men, and the excessive use of titles.[87] It is easy to condemn Duarte Costa's disobedience, but since those days the relationship of *all* Catholics to authority has undergone a complete overhaul. "While many in positions of authority in the church might still demand obedience ... the exercise of authority can never be quite as straightforward in a situation where churchgoers are free to leave and to withdraw their support, both material and spiritual."[88] After all, the Catholic Church has given up the monopoly it previously claimed, as part of the price for engaging successfully with the modern world. Duarte Costa should not be held up as a great villain for anticipating, by a few decades, attitudes which were to become standard Catholic positions.

Conclusions

The Catholic Church is most often studied by insiders of one kind or another, and there is a tendency to ignore the image that the Church projects to non-Catholics. The Catholic Church is widely misunderstood and almost instinctively disliked. It can appear cultish, "extraordinarily conceited and self-absorbed."[89] But no-one struggles with the Church quite like Catholics themselves. "Among the mainstream majority of Catholics in the Western world there is a pervasive sense that the Church has failed them, that it has not listened to their experience and their needs."[90] The post-Vatican II theologians warned the Church to listen to the experiences and needs of Catholics, and one of the most vocal and visible forms that these cries have taken is in the formation of independent micro-church groups. All of the 'big issues' confronting the modern Catholic Church find partial expression in the network of micro-churches, which have been given sacramental and ecclesial form thanks to ICAB. There seems to be no objective reason why the Catholic Church should not reach out and try to heal the wounds. The *dramatis personae* of the 1945 schism are long gone – no currently living person on either side is responsible for the ICAB split itself in any sense, legal or otherwise, and the same institutions would arguably conduct themselves differently today. Retrospect tells us that the rancor and rebellion of these small breakaways tend to highlight real and genuine concerns; renegade groups act as weathervanes for the whole Church. They raise issues which the Church will have to deal with sooner or later. The outrageous reforms that ICAB demanded were ultimately enacted within twenty years, though ICAB's critics in 1945 could not foresee it.

It is not the case that the Church never listens to Catholics' needs and demands and in fact it has shown itself to be capable of responding decisively, not least in the creation of innovative canonical structures to accommodate the ambitions of specific emergent groups. These are official new creations, not part of the two-thousand-year patrimony of the Church. Apostolicity does not actually validate one 'way' over another since being Apostolic means adapting the Apostolic inheritance to the times. Everything visible in the Church is the result of development, held together in a spirit of *in*visible continuity. The Vatican as such is no more a product of the Apostolic age than ICAB – they are both recent developments and yet both share historical continuity with the Apostles. Both 'sides' of the debate have at some stage exaggerated their claims. There would be nothing proper, historically grounded, or faithful to tradition about abolishing the Papacy, as Duarte Costa suggested; but nor is it honest or constructive to pretend that the Papacy has not changed over history, within tradition, and will continue to do so. To compare the reality of the Papacy 500, 1000, 1500 years ago with that of today, and claim that they are effectively the same thing is a preposterous suggestion that would test the poker face of the most humorless Curial official. The Papacy in its various forms has been a means employed to defend the Church when necessary, keep the Church alive, and secure its survival in the world, always adapting to the needs of the day, especially after the security of the Christendom era came to an end.

Most canonical structures, clerical disciplines, and even religious orders started as radical strategies employed to safeguard the Church. Many religious orders began as the renegade fringe groups – the prophetic reformers – of their age. The Church tends to produce strategies appropriate for a particular time and task, but sooner or later they too must adapt. Even the number of sacraments, the number of major Holy Orders, have taken centuries of development to establish. The choice is not between tradition *or* development – they are not opposed – and it is only through misunderstanding or fear that this belief has taken root. The Church's is clearly a tradition *of* development, one which contains all the resources necessary for moving forward in confidence; this is consistent with the etymology of *develop*, to unwrap, or unfold. In recent decades, new canonical structures have strategically 'unfolded' to accommodate 'fringe' conservatives, traditionalists, Latin Mass supporters, conservative Anglicans, specific ethnic and national groups, and Opus Dei. Other communities have actually been brought in from 'fringe' or renegade status into full communion. It is more consistent with and respectful of tradition to see the institutions and organisational structures of the Church, including the current form of the Papacy, as strategic responses to needs, conflicts, and difficulties, rather than as impassive blocks of stone, inscrutable and unchanging over the centuries.

Even the passionately debated obligation of clerical celibacy must historically be seen for what it was, a strategic innovation to address a particular historical situation. This is the more practical and less emotive way of viewing the issue, and allows us to assess both obligatory celibacy and its abandonment according to the whole of their foundations in faith, scripture, tradition, society, and nature. What may be needed is not revolution but constant recalibration. Seeing arguments as opposing sides of a coin may not be helpful, equating one stance with tradition and the other with breaking tradition. The relationship of clerical celibacy to tradition, its past and its future, is evidence of a more complex conversation. The ordination of women, a feature of some emergent micro-church groups, seems to present a more difficult problem on the surface and indeed a problem that is a non-problem from some viewpoints. The temptation arises once more to see two sides; heads or tails, for or against – does the Church have the authority to ordain women or not? But this 'simple' question takes too much for granted, like asking 'Why does Smith's Lemonade taste so good, and why is it better than all the other brands?' Does the Church, for that matter, have the authority to ordain unworthy candidates, candidates with sinister motives, or the unhinged? It clearly *does* sometimes ordain the inept, the dishonest, and the malevolent, so it either a) has the authority to do what is supremely harmful to the Church and society, and objectively wrong, or b) the Church routinely and regularly exceeds its authority; it is clearly not in practice bound by having or not having authority to carry out its acts. To accept the limitations of its authority and ensure that *no* ordinations displease God, the Church would have to give up ordaining people altogether. Ordination, ordained ministry, and priesthood are just more products of development within tradition. As currently understood, their connection to leadership is seamless; the higher leadership roles are reserved to the ordained and therefore to men. "It is not self-evident that the charism of leadership is intrinsically

241

connected to that of pastoral ministry," Paul Lakeland wrote, "but so long as our Church is organized on the *assumption* that the connection is real, women simply cannot take their appropriate places in Church leadership."[91]

In reality, the relationship between ministry, leadership, and sacramental ordination is more flexible than might appear. Considerable numbers of the ordained, priests and bishops, spend part or all of their careers engaged in non-pastoral work – in administrative, managerial, diplomatic, or teaching roles for example. Ordination may be a prerequisite for leadership, but actually doing pastoral ministry is no such prerequisite. Ordination itself does not imply that either pastoral ministry *or* a leadership position will necessarily follow it – not all priests are in ministry and not all those in ministry are priests.[92] It is also evident that roles of responsibility for women, married men, and consecrated laypeople have increased dramatically in recent decades, including leadership roles. Many jobs normally done by ordained men in the past are now more frequently done by women – in colleges and universities, diocesan departments, and chaplaincies for example. The Church repeatedly demonstrates that it does not in practice view the interrelationship of leadership–ministry–ordained roles as set in stone for all eternity. The (deliberately) increasing number of women religious working in Vatican departments,[93] the ongoing expansion of married clergy (deacons, former Anglicans and – imminently – *viri probati*) and the growth of non-diocesan Prelatures and Ordinariates all constitute flexible interpretations of the classic clerical model.

The four bishops ordained by Archbishop Lefebvre in 1988 had their excommunications quashed in 2009. This constitutes a further acknowledgement by the Catholic Church that there may be appropriate ways of doing things outside of the standard ways. The Lefebvre bishops have no jurisdiction or leadership role, but the lifting of the censures opened the door to gradual recognition of the Society of St. Pius X. The Holy Orders, in this case at least, are absolutely not questioned. It is also worth remembering the anomaly of Salomão Barbosa Ferraz, received into the Church as a bishop, though married and a father of seven. Gray areas do officially exist in the theology of priesthood, even while regressive forces nourish the default culture of "docility and obedience [and] reverence for the ordained."[94] The Church is capable of finding solutions to difficult, anomalous, and canonically irregular situations when it wants to. Recourse to simplistic dialectics – 'you are either in or out' – are not helpful and do not in fact express the complex reality of Church membership.

Development has always encountered resistance, especially in the wake of a Council: "There has never been a General Council of the Church which has not been followed by a crisis of Faith for some part of the people, and even by a schism," [95] wrote Bishop George Dwyer, at a time when many feared that another great schism was approaching. But "General Councils are summoned to deal with crises, they are not the cause of them."[96] The theologians of Vatican II certainly attempted to avoid present and future crises, but the Church never seriously heeded the warnings of people like Küng, Rahner, Dulles, and Ratzinger. The ICAB phenomenon is a real feature of their 'future' – our present – Church. ICAB's micro-churches are the incarnation of trends and tendencies which the theologians predicted and understood. They called for these tendencies to be contained and accommodated – a call which was never answered. The Catholic Church is selective in extending its flexible embrace of welcome. God still officially speaks through the hallowed and time-honored institutions of the Church as they stand, with the assumption that "the 'command' structures of the past will persist into the future."[97] But this attitude wilfully neglects the reality of a deeply divided Church.[98] It is almost impossible to talk about being 'in or out' of the Church anyway – the undivided 'mainstream' Church is a myth. The Church's unity is at best a "pluriform unity"[99] and at worst a permanent state of schism.[100] The Church is perhaps most realistically seen as a *collection* of schisms held together in fluctuating accord. Every group within the Church acts as it pleases to some degree. Some schisms are in 'full communion' with others and some are not.

On all sides of the debate, hardly anyone would say that the Church does not need to change at all. "An initial response to the question, 'should the church change,' might well be: 'Why not? Why change the habit of two thousand years?'"[101] Bernard Hoose wrote;

> "After all, over the course of the last two millennia, there have been innumerable changes of various types: changes in how the church is run; changes in attitude; changes in moral quality; changes in teaching; and changes in style. Indeed, one might suggest that change is an important aspect of the church's nature."[102]

Catholic theology has changed as well. The theology that condemned ICAB in the 1940's has been outlived *by* ICAB and the worldwide movement derived from it, and current thinking makes it much harder to condemn the ICAB phenomenon. This phenomenon should be seen as part of the vast experience of the faithful that has continually nudged theology and the Church itself in the direction of adaptation and change. Looking back from our current perspective, the ICAB phenomenon – like it or not, officially or not – is as much a feature of our accumulated Catholic and Apostolic inheritance – or baggage – as the CDF or Opus Dei. Does the ICAB phenomenon, and the lack of a serious response to it, help to unmask a Catholic Church living in denial – denial of its own changing nature, its own need to change? Smaller schisms of the twentieth century – the Mariavites, the Aglipayans, the Lefebvrists – prompted the publication of lengthy and ground-breaking papal documents, but ICAB's half a million to three million Catholics have never received such official attention. The ICAB phenomenon is perhaps too big, too unwieldy, too widespread, too pertinent, and therefore too embarrassing for the Catholic Church to really admit that it exists.

Notes

1   Karl Rahner, *The Shape of the Church to Come*, SPCK, London, 1974, p 108

2   Joseph Ratzinger, *Faith and The Future*, Ignatius Press, San Francisco, 2009, p 116

3   Joseph Ratzinger, 'What will the Church of the Future look like?', 2009, p 116

4   Avery Dulles, *The Resilient Church*, Gill and Macmillan, Dublin, 1978, p 14

5   Avery Dulles, *The Resilient Church*, p 14

6   Karl Rahner, *The Shape of The Church to Come*, p 108

7   Joseph Ratzinger, 'What will the Church of the Future look like?', 2009, p 116 [emphasis added]

8   Joseph Ratzinger, 'What will the Church of the Future look like?', 2009, p 117

9   Joseph Ratzinger, 'What will the Church of the Future look like?', 2009, p 118

10   Karl Rahner, *The Shape of The Church to Come*, p 108

11   Cf. Peter Hebblethwaite, *The Runaway Church*, Collins Fount, Glasgow, 1978, p 242

12   Avery Dulles, *The Resilient Church*, p 15

13   Cf. Pontifical Council for the Pastoral Care of Migrants and Itinerant People, *Erga Migrantes* No. 19 http://www.vatican.va/roman_curia/pontifical_councils/migrants/documents/rc_pc_migrants_doc_20040514_erga-migrantes-caritas-christi_en.html [accessed 10th May 2018]

14   Canons 294 to 297 – http://www.vatican.va/archive/ENG1104/_P10.HTM [accessed 10th May 2018]

15   Cf. Clarence Kelly, *The Sacred and the Profane*, Seminary Press, Round Top, New York, 1997, p 231

16   Vatican Congregation for Bishops, *Animarum Bonum*, 18th January 2002, at www.adapostolica.org, http://www.adapostolica.org/wp-content/uploads/2014/01/Decreto-de-Ere%C3%A7%C3%A3o-da-Administra%C3%A7%C3%A3o-Apost%C3%B3lica-Animarum-Bonum.pdf, [accessed 9th May 2018]

17   Cf. Pastoral Letter of the Bishops of the Ecclesiastical Province of São Paulo, December 1972, p 94

18   Johann A. Möhler, *Unity in the Church*, Catholic University of America Press, Washington, 1996, p 210

19   Cf. Rahner, in Vorgrimler (ed), *One, Holy, Catholic, and Apostolic*, Sheed & Ward, London, 1968, p 4

20 Cf. Gerard Mannion, *Ecclesiology and Postmodernity*, Liturgical Press, Collegeville, 2007, p ix

21 Gerard Mannion, *Ecclesiology and Postmodernity*, p x

22 F.W. Faber, *The Precious Blood*, John Murphy, Baltimore, (10th American Edition), 1868 [?], pp 352-353

23 Cf. Mark Chapman, 'Authority', in Gerard Mannion and Lewis S. Mudge, (eds), *The Routledge Companion to the Christian Church*, Routledge, Abingdon, 2008, [pp 497-510], p 497

24 Karl Rahner, *The Shape of the Church to Come*, p 108

25 Karl Rahner, *The Shape of the Church to Come*, p 108 [emphasis added]

26 Karl Rahner, *The Shape of the Church to Come*, p 108

27 Karl Rahner, *The Shape of the Church to Come*, p 109

28 Karl Rahner, *The Shape of the Church to Come*, p 109

29 Cf. Karl Rahner, *The Shape of the Church to Come*, p 108

30 Karl Rahner, *The Shape of the Church to Come*, p 111

31 Karl Rahner, *The Shape of the Church to Come*, p 114

32 Karl Rahner, *The Shape of the Church to Come*, p 111

33 Karl Rahner, *The Shape of the Church to Come*, p 110

34 Cf. John E. Lynch, 'The Changing Role of the Bishop', *Jurist*, Vol. 39, 1979, [pp 289-312], pp 291-292

35 Johann Adam Möhler, pp 188-189

36 Cf. Paul Lakeland, *Church – Living Communion*, Liturgical Press, Collegeville MN, 2009, p 32

37 Paul Lakeland, *Church – Living Communion*, p 32

38 Cf. Gerard Mannion, *Ecclesiology and Postmodernity*, pp 34-35

39 Cf. Gerard Mannion, *Ecclesiology and Postmodernity*, p 35

40 Gerard Mannion, *Ecclesiology and Postmodernity*, p 35

41 Schism, according to Canon 751 of the 1983 Code of Canon Law

42 John E. Lynch, 'The Changing Role of the Bishop: A Historical Survey', pp 291-292

43 Cf. John E. Lynch, 'The Changing Role of the Bishop: A Historical Survey', pp 291-292

44 Johann Adam Möhler, p 218

45 Johann Adam Möhler, p 221

46 Johann Adam Möhler, p 226

47 Johann Adam Möhler, p 226

48 Michael J. Buckley SJ, 'Resources for Reform from the First Millenium', in Stephen J. Pope (ed), *Common Calling*, Georgetown University Press, Washington DC, 2004, [pp 71-86], p 72

49 Michael J. Buckley SJ, 'Resources for Reform from the First Millenium', p 74

50   Michael J. Buckley SJ, 'Resources for Reform from the First Millenium', p 74
51   Michael J. Buckley SJ, 'Resources for Reform from the First Millenium', p 74
52   Michael J. Buckley SJ, 'Resources for Reform from the First Millenium', p 72
53   Johann Adam Möhler, p 220
54   Michael J. Buckley SJ, p 76, "the Council of Nicaea, the fifth canon of Chalcedon, and many regional councils insistently enjoined bishops—or priests and deacons—from moving from one see to another."
55   Michael J. Buckley SJ, 'Resources for Reform from the First Millenium', p 76
56   Michael J. Buckley SJ, 'Resources for Reform from the First Millenium', p 76
57   Francis A. Sullivan SJ, *From Apostles to Bishops,* The Newman Press, New York/Mahwah, 2001, p 14
58   Mark Chapman, 'Authority', p 498
59   Michael J. Buckley SJ, 'Resources for Reform from the First Millenium', pp 75-76
60   Padre Florence Marie [Florêncio Maria] Dubois, *O Ex-Bispo de Maura e o Bom Senso [The Ex-Bishop of Maura and Common Sense],* Ed. Vozes Limitada, Petrópolis–Rio de Janeiro–São Paulo, 1945, p 16
61   Mark Chapman, 'Authority', p 498
62   Johann Adam Möhler, p 220
63   Francis A. Sullivan SJ, *From Apostles to Bishops,* p 14
64   Francis A. Sullivan SJ, *From Apostles to Bishops,* p 14
65   Michael J. Buckley SJ, 'Resources for Reform from the First Millennium', p 75-76
66   Johannes L. Witte SJ, 'One, holy, catholic, and apostolic', p 3
67   Johannes L. Witte SJ, 'One, holy, catholic, and apostolic', p 5
68   Johannes L. Witte SJ, 'One, holy, catholic, and apostolic', p 5
69   John J. Burkhard OFM Conv, *Apostolicity Then and Now,* Liturgical Press, Collegeville, 2004, p 24-25
70   John J. Burkhard OFM Conv, *Apostolicity Then and Now,* p 25
71   Cf. Paul Lakeland, *Church – Living Communion,* p 58
72   John E. Thiel, *Senses of Tradition,* Oxford University Press, Oxford, 2000, p 44
73   Paul Lakeland, *Church – Living Communion,* p 58
74   A.M. Ramsey, *The Gospel and the Catholic Church,* Longmans, Green & Co., London, 1936, p 129
75   Karl Barth, *The Epistle to the Romans,* Oxford University Press, Oxford, 1968, p 301

[76] Cf. Paul Lakeland, *Church – Living Communion,* pp 10-11

[77] Paul Lakeland, *Church – Living Communion,* pp 10-11

[78] Paul Lakeland, *Church – Living Communion,* pp 52-53

[79] Mark Chapman, 'Authority', p 504

[80] Michael J. Buckley SJ, 'Resources for Reform from the First Millennium', p 75

[81] Mark Chapman, 'Authority', p 504

[82] Michael J. Buckley SJ, 'Resources for Reform from the First Millennium', pp 75-76

[83] John E. Lynch, 'The Changing Role of the Bishop: A Historical Survey', pp 291-292

[84] John E. Thiel, *Senses of Tradition: Continuity and Development in Catholic Faith,* p 47

[85] John E. Thiel, *Senses of Tradition: Continuity and Development in Catholic Faith,* p 47

[86] Leo Joseph Cardinal Suenens, *The Tablet,* 17th May 1969, p 14

[87] Cf. Gerard O'Connell, *La Stampa,* 1 Apr. 2014 'Pope abolishes honorary title of Monsignor for Diocesan Priests' http://vaticaninsider.lastampa.it/en/the-vatican/detail/articolo/31027/ [accessed 9th May 2018]

[88] Cf. Mark Chapman, 'Authority', p 498 [emphasis added]

[89] Paul Collins, *Papal Power,* Fount / Harper Collins, London, 1997, p x

[90] Paul Collins, *Papal Power,* p x

[91] Paul Lakeland, *Church – Living Communion,* p 75 [emphasis added]

[92] Cf. George B. Wilson SJ, *Clericalism,* Liturgical Press, Collegeville, 2008, p xvi

[93] Cf. *The Tablet,* 29th March 2014, p 12

[94] Avery Dulles, *The Resilient Church,* p 9

[95] George Dwyer, in Yves Congar, *Challenge to the Church,* Collins Liturgical, London, 1977, p 6

[96] Bishop George Dwyer, in Yves Congar, *Challenge to the Church,* p 6

[97] Mark Chapman, 'Authority', p 498

[98] Cf. Joseph Ratzinger, *Salt of the Earth,* Ignatius Press, San Francisco, 1997, pp 242-243

[99] Avery Dulles, *The Catholicity of the Church,* Clarendon Press, Oxford, 1987, p 77

[100] Avery Dulles, *The Catholicity of the Church,* p 77

[101] Bernard Hoose in Mannion, *Church and Religious 'Other,'* T&T Clark, London 2008 [221-231] p 221

[102] Bernard Hoose, p 221

IX
GOD, LAND AND FREEDOM?
— Conclusions —

"He shall also judge those who give rise to schisms, who are destitute of the love of God, and who look to their own special advantage rather than to the unity of the Church; and who for trifling reasons, or any kind of reason which occurs to them, cut in pieces and divide the great and glorious body of Christ."

St. Irenaeus, *Adversus Haereses*
(On the Detection and Overthrow of the So-Called Gnosis)
Book IV, Chapter XXXIII, Number VII

What really motivated Carlos Duarte Costa? He has understandably been called "a revolutionary"[1] but he was not alone in wanting to see the Church adapt and develop both a distinctive role and a distinctive voice in post-Christendom society. The challenge for his generation of bishops was to "come to grips with the death of Christendom without simply acquiescing in the privatization of the church."[2] And the Church itself did seem to acquiesce, which was perhaps "strange from the point of view of theology, but perfectly understandable [and desirable] from the point of view of politics."[3] But this is less strange when viewed as a strategy to survive in the new political order, which was not without potent elements of anticlericalism.[4] Duarte Costa's near-contemporary, the head of the Catholic Church in Brazil, Cardinal Silveira Cintra, accepted what may be called the "political marginalization of the church"[5] only so far. While it is true that Silveira Cintra did not violently denounce the authoritarian Vargas regime, he only tolerated it just enough to win the desired concessions, and to allow the Church to become a moderating influence on the dictatorship. As a result the Church in Brazil endured dictatorship better than the Church in Fascist Italy, for example, even though the members of Vargas's junta were not particularly sympathetic to Catholicism.

With the dictatorial regimes of the 1930's representing the extreme version of the modern nation-state, it was clear that they strove to inherit the all-embracing hold that religion had once had. The nation-state was to be the new religion in some senses, the new Christendom. Somewhere in this new state of affairs Duarte Costa became committed to the idea of a National Church. In being National, his idea was not to prop up the Nationalist regime – on the contrary – but rather to pull back the nation-state ethos into the domain of religion; if the 'New State' could be all-embracing then so could the Church. ICAB was envisioned as being the aggregate of all Brazilian beliefs, values, rituals and customs – a sort of Church–Nation–State – since "the base of religion in Brazil is in the culture itself ... [which is of a] sacral nature."[6] ICAB would embrace Freemasonry, Theosophy, Protestantism, Positivism, Communism, Spiritualism, Umbanda, Macumba and Candomblé, all under one roof. Though Duarte Costa's aim was to "democratize the Church"[7] and although he accused others of fascism – the Pope, the Nuncio, the bishops, the foreign clergy – ICAB was fundamentally totalitarian in principle[8] – everything within ICAB, nothing of value outside of ICAB – and even slightly fascist in its persecution complex and nationalism. And for all his condemnations of fascism, Duarte Costa's leadership style was absolutely authoritarian and utterly opposed to delegation, consultation or collegiality.[9]

Christendom, which "finally and definitively crumbled in the twentieth century,"[10] is widely regarded as an unedifying and embarrassing quirk of history, but it does demonstrate that the form and role which religion takes in society are not inevitable.[11] Duarte Costa's politics were perhaps not very well worked-out, but his vision for ICAB was certainly not detached from reality. Brazil is on the whole a deeply religious nation, but its Catholicism is an "extremely heterogeneous"[12] version of it. Brazilian Catholicism is more like, as Thomas C. Bruneau wrote, "a cultural repertoire of [rituals,] customs, [and] sacraments"[13] – a phrase that would serve well as a description of ICAB. In spite of inconsistencies and contradictions,[14] Duarte Costa's ICAB idea was not inconsistent with the character of Brazilian Catholicism. ICAB was intended to combine this character with the all-embracing, universalizing purpose of the modern nation-state, "encompassing all citizens regardless of their other affiliations."[15]

Carlos Duarte Costa – Courageous and Democratic?[16]

Though his own style tended towards the authoritarian and totalitarian, Duarte Costa took an uncompromisingly critical stance against Fascism at a time when sectors of the Church hierarchy were in collusion with right-wing regimes. This is also, however, one of the most grossly over-inflated and fallacious aspects of the ICAB story. Pope Pius XII's role in World War Two continues to be a controversial topic, though the more sensationalist interpretations of Pius as 'Hitler's Pope' have been largely laid to rest. It is ironic that the Vatican excommunicated Duarte Costa just one week after Hitler's death and nine days after Mussolini's death, both of whom were Catholics who were never excommunicated. Cardinal Bertram of Breslau (Wrocław) was even rumored to have ordered a Requiem Mass to be said for Hitler. But the question is not whether it ever crossed Pope Pius XII's mind to excommunicate Hitler and Mussolini, but rather what good it would have done. The Church in Germany and Italy, just like the Church in Brazil, took measures to ensure its survival; it may have been easier for Duarte Costa to criticize because Rio de Janeiro was not occupied by the Nazis. In terms of the Pope's concrete actions during the Nazi occupation, the wartime Chief Rabbi of Rome, Israel Zolli, became one of Pius XII's most vehement defenders. Zolli himself was among the Jews saved by the Pope, and when he converted to Catholicism in 1945 he took Pius XII's Christian names, Eugenio Maria.

Duarte Costa's own anti-Nazi stance remains a powerful and enduring part of the ICAB myth.[17] When Duarte Costa makes occasional, brief appearances in books dealing with Independent Catholicism and ICAB micro-churches, this part of the myth is usually uncritically repeated. A central part of the myth is that Duarte Costa supposedly spoke out against the 'Ratlines' – clandestine assistance networks for Nazi war criminals fleeing to countries including Brazil, using or abusing agencies of the Catholic Church or the Red Cross. This denunciation is often cited as one of the reasons for Duarte Costa's excommunication.[18] This would date Duarte Costa's 'speaking out' against the Ratlines to the first half of 1945 at the latest, since he was excommunicated on 4th May 1945. The first problem is obvious – Ratlines to Brazil had not started by May 1945.[19] The South American Ratline was in operation from 1946, much facilitated by the accession to power of Juan Domingo Perón in February of that year.[20] The first confirmed South American 'Rats' were Nazi collaborating journalists connected to the Catholic *Action Française* (AF) movement, and their destination was Argentina, not Brazil.[21] The most notorious war criminals to flee to Brazil – Franz Stangl and Gustav Wagner – arrived in 1950-1951 by regular travel means, and Josef Mengele arrived in Brazil in 1960. The very early Ratlines operating solely within Europe were not common knowledge in 1945, and Duarte Costa was no Church insider by that stage. Most conclusively, Duarte Costa never even *mentioned* the Ratlines, in spite of the many negative things he said and wrote about the Vatican. Duarte Costa's lengthy 1945 *Manifesto* actually gives the reasons, as he saw them, for his excommunication, and he does not even hint at anything about denouncing escaping Nazis. He was not exercising discretion; he openly accused the Church of orchestrating at least two cold-blooded murders (not Nazi-related) and of colluding with the Franco and Salazar regimes to plan a joint right-wing Iberian takeover of Latin America. Duarte Costa never presented firm evidence for any of these accusations, so there was no reason for him not to mention the European Ratlines if he knew about them.

Could it be that Duarte Costa's supposed denunciations of the Ratlines came later when they were common knowledge? No, because throughout 25 editions and hundreds of pages of *Luta!* written, produced and published under his personal guidance, Duarte Costa repeated his entire list of complaints against the Roman Catholic Church and never once mentioned the Ratlines. The fact is that we simply do not know what he thought about the thousands of immigrants from Germany after 1945 – many of them no doubt had served in the war and some, perhaps many, could have been former Nazis – which is not the definition of a war criminal in any case. It may be recalled that ICAB considered the Roman Catholic bishop of Lages, who was born in Brazil, to be a 'Nazi' because he joined the German branch of the Franciscans, and this kind of sensationalism endures. The 'Ratline denouncing' myth is a careless and irresponsible embellishment to the ICAB story, which should cease to be repeated. Surely, respect for the victims of Nazism demands that the utmost veracity be painstakingly established in the telling of history.[22]

A similar problem arises with the uncritical description of Duarte Costa as an outspoken supporter of social and political reform. Which reforms was he outspoken about? Rather than reforming, perhaps he was in favor of conserving the democratic constitution of the First Republic when this was threatened and later thrown out. Ten years later he was more for revolution than reform, with his support of Stalin and the Soviet Union – in 1943 of course practically everyone in the 'free world' supported Stalin. It is not clear how much of a committed ideological communist Duarte Costa really was, not least because his views and opinions were fairly fluid over the years. There is no evidence that he ever joined Brazil's influential Communist Party. Duarte Costa did intervene directly in politics with the foundation of his short-lived Christian Socialist Party, but its impact was negligible. Pelypenko longed to find solid proof of "ICAB and its links with the agents of Moscow"[23] but he did not get very far – he did much better establishing ICAB's ties to the Freemasons.[24] Duarte Costa was certainly outspoken in support of allowing civil divorce, as well as religious divorce, but the best examples of attempts at social reform are his efforts to provide free elementary education for the poor. The first ICAB churches, he decreed, also had to have a school attached to them. This was in the context of the Roman Catholic Church having dismally failed to establish good provision of elementary education, instead concentrating its efforts on high school and university education, which is the preserve of the children of the elite.

Carlos Duarte Costa – the Rebel in Rio

"Hatred towards the Supreme Pastor is the spinal column of heresy,"[25] Dubois wrote, but he claimed that Duarte Costa's rejection of the Papacy was more visceral than theological: "The pain of rejection is at the heart of Dom Carlos's anti-papalism."[26] Duarte Costa had longed to become Auxiliary Bishop of Rio de Janeiro and resented having to make do with being Bishop of Botucatu. What was Duarte Costa like as a bishop? His performance received mixed reviews: he apparently "allowed the property of the diocese to fall into ruin. … [but] there have been holy bishops who were not good administrators."[27] In spite of criticizing the Roman Catholic Church as an "institution dominated by pomp,"[28] he was known for his "love [of] miters, rings, and pastoral staffs."[29] It was felt that without his family connections he would never have been ordained priest or bishop.[30] It is surely not necessary to speculate too much about Duarte Costa's mental state and apparent nervous condition. His contemporaries Fathers Bettencourt and Dubois were not unkind or unsympathetic, but Pelypenko considered Duarte Costa "disturbed"[31] and worried that his mental health made him capable of anything, like Bishop Vargas, whose church mysteriously burnt down.[32]

Duarte Costa led ICAB for almost sixteen years before his death in April 1961, but after the drama of his initial break with Rome his achievements were modest. He ordained many priests and bishops, it is true, but he was forever feuding with most of them. This was particularly the case with Luis Fernando Castillo Mendez, whom he denounced as a fraud, a conman, a thief, a liar etc. and Salomão Barbosa Ferraz, whom he considered an opportunist in league with the Vatican to undermine ICAB. Defections, desertions, and denunciations were constant. Duarte Costa at least tried, in fairness, to maintain contact with all his priests, even by-passing the other bishops to do so;[33] "all our priests, as also bishops, are under the direct authority of Dom Carlos ... since Dom Carlos does not trust any of our bishops and does not concede them more authority than to the priests."[34]

So much for Duarte Costa's leadership style. His intellectual output was unfortunately also meager, consisting of short, quite repetitive articles appearing in *Luta!* The articles often take the form of an 'attack' on some aspect of Roman Catholic teaching; he repeated that celibacy is wrong because it is unnatural – "a factor in sexual aberrations"[35] – though he himself ostensibly remained celibate throughout his life. Some, including ICAB bishops and clergy, have disputed this. Pelypenko tantalized his readers by mentioning "a lady in middle-age, of quite pleasant appearance, who lives in [Duarte Costa's] apartment with him"[36] – but she is not mentioned anywhere else. Duarte Costa claimed that Roman Catholic priests are only interested in money. He called the Roman Catholic Church "a highly commercialized institution,"[37] but his own institution would become known for its simony[38] and as "a vast dispensary of ecclesiastical services,"[39] alongside the small matter of counterfeiting money in the ICAB seminary.[40] But it is the Jesuits, according to *Luta!* who are a secretive, avaricious, and corrupt sect. Roman Catholicism is just another form of colonization, the Vatican is Fascist, papal control is parasitical and undermines the fatherland, the true Church should unite all religions into one, and Duarte Costa himself is always beyond reproach. *Luta!* published articles by Spiritualists and Freemasons uncritically, never conceding the possibility of ideological or spiritual conflicts with Christianity; only Roman Catholicism was flawed.

Duarte Costa wanted to "revive primitive Christianity"[41] by restoring the "autonomous, self-sufficient, and insular"[42] character of the early Church. Even in the view of its senior clergy, however, ICAB remained "identical to the Roman [Catholic Church], with the only difference that it has no Pope."[43] Duarte Costa and his bishops had no intention of giving up "the honours of the episcopacy"[44] in accordance with "the late medieval or post-Tridentine conception of prelacy [including] wearing vestments and other regalia in the Baroque, Gothic Revival, or Oriental fashions."[45] While the Roman Catholic Church began to evolve and adapt to the twentieth century, ICAB ever more vehemently stuck to this same old "ritual-based image of the ordained ministry."[46] But the early Church to which Duarte Costa aspired not only did not recognize a bishop's supposed freedom to ordain and consecrate anyone he pleased, it vehemently and expressly condemned it as false. The Council of Chalcedon (451) emphasized that the call to ordained ministry springs from the community, and not from the initiative of the ordaining bishop.[47] It is not clear to what extent Duarte Costa was able to disseminate his original proposal for the election of ICAB bishops and priests, but it never became the norm in the wider movement.

Serious reform was never truly on ICAB's agenda, but in its defense, it sprang from a form of Catholicism concerned mainly with imparting "spiritual verities,"[48] "pretty words and exterior acts."[49] The Roman Catholic Church found itself unprepared for modern urban society, and in contrast to this state of paralysis, ICAB – in part at least a genuinely grass-roots movement – managed to look more like the real Church of the people. ICAB assumed the mantel of 'the church of the poor,' though this actual phrase only seems to have acquired popularity later, and there is no evidence that it was used in Duarte Costa's day. After Duarte Costa's death, ICAB was subject to the whim and opportunism of whichever bishop temporarily held sway, and the supposed reformist movement resisted modernization, theological reflection, intellectual engagement, and dialogue. ICAB's fortunes had always to some extent been guided by opportunity and convenience – some branches allied themselves to oppressive governments and others were used as stooges to discredit the Catholic Church. Fame and notoriety can also project a strange appeal, recalling sensationalist reports in recent years of same-sex marriages, UFO's, and the extraterrestrial origins of Jesus. ICAB always garnered accusations of questionable behavior, though there is no doubt that a wide range of motivations were represented.

Did ICAB preempt Liberation Theology?

The experience of Catholicism in the post-war and Cold War world, particularly in Latin America, gave rise to Liberation Theology, which drew new attention to the undeniable political dimension of practising the Christian faith. Duarte Costa certainly recognized this dimension, but he never had any carefully worked-out philosophy. The 'national church' idea he espoused was completely analogous to Liberation Theology; ICAB was designed to mark the passing of Christendom by creating a new all-embracing religious force in society. Liberation Theology, on the other hand, rejected anything reminiscent of the Christendom era "when the church directly wielded political power,"[50] especially rejecting alliances with governments which ICAB sought to cultivate. Similarly, the 'national church' as an instrument of pageantry and ceremony only helps to emphasize the Church's exile to "the apolitical realm of values and ideals,"[51] safely away from real politics. But the potential contradictions inherent in the idea of a national or nationalist Catholic Church never troubled Duarte Costa. Pelypenko surmised that being called the 'igreja brasileira' was either meant to appeal to people's basic patriotism, to attract as many people as possible, or that the word 'Brazilian' was more or less arbitrarily chosen to replace 'Roman.'[52] Dubois called ICAB "misdirected patriotism."[53]

Being a 'national church' effectively means the abandonment of a political dimension, because any political stance it takes is bound to exclude some section of society. The national church would aim to be culturally all-embracing and representative, and it would become divisive if it ever took a side in politics. This echoes Cardinal Silveira Cintra's old objection to the idea of a Catholic political party, which Duarte Costa ignored. ICAB could only claim to represent the whole nation by focusing on shared customs and rituals – much like the old Catholic Church of "pretty words and exterior acts."[54] This rather vacuous conception of a National Church – "formal ritualistic allegiance to Christianity"[55] blended with national custom and culture – was the most that ICAB ever could, or in fact ever did, achieve. Even so, the post-Vatican II period saw ICAB move significantly to the right politically and even directly collude with right-wing dictatorships. This was clearly a rejection of the founder's political orientation, but Duarte Costa himself was politically volatile: he signed Silveira Cintra's pastoral letter against Communism and then eagerly prefaced Hewlett Johnson's *The Socialist Sixth of The World / The Soviet Power*, praising Stalin; he campaigned against President Vargas and then vowed solidarity and national unity with him; he welcomed priests and religious from Mussolini's Italy before 1937 and later condemned all 'Axis' clergy as 'fascist.' Everyone has the right to change their mind of course, but for Duarte Costa it was clearly a regular occurrence.[56] He was no doubt imbued with a certain "spirit of contradiction."[57]

Did ICAB preempt Vatican II?

The flagship of ICAB was the "use of Portuguese instead of Latin"[58] and reform did not initially go further than an expedient translation.[59] Duarte Costa's clergy were under no illusions; apart from the fact that "Dom Carlos renounced Latin,"[60] ICAB "retained everything that is Roman, only ... religious services are

258

celebrated not in Latin but in Portuguese."[61] Equally salient was Duarte Costa's take on interreligious dialogue; critics called ICAB an "amalgamation of sects"[62] because of his attempts to draw all religions into one very broad definition of Catholicism. "Dom Carlos told reporters that there is no incompatibility between the Igreja Brasileira and other religions. There are 'delicate differences' of theological and philosophical concepts. But that is all."[63] The Archbishop of Belém, Mario de Miranda Vilas Boas, commented that a complete apostasy is at least preferable to a partial apostasy; the first is more sincere and the apostate does not risk being accused of repudiating all that which is inconvenient only to hold onto all that which suits him.[64] Much later, critics of Vatican II – who do not stop short of calling that Council apostasy – could recognize parallels between ICAB and the reformed Catholic Church which "surrendered its distinctive vision of the world and its role in it,"[65] proving perhaps that the opposing ecclesial mindsets have by no means disappeared.[66] Beyond these initial innovations though, the Roman Catholic Church would lament the fact that ICAB otherwise endeavored to keep faith in the dark ages, especially in the context of Vatican II: "[ICAB] contradicts and prejudices everything that the Council desires."[67]

Pelypenko was shocked at ICAB's 'reformed' disciplines – priests and bishops marrying, separating, living in partnership, unofficially adopting children, divorcing, remarrying; "This is the most crass contradiction of the Holy Scriptures and the violation of the precepts of the Holy Church."[68] In fact these were hardly Vatican II-style reforms, but simply the wholesale lifting of restrictions and taboos. The fundamental distinction between the reforms of Vatican II and the reforms of ICAB is that very little reflection, consultation, colloquy, or research sat behind the axe-fall decisions of Duarte Costa. The 'ICAB as Vatican II precursor' myth, like so many of the legends surrounding ICAB, is ripe for clarification. ICAB did not preempt Liberation Theology *or* Vatican II in any substantial sense that can be pinpointed. Understandably there is a tendency to try to interpret the ICAB story by 'pegging' it to the more noteworthy events of the time: the Ratlines, Vatican II, Liberation Theology; but the ICAB connections to all of these are at best circumstantial and at worst, as with the Ratlines-denouncing myth, fabricated. The same thing occurs with the comparison between ICAB and the Worker Priests movement, or describing ICAB priests as Worker Priests, simply because they have jobs. This description deliberately ignores what the principles of the Worker Priest movement are. The (real) Worker Priests have a history, methodology, theology, philosophy of work, and praxis that suggest no comparison whatsoever with ICAB priests. This is not to denigrate ICAB priests for simply earning money to support their families, obviously. ICAB priests, for the most part, are working priests, or working men who are also priests, and are in no way connected to the Worker Priest movement. ICAB itself has not always appreciated the working efforts of its priests; Father Raúl Clementino Smania was made to choose between his job and the Church, and when he chose his career over ICAB he was branded a "traitor."[69]

Conclusions – ICAB and theology – what about Catholicity?

Duarte Costa was openly and repeatedly recognized as the 'founder' of ICAB; there was never any pretense that this was a Church founded by Jesus Christ. Consequently Duarte Costa deserves the credit for 500,000 adherents in Brazil, 50 years after his death, and an incalculable number of supporters – conceivably many thousands – through ICAB's branches and offshoots in other countries. Duarte Costa grasped some truths about Brazilian Catholicism that his fellow Roman Catholic bishops may not have wanted to acknowledge: the Brazilian clergy simply did not have a long history of maintaining celibacy or putting the concerns of the Church before those of self, family, society, or fatherland; Brazilian Catholics in general did not regard Catholicism as exclusive or incompatible with Afro-Brazilian religions, Spiritualism, Freemasonry, superstition, or magic. Duarte Costa, far from cowering from these unpalatable truths, incorporated them all into ICAB's repertoire. For Pelypenko, it was all "completely misguided."[70]

Perhaps sensing, in Duarte Costa's pluralist attitude, a threat to their Catholic identity, over the decades the clergy of ICAB and its offshoots have tended to place more and more faith in apostolic succession. As well as furnishing "implacable theological truth [and] legitimacy"[71] it is often felt that apostolic succession – valid Holy Orders – acts as a guarantee of Catholicity as well. But the idea that during ordination the bishop transmits a sort of 'being Catholic' is not grounded in theology. To outsiders this idea may not seem less reasonable than the idea of apostolic succession itself, but the two things are different. In fact, for Catholic theology the ordaining bishop's faith, or lack of faith, or heresy for that matter, have no bearing on the ordination transmitted. The idea that ordination by a Catholic makes you Catholic is like the idea that eating a vegetarian meal prepared by a vegetarian chef makes you a vegetarian – the things are no doubt related, but being a vegetarian, or a Catholic, involves decisions and factors of ongoing commitment and assimilation which cannot be transmitted by carrying out certain actions or rituals. This impoverished understanding of being Catholic can be observed in practice in a lot of micro-church material and websites. They often list their apostolic *successions* – plural – giving lists of accumulated genealogical lines described as Chaldean, Orthodox, Old Catholic, Syro-Malabaric, Celtic, and the all-important Roman Catholic. At least one Independent Catholic bishop boasts of having received every variety of Holy Orders available on the market, thus magically equipping him to perform all and any religious rites (or none at all) as requested. It is as if his multiple ordinations have made him simultaneously Orthodox, Anglican, Coptic, Mariavite, and Old Catholic. The ICAB phenomenon, founded by a Catholic bishop but widely and wildly deviating from Catholicism, illustrates the logical conclusion that being ordained by a Catholic does not make someone Catholic. The suggestion that ICAB or ICAB bishops are 'obviously Catholic' because Duarte Costa was Catholic is utterly baseless.

Conclusions – ICAB and ecclesiology – what about 'Dominus Iesus'?

In terms of understanding and explaining ICAB's place in the universal Church, some have tended towards applying the non-Catholic 'branch theory,' which is discarded mainly for not being mirrored by anything in the Gospel. Michael Ramsey called it "an unconscious attempt to make the best both of unity and of schism, and the relation between Church order and the Gospel is obscured."[72] Members of the ICAB movement found hope in a Vatican document published in August 2000, *'Dominus Iesus' – on the unicity and salvific universality of Jesus Christ and the Church,*[73] particularly Part IV, Paragraph 17. The sentence of most interest in the all-important paragraph reads:

> "The Churches which, while not existing in perfect communion with the Catholic Church, remain united to her by means of the closest bonds, that is, by apostolic succession and a valid Eucharist, are true particular Churches."[74]

For the ICAB phenomenon, it is argued, this is clear and total vindication and explicit recognition by the Roman Catholic Church; the document states two criteria for being a true particular Church (in effect two elements of one criterion) and ICAB possesses them. The opposing argument is composed as follows:

a) The key sentence in *Dominus Iesus* begins 'The Churches' – it is talking about Churches, and ICAB is not a Church in the understanding of the Catholic Church and Catholic theology, and the micro-church offshoots even less so; they may or may not be Churches according to various domestic legal definitions, or the definitions used by other organizations and denominations, but this is obviously of no concern here to the Congregation for the Doctrine of the Faith (CDF).

b) The context of the document, the specific biblical references, and the specific references to documents of the Second Vatican Council, all make it clear that the Churches being referred to are the Eastern Orthodox Churches, including the ancient sees of Constantinople, Alexandria, Antioch, and Jerusalem; these are the Churches not 'in *perfect* communion with the Catholic Church,' whereas ICAB and its offshoots are not in *any* kind of communion with the Catholic Church. The phraseology of the rest of the document – 'particular Churches' – also typifies previous discussion of the historical non-Latin Rite Churches.

c) The document makes reference to apostolic succession as a criterion for being a true particular Church and then clarifies this by making reference to a sub-criterion, a valid Eucharist. A valid Eucharist would imply a valid apostolic succession, as opposed to an apostolic succession that is recognized as such but not recognized as valid. However, the Roman Catholic Church has repeatedly stated that *none* of the sacraments of ICAB or its offshoots are to be considered valid, regarded as valid, or treated as valid. They are to be absolutely avoided. If *Dominus Iesus* had intended to include the ICAB movement they could easily have used the phrase 'and a possibly valid Eucharist' or similar wording.

In fairness to the ICAB movement and Independent Catholics in general, the more generous interpretation of *Dominus Iesus* is not entirely unreasonable. The difficulty lies in the terminology used – 'the Churches' is not a universal-use term but a specific-use one, and the document does not define it. The document in fact "assumes a select audience of theologically competent Catholics familiar with the curial style"[75] who do not need any clarifications of the terms used. It cannot have occurred to the CDF that *Dominus Iesus* would be of great interest to those Catholics not in perfect, or not in any, communion with Rome. This further demonstrates that for the Roman Catholic Church the ICAB or Independent Catholic phenomenon simply does not exist. The Vatican did not anticipate that the issues of *Dominus Iesus* could be of broader relevance, or even that "documents coming from Rome are not purely church documents"[76] any more, and will reach a wider audience beyond "those in the know."[77] The intended audience of the document, incidentally, is not specified.

The Roman Catholic Church's actual position on the ICAB phenomenon is not universally known. ICAB supporters have generally worked hard to publicize the example of Salomão Barbosa Ferraz's recognition by the Vatican, while preferring to overlook official declarations of the doubtfulness, illicitness, or invalidity of ICAB sacraments, and the fact that it is not regarded as a Church. Considering *Dominus Iesus* in its entirety, its purpose, its background, and the wider context of other documents, the only possible conclusion is that the 'recognition' contained in the document has nothing to do with the ICAB phenomenon. The document does have some incidental and unintended bearing on the ICAB case, but for the problems highlighted above the outcome is still negative. It is evident that as far as *Dominus Iesus* – and its authors – are concerned, the ICAB phenomenon does not exist.

Conclusions – is ICAB heresy, schism, apostasy?

Is it still helpful to talk about the ICAB movement in terms of a 'schism'? Many of the communities emerging from ICAB correspond to the description of the future Church offered by the theologians of Vatican II – Rahner, Ratzinger, Dulles, Küng – though they may have failed to predict all of the ICAB movement's flaws. Duarte Costa's timing meant that he was judged according to Vatican I theology, whereas Vatican II theology seems to largely vindicate him. It remains difficult to evaluate exactly how much ICAB influenced Catholic Church reform and how much ICAB was inspired and motivated by reforms already in progress. In the case of Luigi Mascolo, studying at the Angelicum in the late 1950's, he seemed to find in ICAB the full expression of the reformable Catholicism he had learnt about in Rome. Even Duarte Costa's extreme take on ecumenical dialogue becomes less of a scandal, since "the dogma of the Fourth Lateran Council (1215) and of the Council of Florence (1442), *'extra ecclesiam nulla salus,'* has no longer been held even by the Catholic Church since Vatican II."[78] The Catholic Church itself renders it difficult to make charges of heresy stick.

If the Vatican were to reach out and show some sign of recognition or acceptance towards ICAB, what would happen – would the dome of St. Peter's cave in? Having ICAB in the fold could arguably make the Catholic Church more fractious – but could it really be more fractious than it already is, permanently teetering on the brink of splitting in two, or three? The real challenge, as the theologians warned, is surely not just to survive in willful ignorance of effective schisms, but to identify the fractures and repair them. The Church's response to Independent Catholicism has never been clear or uniform. The various responses to ICAB – from diocesan level, from the national bishops' conference, and from the Vatican – have not only been uncoordinated but actually at odds with each other. Misinformation and mystification are not just the fault of the ICAB movement. This failure to properly address the phenomenon has contributed to offshoot communities going further into a sect-like mentality and defensive stance.[79] Allowing schisms to happen and persist is possibly a two-way street; did the Catholic Church do everything it could – or indeed anything – to prevent or remedy the ICAB schism? What options did it explore? What a contrast with the Church's imaginative multi-layered response to the Lefebvre case of 1988, to the Heralds of the Gospel, and to the Anglican traditionalists. Even the Mariavites, the Aglipayans, and the SSPX, though condemned, prompted the highest levels of response from the Vatican. But where is the papal encyclical dealing with the vast international community of Independent Catholics – Catholics who cannot even boast of 'imperfect' communion with Rome? The

ICAB phenomenon was arguably not inflicted upon the Church, but allowed to happen, and it is being allowed to continue.

Pelypenko doubted that more than a "handful of deceived people"[80] really felt they belonged to ICAB and assimilated its precepts, opining that they would probably run a mile if they knew what they were getting involved with.[81] The Roman Catholic Church also denied that ICAB really had an exclusive faithful of its own, rather than co-opting regular Roman Catholics: "Their 'ministers' operate among people who are already committed to the [Roman] Catholic Church ... who do not realize the error they are being drawn into, nor are they contemplating abandoning the Church of their baptism!"[82] Broadly speaking the modern-day offshoots of ICAB tend to appeal not so much to mainstream Catholics as to disgruntled Catholics, Catholics who for some reason feel that they do not 'fit' in the mainstream Church, and those who have met with obstacles in their careers as seminarians or priests. Offshoots have frequently retained the least edifying characteristics of the ICAB mother church, focusing on rituals, blessings and ceremonies rather than authentically witnessing the Gospel. Bearing in mind, however, that many in the ICAB offshoot movement are at least sincere and genuine in striving to form a Christian community, it is difficult to say which model is the exception and which is the rule.

Conclusions – is ICAB sinful?

Above and beyond any claim that ICAB may be truly Catholic, truly Apostolic, and truly concerned for unity, there is another classic identification mark of the Church to consider – arguably the least scientifically verifiable and the hardest to discuss: Holiness. Setting out to discuss holiness must begin with recognizing that being holy does not equate to never breaking the rules – Jesus, after all, "was executed by the legitimate authorities of his day for acts he actually committed."[83] Ultimately, neither civil nor religious laws can take precedence over doing the will of God. The point of

Jesus's 'wrongdoing,' however, was not to overturn civil or religious laws but to challenge civil and religious authorities. The Temple is much better remembered as the location of Jesus's most famous demonstration than for Jesus's preaching. The Temple authorities were certainly breaking no laws – they were keeping the temple running smoothly in the busy Passover season, ensuring essential currency exchange services and the convenient sale of sacrificial doves for pilgrims travelling from far and wide. Jesus did not simply speak out against the authorities, rightfully exercising his freedom of speech; he "disrupted the legitimate, even necessary, functioning of the temple – and during Passover week!"[84] Not appreciated by the pilgrims, surely. Jesus's protests could understandably have been called extreme, sectarian, schismatic, with no shortage of "confusion and disorientation"[85] for the ordinary faithful.

Jesus, furthermore, "is not simply calling for temple reform. He fundamentally opposes the temple. He looks forward to its destruction."[86] The religious authorities – certainly legitimate, certainly rightful – are not sacrosanct. They are challengeable and changeable, not immune to radical alteration. And of course Jesus the 'extremist schismatic' was not alone in his attitude, though clearly more vocal than most: "Many Jews (we cannot know how many) regarded the temple authorities as fully corrupt."[87] Religious authorities, we must appreciate, can be legitimate and corrupt – or holy and sinful, infallible and fallible – at one and the same time. It appears from his actions that Jesus really wants this recognition of the sinful nature of the religious institutions. As Charles Curran wrote, "The recognition of the sinfulness of the church not only calls for a constant scrutiny of the structures and institutional aspects of the church, but also gives some indication of the type of structures we need."[88] This recalls Küng's question: "is this Church or that, which calls itself the Church of Christ, really Christ's Church?"[89] The urgent need emerges to not only question the legitimacy of the institution but to develop a culture in which the institution itself boldly and openly leads the questioning.[90]

The Church's ongoing history is full of potential sinful pitfalls, shot-through with "false developments … fanaticism and heresy, even the possibility of a pseudo-Church."[91] It takes some Jesus-style radicalism every so often to force the Church to be true to itself. Change and conflict are hardly strangers to each other in the Church's history. Robert Schreiter wrote that "change, conflict and transition"[92] tend to prompt discussion of the four marks of the Church, and this includes reflection about a possible fifth mark of the Church.[93] Suggestions of a fifth mark have included dialogical, discerning, immigrant, marked by suffering, marked by sexuality[94] and, of course, sinful.[95] The Church's "call to conversion"[96] sits alongside "the sinfulness that affects the church and all its members."[97] These fifth marks place imperfection at the heart of Catholic identity, to balance and challenge the historic exaltation of the *societas perfecta*. Actively challenging the institutions of the Church, protesting and demanding authenticity and transparency from them, is consistent with the call to holiness while recognizing sinfulness. It may also be considered part of the duty – and even the human rights – of the Church member.

Conclusions – ICAB and the human rights of the Catholic

The demand for human rights inside the Catholic Church has been called the "implicit legacy"[98] of the development of Catholic Social Teaching, much of which Duarte Costa dismissed as 'fascism' incidentally, without elaborating. But Duarte Costa unfortunately just missed out on Pope St. John XXIII's pivotal 1963 encyclical *Pacem in Terris*. It upholds "the supreme right of humans to be able to follow their conscience,"[99] which might have sat well with the founder of ICAB. The ICAB movement's struggle may be looked upon as part of the dialogue between Catholicism and social and religious ethics – including the very right to dissent. It is not a question of contriving a moral hierarchy composed of secular and ecclesiastical rights and powers, but rather identifying harmony in the two sources of rights: the "rights given by God" [100] justifiably limit the temporal powers of the Church, as Walter Kasper acknowledged. The pace of the debate accelerated during the 1960's, with Vatican II and the rise of secular human rights and civil rights movements, and it has not abated since then.

The ongoing revolution in media and communications helps to nourish the desire for freedom and development throughout the religious universe, demanding concrete responses from the Catholic Church. The significance of media and the Internet for religion – not least Independent Catholicism – is a vast topic in its own right. Independents' communication skills are sometimes far superior to their regular Catholic counterparts,' incidentally, which posits interesting possibilities for the future. What it means to be Catholic faces direct everyday challenges not only from phenomena such as the ICAB movement, but also from the whole range of changing and competing online and offline contexts in which Catholics live and work. As Julie Byrne wrote, we may become "less interested in who is really Catholic, and more interested in how the word Catholic functions, how it is claimed and changed by various self-described Catholics."[101]

For God, Land and Freedom?

Christ the Redeemer, the indisputable symbol of Brazil, looks out inscrutably over Rio de Janeiro. The immense *Cristo Redentor* statue took ten years to build, but at the time of its inauguration in 1931 the Catholic Church in Brazil – the world's largest Catholic population, in the world's largest Catholic continent – had no influence. Its fortunes had been so bound up with those of the State that after separation the Church had no voice of its own. In contrast with the Church's size, furthermore, committed Catholics were almost completely unrepresented in public life. The process of Romanization, rebuilding links with Rome and becoming more clearly *Roman* Catholic, was fairly successful. Then Cardinal Silveira Cintra aimed to re-establish the Church as an influential mover in society and 'reclaim' Brazil for Catholicism – though it is questionable whether Brazil had ever truly been converted to begin with. The inauguration of *Cristo Redentor* was part of Silveira Cintra's strategy to reaffirm the Church's power.

But Romanization, as Duarte Costa saw it, was just colonization by another name. That the colonizing principle had not disappeared seemed to be borne out as the Church increasingly forged alliances with undemocratic regimes. The presence of foreign clergy in Brazil, especially from Franco's Spain and Mussolini's Italy, looked like evidence of the impending Vatican-backed Fascist world takeover. For Duarte Costa, the Catholic Church had at best been duped. It seemed to him to be high time to take back both nationhood and Christianity from dangerous usurpers. Duarte Costa may well be revered by some, but he was surely more revolutionary than saint: "Guided by the pride of his ambition, he decided to found his own Church."[102] He stood up to an organization which most people perceived as untouchable; he fought against a power that often inspires fear. He was a David against a Goliath. He claimed to be returning the Church to the third century, but he really meant the sixteenth – when Catholicism developed into its original Brazilian version, with all its flaws and contradictions, and its divergence from the Roman brand.

The Roman Catholic Church, Dubois contended, "is accustomed, as of almost two thousand years, to smiling in the face of attackers. The path of Church history is littered with the detritus of a thousand anti-Churches."[103] Even so, Dubois warned that "The anti-Church of Dom Carlos may grow."[104] Though "bitterly persecuted," [105] Duarte Costa soon claimed "several hundred thousand members ... in Brazil – and about 150,000 members in Venezuela."[106] He used his sacramental powers to empower and encourage those who shared his consternation with the Roman Catholic Church. Though he may not have envisaged it, his sacramental 'descendants' have taken the fight to the Vatican again and again, in the name of everything from abolishing celibacy, women's ordination, LGBT rights, to extreme conservative traditionalism. Duarte Costa's lasting legacy consists of giving many and varied renegade Catholics a potentially valid claim to Holy Orders, though the claim relies on a benevolent application of theology and much benefit of the doubt. His legacy also consists, of course, in leaving behind a Church that still exists, though it has evolved considerably from what it originally set out to be.

Whatever Duarte Costa's good intentions, within his lifetime ICAB became a refuge for characters who quite rightly could not find a place in the Roman Catholic Church; those with 'erroneous concepts of priestly vocation' and 'priesthood-mania." ICAB is unlikely to ever shake off the reputation for simony, opportunism, and superficiality, but as long as such accusations come from the Roman Catholic Church they can be derided as persecution, fascism, and religious monopolism. Pelypenko concluded that "ICAB exists for the sole purpose of undermining the authority of the Roman Catholic Church,"[107] and the Roman Catholic position never shifted from that expressed in the 1948 Court case against ICAB, for its "malicious intent to create confusion among the faithful."[108] But the Roman Catholic Church also realized that it could learn something from ICAB, and an unspoken dialogue of ideas was already underway within Catholicism.

The Church that Duarte Costa rebelled against has been reformed beyond recognition. Its current theology not only accepts much of what ICAB wanted to do but embraces it. The ICAB story reveals how much the Catholic Church has undergone change, which is "an important aspect of the [its] nature."[109] Duarte Costa rebelled against Pope Pius XII – it is hard to say whether he would have clashed in the same way with Pope St. John XXIII, but Salomão Ferraz certainly found Pope John's pontificate more amenable. Ferraz's acceptance into the Roman Catholic Church did not immediately go down well in Rome – there is every possibility that it came about amid misunderstandings or misinformation, especially concerning his precise marital status – at least one Cardinal was under the impression that Ferraz was a widower. Furthermore, no-one ever checked Ferraz's theology: he did not cease to concelebrate with Protestants or quit using Portuguese, and at the close of the Third Session of Vatican II Ferraz wrote of "the Holy Father as the visible head of the Church, not as the *alter-Christus*."[110] Little wonder they did not want Ferraz speaking in public too much. But, in reality, are not most Catholics, even bishops, guilty of selective obedience to the Pope? At this moment some senior Catholics are no doubt 'sitting out' the Francis Papacy in the hope of getting someone more conservative next time. But in general Catholic theology has mellowed, and in some quarters the practice has too. We know that some 'mystery' Roman Catholic bishops have consecrated Women-priests, and that Pope Francis has been on friendly terms with more than one Independent Catholic bishop. Perhaps things are coming full circle – Duarte Costa called the Pope 'my brother in the episcopate' and the current Pope referred to an Independent prelate as 'my brother bishop.'"[111] Surely we are closer than ever to the realization of Duarte Costa-style "diversity in unity."[112]

It is fair to say that a complete understanding of Catholicism in Brazil cannot be achieved without understanding ICAB – one man's attempt to incarnate the authentically Brazilian take on Catholicism as an official, all-inclusive 'national church." For the Roman Catholic Church, ICAB remains simply the fomenter of "confusion and disorientation"[113] under a mask of appealing to religious freedom. Rome dismisses this appeal, saying that "the *'igrejas brasileiras'* do not respect religious freedom; rather they are a threat to it."[114] The Roman Catholic Church's commitment to ecumenical dialogue and "fraternal cohabitation, in accordance with the [Second Vatican] Council"[115] is beyond question, they say,[116] so why has the tree produced so little fruit? The demand from Brazilian Catholics today seems to be for an uncomplicated appearance of Catholicism *on* demand – weddings and baptisms – but without *the* demands of assimilating the faith or committing to the Church. If indeed ICAB has become a "dispenser of ecclesiastical services for those people who cannot obtain them from the Roman Church,"[117] then perhaps that says more about the Roman Church than it does about ICAB. The Roman Catholic Church frequently encounters cases of its members who, at the moment of needing to present a certificate of baptism, discover that they were actually baptized in an ICAB church, unbeknownst to them. Do most Brazilian Catholics really care? ICAB certainly demonstrates how to listen to the voice of the laity.

It took a Latin American Pope to say a lot of the things that Catholics had been thinking for years – more compassion for the divorced, the separated, the remarried, the gay, the poor, the agnostic, the doubting, and the non-Catholic; let us finally address the issues of roles for married men, roles for women, and may life choices, including celibacy, be made with openness, simplicity, and fairness. Suddenly it was time to throw out the trash in the Roman Curia, to shake up the loafing bureaucrats, the careerists and wealth-seekers; to call out corruption for what it is, involve the laity in the Church's toughest challenges, and engage with the Church's victims. The debates ultimately merge into one urgent project – the continued construction of a Kingdom that is just, here on Earth as it is in Heaven. Christians of every hue are ultimately united in the same objective – achieving Heaven. In the meantime they wrestle with the very human longing to understand where we come from, where we belong, and to where we are headed on our pilgrimage. And this is the essence of the ICAB story – it is a fundamentally human story of the ambitions and hopes which tumble around within the human soul hungering for expression – the longing to embrace and reconcile our faiths, our origins, and our aspirations: the quest to find God, Land and Freedom.

Notes

[1]   *New York Times*, 3rd August 1973, p 4
[2]   William T. Cavanaugh, 'Church,' Chapter 27 in Peter Scott and William T. Cavanaugh (eds), *The Blackwell Companion to Political Theology*, Blackwell, Oxford, 2004, [pp 393-406], p 393

3   William T. Cavanaugh, 'Church,' p 393
4   Cf. Gregory D. Gilson and Irving W. Levinson (eds), *Latin American Positivism – new historical and philosophic essays,* Lexington Books, Plymouth UK 2013, p 128 (note 25), and Cf. Heiko Spitzeck et al (eds), *Humanism in Business,* Cambridge University Press, Cambridge, 2009, p 41
5   William T. Cavanaugh, 'Church,' p 393
6   Thomas C. Bruneau, *The Political Transformation of the Brazilian Catholic Church,* Cambridge University Press, London and New York, 1974, p 60
7   Father [Florence Marie | Florêncio Maria] Dubois, *O Ex-Bispo de Maura e o Bom Senso [The Ex-Bishop of Maura and Common Sense],* Ed. Vozes Limitada, Petrópolis–Rio de Janeiro–São Paulo, 1945, p 16
8   Cf. Dubois, p 36
9   Cf. Obispo Alejo Pelypenko, *Infiltración Comunista en las Iglesias de América,* Pia Sociedad de San Pablo, Buenos Aires, 1961, p 140. Henceforth 'Pelypenko'
10   William T. Cavanaugh, 'Church,' p 397
11   Cf. William T. Cavanaugh, 'Church,' p 397
12   Thomas C. Bruneau, p 60
13   Cf. Thomas C. Bruneau, p 60
14   Dubois, p 22
15   William T. Cavanaugh, 'Church,' p 393
16   Cf. Kenneth Leslie, 'Protestant Digest', Vol. 6, Issue 7, Protestant Digest Inc. New York, 1945, p 14
17   Cf. *Diário do Grande ABC* newspaper, 10th March 2013, 'Eles são católicos mas ignoram o papa' [They are catholic but they ignore the pope], by Fábio Munhoz, http://www.dgabc.com.br/Noticia/91241/eles-sao-catolicos-mas-ignoram-o-papa [accessed 12th May 2018]
18   Cf. Julie Byrne, *The Other Catholics: Remaking America's Largest Religion,* Columbia University Press, New York, 2016, p 97
19   Cf. Michael Phayer, *Pius XII, the Holocaust, and the Cold War,* Indiana University Press, Bloomington IN, 2008, p 182, and Cf. Uki Goñi, *The Real Odessa: Smuggling the Nazis to Perón's Argentina* (revised edition), Granta, London, 2003, p 100
20   Cf. Uki Goñi, *The Real Odessa: Smuggling the Nazis to Perón's Argentina,* p 100
21   Cf. Michael Phayer, *Pius XII, the Holocaust, and the Cold War,* p 182
22   In the course of my research, two ICAB priests showed me a photograph of 'Nazi' bishops – actually Spanish bishops, giving a half-hearted salute – and a ludicrous doctored photograph of a young Joseph Ratzinger apparently giving the Nazi salute – in fact giving a blessing with both hands, but the photograph was cut. The ICAB priests handed me these

photographs with grave expressions, in all seriousness treating them as ICAB's archival 'exhibits' in the case against the Vatican's Nazi links. This exemplifies the state of the evidence in the case for Duarte Costa supposedly campaigning against Nazis in Brazil.

23 Pelypenko, p 120

24 Cf. Pelypenko, p 128

25 Dubois, p 39

26 Dubois, p 41

27 Dubois, p 11

28 Act of Foundation of the Brazilian Catholic Apostolic Church, Department of Justice of the State of Rio de Janeiro, Registry of Titles and Documents, Notarial Office Number 2, Book B28, Number 39,026, Protocol Number 107,965, 26th July 1945 ['Ata de Fundação da Igreja Católica Apostólica Brasileira,' Justiça do Estado do Rio de Janeiro, Registro de Títulos e Documentos, Cartorio do 2° Oficio, Livro B28, número 39.026, protocolo n° 107.965]

29 Dubois, p 9

30 Cf. Irmã [Sister] Maria Regina do Santo Rosário [Laurita Pessôa Raja Gabaglia], *O Cardeal Leme*, J. Olympio, Rio de Janeiro, 1962, p 467

31 Pelypenko, p 170

32 Cf. Pelypenko, p 170

33 Cf. Pelypenko, p 140

34 Pelypenko, p 126

35 *Luta!* issue 4, January-February 1948, pp 7-12

36 Pelypenko, p 225

37 Act of Foundation of the Brazilian Catholic Apostolic Church, Department of Justice of the State of Rio de Janeiro, Registry of Titles and Documents, Notarial Office Number 2, Book B28, Number 39,026, Protocol Number 107,965, 26th July 1945

38 Aloísio Cardinal Lorscheider, '"Igreja Brasileira," Esclarecimento e Procedimento,' in *Convergência* (Journal of the Conference of Religious of Brazil – CRB), Yr. 25, No. 231, Apr. 1990 [pp 137-142] p 141

39 Wagner Pires da Silva, 'An Other Catholicism: The Bishop of Maura and the Brazilian Catholic Apostolic Church', *Revista de História Bilros*, Vol. 5, No. 8, Jan.-Apr. 2017, [pp 106-125], pp 122-123

40 Cf. Dom Estêvão Bettencourt OSB, in *Pergunte e Responderemos*, Number 55, July 1962, online version at http://www.pr.gonet.biz/revista.php [accessed 05/04/2018]

41 Peter F. Anson, *Bishops At Large*, Faber and Faber, London, 1964, p 27

42 John E. Lynch, 'The Changing Role of the Bishop,' *Jurist*, Vol. 39, 1979, [pp 289-312], pp 291-292

43 Pelypenko, p 115

44 Dubois, p 75
45 Peter F. Anson, *Bishops At Large,* p 27
46 Michael Richards, *A People of Priests,* Darton, Longman and Todd, London, 1995, p 113
47 Cf. Richard P. McBrien, *Ministry,* Harper & Row, San Francisco, 1988, pp 37-38 and pp 45-46
48 Daniel M. Bell Jr., 'State and Civil Society,' Ch 29 in Peter Scott and William T. Cavanaugh (Eds), *The Blackwell Companion to Political Theology,* Blackwell, Oxford, 2004, [pp 423-438], p 430
49 Thales de Azevedo, *O Catolicismo no Brasil,* Govt. of Brazil, Min. of Ed. & Culture, RJ, 1955, p 21
50 Daniel M. Bell Jr., 'State and Civil Society,' p 430
51 Daniel M. Bell Jr., 'State and Civil Society,' p 430
52 Cf. Pelypenko, p 116
53 Dubois, p 20
54 Thales de Azevedo, *O Catolicismo no Brasil,* p 21
55 Michael Amaladoss SJ, *Life in Freedom,* Orbis, Maryknoll, 1997, p 95
56 Cf. Dubois, p 90, and Cf. pp 89-91
57 Dubois, p 22
58 Cf. Dubois, p 19
59 Dubois, p 19
60 Dubois, p 75
61 Pelypenko, p 116
62 Cf. Dubois, p 19
63 *Diario da Manha,* Tuesday 12th June 1956, p 8
64 Cf. Dubois, p 19
65 Joseph A. Komonchak, 'Interpreting the Council,' in Mary Jo Weaver and R. Scott Appleby (eds), *Being Right,* Indiana University Press, Bloomington, 1995, [pp 17-36] see p 19
66 Cf. Gerard Mannion, *Ecclesiology and Postmodernity,* Liturgical Press, Collegeville, 2007, p.15-16 and Ch 3 [pp 43-74] 'From the "Open Church" to Neo-Exclusivism?'
67 Pastoral Letter of the Bishops of the Ecclesiastical Province of São Paulo on the "Igreja Brasileira," in CNBB, 'Comunicado Mensal' [Monthly Communiqué] number 243, December 1972, [pp 90-97], p 91
68 Pelypenko, p 171
69 Pelypenko, p 193
70 Pelypenko, p 170
71 Frédéric Luz, *Le Soufre et L'Encens [Sulphur and Incense],* Claire Vigne, Paris, 1995, p.25
72 A.M. Ramsey, *The Gospel and the Catholic Church,* Longmans, Green & Co., London, 1936, p 218

73   Congregation for the Doctrine of the Faith, *'Dominus Iesus'*, 6th August 2000, at www.vatican.va http://www.vatican.va/roman_curia/congregations/cfaith/documents/rc_con_cfaith_doc_20000806_dominus-iesus_en.html [accessed 12th May 2018]

74   Congregation for the Doctrine of the Faith, *'Dominus Iesus'* – at www.vatican.va, Part IV, Paragraph 17

75   Peter Chirico, 'Dominus Iesus as an Event,' in *America: The Jesuit Review*, 26th March 2001 https://www.americamagazine.org/issue/332/article/dominus-iesus-event [accessed 12th May 2018]

76   Peter Chirico, 'Dominus Iesus as an Event,' 26th March 2001

77   Peter Chirico, 'Dominus Iesus as an Event,' 26th March 2001

78   Hans Küng, 'Towards an Ecumenical Theology of Religions: Some Theses for Clarification,' in Hans Küng and Jürgen Moltmann (Eds), *Concilium: Religion in the Eighties; Christianity Among World Religions*, T. & T. Clark Ltd, Edinburgh, 1986, [pp 119-125], p 119 [capitalization replaced by italics]

79   Cf. Kathleen Kautzer, *The Underground Church*, Haymarket Books, Chicago, 2013, p 15

80   Pelypenko, p 172

81   Cf. Pelypenko, pp 172-173

82   Pastoral Letter of the Bishops of the Ecclesiastical Province of São Paulo, December 1972, p 94

83   Greg Carey, *Sinners: Jesus and his earliest followers*, Baylor University Press, Waco TX, 2009, p 79

84   Greg Carey, *Sinners*, p 90

85   Pastoral Letter of the Bishops of the Ecclesiastical Province of São Paulo, December 1972, p 91

86   Greg Carey, *Sinners*, p 91

87   Greg Carey, *Sinners*, p 91

88   Charles E. Curran, 'The Church is Sinful,' in William Madges and Michael J. Daley (eds), *The Many Marks of the Church*, Twenty-Third Publications, New London CT, 2006, p.209

89   Hans Küng, *The Church*, Search Press, London, 1978, p 264

90   Hans Küng, *The Church*, p 264

91   Hans Küng, *The Church*, p 264

92   Robert J. Schreiter, *The New Catholicity*, Orbis Books, Maryknoll NY, 1997, p 119

93   Paul Lakeland, *Church – Living Communion*, Liturgical Press, Collegeville MN, 2009, p 2

94   Cf. William Madges and Michael J. Daley (eds), *The Many Marks of the Church*

95   Cf. Charles E. Curran, 'The Church is Sinful,' in William Madges and Michael J. Daley (eds), p 208

96   Charles E. Curran, 'The Church is Sinful,' p 209

97   Charles E. Curran, 'The Church is Sinful,' p 209

98   Gerard Mannion, *Solidarity and Human Rights Implications of Pacem in Terris,* lecture at Georgetown University, 12th April 2013, https://www.youtube.com/watch?v=gARHjPtu5WI [accessed 9th May 2018]

99   Gerard Mannion, *Solidarity and Human Rights Implications of Pacem in Terris,* 2013

100   Walter Kasper, *That They May All Be One,* Burns and Oates (Continuum), London, 2004, p 146

101   Julie Byrne, "Catholic But Not Roman Catholic," in *American Catholic Studies* Volume 125, Number 3, Fall 2014, [pp 16-19], p 17

102   Pelypenko, p 119

103   Dubois, p 89

104   Dubois, p 89

105   *The Churchman,* Volume 162, June 1948, University of Michigan, p 25

106   *The Churchman,* June 1948, p 25

107   Pelypenko, p 122

108   *Luta!* issue 8, July 1949, p 3

109   Bernard Hoose, 'Should the Church Change?,' in Gerard Mannion (ed), *Church and Religious 'Other,'* T&T Clark, London, 2008, [pp.221-231], p 221

110   Dom Raimundo Augusto de Oliveira, *Dom Salomão Ferraz e o Ecumenismo [Dom Salomão Ferraz and Ecumenism],* Feira de Santana, Bahia, undated, p 77

111   Cf. *The Tablet,* 1st March 2014, p 24, referring to the late Bishop Tony Palmer.

112   Ladislas Orsy SJ, 'The Church of the Third Millennium: In Praise of *Communio,*' in Stephen J. Pope (ed), *Common Calling,* Georgetown University Press, Washington DC, 2004, [pp 229-251], p 235

113   Pastoral Letter of the Bishops of the Ecclesiastical Province of São Paulo, December 1972, p 91

114   Pastoral Letter of the Bishops of the Ecclesiastical Province of São Paulo, December 1972, p 93

115   Pastoral Letter of the Bishops of the Ecclesiastical Province of São Paulo, December 1972, p 92

116   Cf. Pastoral Letter of the Bishops of the Ecclesiastical Province of São Paulo, December 1972, p 92

117   Wagner Pires da Silva, p 123

ACKNOWLEDGEMENTS

It is a great pleasure to be able to offer my thanks to those who have contributed in many ways to the realization of this book, including Prof. Paul D. Murray and Dr Marcus Pound at the Centre for Catholic Studies at Durham. I am indebted to the following Bishops and Archbishops: their Most Reverend Excellencies Oscar Pereira Andrade, Luis Bergonzi Moreno, Rómulo A. Braschi, Alicia Cabrera Braschi, Gustavo A. Gabucci, David J. Kalke, Dr Felismar Manoel, Dr William J. Manseau, Christine Mayr-Lumetzberger, Harold J. Norwood, Raimundo A. de Oliveira, and James A. Wilkowski, and in Memoriam: Peter Paul Brennan, Horacio Clark and Gustavo Navarro.

My heartfelt appreciation goes to Dr Luca Badini Confalonieri and Dr John Wijngaards at the Wijngaards Institute. Many thanks to Yosmar I. Ferrer and Natalia Hidalgo at the Universidad Católica Andrés Bello, Miguel A. Araujo and Araceli Noguez at Universidad Nacional Autónoma de México, and Priscila Medeiros de Oliveira at the Documentation and Information Centre of the CNBB. I am very grateful to the Bodleian Library, Heythrop College, the Library of Congress (Buenos Aires), the Archdioceses of Rio de Janeiro, Caracas, Matera-Irsina, and the Diocese of Solsona. For many and varied pieces of assistance and encouragement I warmly thank Prof. Julie Byrne, Cathy Caridi, Nelson Ferrara Gomes, Peter Harvey, Prof. Edward N. Peters, Fr. James Radloff, and Br. Tim Raible. Very many thanks to Rev Dr John R. Mabry and Apocryphile Press.

And all would be impossible without the support and encouragement of brilliant family and friends: Sr. Dr Margaret Atkins OSA, Andrew Brady, James Brady, Dr Simon Bryden-

Brook, Patrizia Della Rosa, Christine Jarvis Hall, Robert Hall, Stella Hall, Ted Jarvis, Martin McManus, Emily Manis, Fr. Giuseppe Nardozza, Patricia Guitti Pollastri, Tatiana Guitti Pollastri, Dr Giorgio Scalici, Gabriel Seisdedos, and Rachanee Surintharat – source of endless patience and help.

Edward Jarvis
25th May 2018, Feast of the Venerable Bede

ABOUT THE AUTHOR

EDWARD JARVIS was born in Yorkshire, England, in 1975. He studied philosophy, theology, and religious studies, first in Italy and then in England. He graduated top of his Department in 2004 and went on to take advanced degrees and conduct postgraduate research. He is fluent in several languages and currently teaches and writes in Southeast Asia.

SOURCES

Bibliography

ALLEN John L. Jr., *The Future Church – How ten trends are revolutionizing the Catholic Church*, Image, New York, 2009

AMALADOSS Michael SJ, *Life in Freedom – Liberation Theologies from Asia*, Orbis, Maryknoll, 1997

ANSON Peter F., *Bishops At Large*, Faber & Faber, London, 1964 / Apocryphile Press, Berkeley CA, 2006

AZEVEDO Thales DE, *O Catolicismo no Brasil [Catholicism in Brazil]*, Government of Brazil, Ministry of Education and Culture, Rio de Janeiro, 1955

BADANELLI Pedro, *Perón: la iglesia y un cura [Perón: the church and a priest]* Editorial Tartessos, Buenos Aires, 1960

BAIN Alan M. (ed) *Bishops Irregular: An International Directory of Independent Bishops*, A.M. Bain, Bristol UK, 1985

BARRETT David V., *Sect, 'Cults' & Alternative Religions*, Blandford (a Cassell imprint), London, 1998

BARTH Karl, *The Epistle to the Romans*, Oxford University Press, Oxford, 1968

BEAL John P., James A. CORIDEN, Thomas Joseph GREEN (eds), *New Commentary on the Code of Canon Law*, Paulist Press, New York/Mahwah NJ, 2000

• PAPROCKI Thomas J., 'Part V: The Method of Proceeding in Administrative Recourse and in the Removal or Transfer of Pastors (cc. 1732-1752)' [pp 1818-1847] in BEAL John P. et al (eds), *New Commentary on the Code of Canon Law*

BELL Daniel M. Jr.—see SCOTT Peter and William T. CAVANAUGH

BEOZZO José Oscar, *Padres Conciliares Brasileiros no Vaticano II: Participação e Prosopografia – 1959-1965, [Brazilian Council Fathers of Vatican II: Participation and Prosopography – 1959-1965]*, Faculdade de Filosofia, Letras e Ciências Humanas, Universidade de São Paulo, São Paulo, 2001

BENEDICT XVI—see RATZINGER Joseph

BEST Thomas F.—see MANNION Gerard and Lewis S. MUDGE

BRANDÃO Carlos RODRIGUES, *Memória do Sagrado: religiões de uma cidade do Interior [Memory of the Sacred: religions of a hinterland city]* Tempo e Presença Editora, Itapira SP, 1980

BRANDRETH Henry R.T., *Episcopi Vagantes and the Anglican Church*, SPCK, London, 1961 / Apocryphile Press, Berkeley CA, 2006

BRUNEAU Thomas C., *The Political Transformation of the Brazilian Catholic Church*, Cambridge University Press, London and New York, 1974

BUCKLEY Michael J.—see POPE Stephen J.

BURKHARD John J. OFM Conv., *Apostolicity Then and Now – An Ecumenical Church in a Postmodern World*, Liturgical Press, Collegeville MN, 2004

BYRNE Julie, *The Other Catholics: Remaking America's Largest Religion*, Columbia University Press, New York, 2016

CAREY Greg, *Sinners: Jesus and his earliest followers*, Baylor University Press, Waco TX, 2009

CAVANAUGH William T.—see SCOTT Peter

CHAPMAN Mark—see MANNION Gerard and Lewis S. MUDGE

CLARKE Peter B. (ed), *Encyclopedia of New Religious Movements*, Routledge, London, 2006

COLLINS Paul, *Papal Power – A proposal for change in Catholicism's third millennium*, Harper Collins / Fount, London 1997

CONGAR Yves, *Challenge to the Church: The Case of Archbishop Lefebvre [La Crise dans l'Eglise et Mgr Lefebvre]*, Collins Liturgical Publications, London, 1977

COOKE Bernard J.—see WEAVER Mary-Jo and R. Scott APPLEBY

CUNEO Michael W., *The Smoke of Satan: Conservative and Traditionalist Dissent in Contemporary American Catholicism*, Johns Hopkins University Press, Baltimore MD, 1999

CURRAN Charles E.—see MADGES William and Michael J. DALEY

DUBOIS (Padre) Florêncio Maria [Florence Marie] B [Barnabite], *O Ex-Bispo de Maura e o Bom Senso [The Ex-Bishop of Maura and Common Sense]*, Editora Vozes Limitada, Petrópolis RJ – Rio de Janeiro – São Paulo, (Biblioteca Apologetica, Dirigida pelo Padre Agnelo Rossi, Volume V), 1945

DULLES Avery SJ
– *The Resilient Church*, Gill and Macmillan, Dublin, 1978
– *The Catholicity of the Church*, Oxford University Press, Oxford, 1987

FABER Frederick William CO, *The Precious Blood: or The Price of Our Salvation*, John Murphy, Baltimore (10th American Edition), [undated – c.1868]

FAUSTINO Oswaldo, *A Legião Negra: A Luta dos Afro-Brasileiros na Revolucão Constitucionalista de 1932 [The Black Legion: The Struggle of Afro-Brazilians in the Revolution of 1932]*, Selo Negro Edições, São Paulo SP, 2011

FERRAZ Salomão BARBOSA, *A Fé Nacional [National Faith]* O.S.A., São Paulo, 1932

FILHO João DORNAS, *O Padroado e a Igreja Brasileira [Patronage and the Brazilian Church]*, Companhia Editôra Nacional, Rio de Janeiro, 1937

FILHO Arnaldo LEMOS, *Os Catolicismos Brasileiros [Brazilian Catholicisms]* Editora Alinea, Guanabara; Campinas SP, 1996

FLANNERY Austin OP (ed), *Vatican Council II, The Conciliar and Post-Conciliar Documents*, Dominican Publications, St. Saviour's, Dublin, 1975

FLINN Frank K., *Encyclopedia of Catholicism*, Checkmark Books, New York, 2008

FREITAS (Dom) Gerardo Albano DE, *Igreja Brasileira – Abençoada Rebeldia [Brazilian Church – Blessed Rebelliousness]*, Centro de Estudos Teológicos ICAB, São Paulo, 1987

GABAGLIA (Irmã) [Sister] Maria Regina do Santo Rosário [Laurita Pessôa Raja Gabaglia], *O Cardeal Leme [Cardinal Leme]*, J. Olympio, Rio de Janeiro, 1962

GAILLARDETZ Richard, *Ecclesiology for a Global Church: a people called and sent*, Orbis, Maryknoll, 2008

GARCIA RODRIGUEZ José Carlos, *Pedro Badanelli – La Sotana Española de Perón [Pedro Badanelli – Perón's Spanish Priest]*, Editorial Akrón, Astorga, León, 2008

GILL Anthony, *Rendering Unto Caesar – the Catholic Church and the State in Latin America*, Chicago University Press, Chicago, 1998

GILSON Gregory D. and Irving W. LEVINSON (eds), *Latin American Positivism – new historical and philosophic essays*, Lexington Books, Plymouth UK, 2013

GOLDENBERG Naomi R., *Resurrecting the Body: Feminism, Religion, and Psychoanalysis*, Crossroad, New York, 1990

GOÑI Uki, *The Real Odessa: Smuggling the Nazis to Perón's Argentina* Granta, London, (revised edition), 2003

HAAG Herbert, *Clergy and Laity – did Jesus want a two-tier church?* Tunbridge Wells: Burns & Oates, 1998)

HAIGHT Roger SJ
– *Christian Community in History; Volume I, Historical Ecclesiology*, Continuum, New York, 2004
– *Christian Community in History; Volume II, Historical Ecclesiology*, Continuum, New York, 2005

HALLS W.D. (Wilfred Douglas) *Politics, Society and Christianity in Vichy France*, Berg, Oxford, 1995

HEBBLETHWAITE Peter
– *The Runaway Church*, Collins Fount, Glasgow, 1978
– *The Year of Three Popes*, Collins, London, 1978

HIND John—see PUGLISI James F.

HOOSE Bernard—see MANNION Gerard

JOHNSON Hewlett, *O Poder Soviético*, Editorial Calvino, Rio de Janeiro, 1943

KASPER Walter
- *Theology and Church*, Crossroad, New York, 1989
- *Leadership in the Church*, Crossroad, a Herder and Herder book, New York, 2003
- *That They May All Be One*, Burns and Oates (a Continuum imprint), London, 2004

KAUTZER Kathleen, *The Underground Church: nonviolent resistance to the Vatican Empire*, Haymarket Books, Chicago, 2013

KELLY (Most Rev.) Clarence, *The Sacred and the Profane*, Seminary Press, Round Top NY, 1997

KÜNG Hans, *The Church*, Search Press, London, 1978

LAKELAND Paul
- *The Liberation of the Laity*, Continuum, New York / London, 2004
- *Church – Living Communion*, Liturgical Press, Collegeville MN, 2009

LAPIDE Pinchas E. *The Last Three Popes and the Jews*, Souvenir Press, London, 1967

LENNAN Richard, *The Ecclesiology of Karl Rahner*, Clarendon Press, Oxford, 1995

LÖBINGER Fritz, *Like His Brothers and Sisters: Ordaining Community Leaders*, Claretian Publications, Quezon City; Philippines, 1998

LOPES Rose, *Dimensões dos Aliens [Dimensions of the Aliens]* Club de Autores [self-publishing], 2015

LUZ Frédéric, *Le Soufre et L'Encens – Enquête sur les Églises parallèles et les Évêques Dissidents [Sulphur and Incense – A study of parallel churches and dissident bishops]*, Claire Vigne, Paris, 1995

McBRIEN Richard P., *Catholicism*, Geoffrey Chapman, London, 1994

McMILLAN Sharon L., *Episcopal Ordination and Ecclesial Consensus*, Liturgical Press (a Pueblo book) Collegeville MN, 2005

MADGES William and Michael J. DALEY (eds), *The Many Marks of The Church*, Twenty-Third Publications, New London CT, 2006

- CURRAN Charles E., 'The Church is Sinful,' in William MADGES and Michael J. DALEY (eds), *The Many Marks of The Church* [pp 207-211]

MANDATTO Jácomo, *Relíquias da Terra Natal [Relics of my Native Land]* Grupo Pedra, Itapira, 1959

MANNION Gerard (ed)

- *Readings in Church Authority: gifts and challenges for contemporary Catholicism*, Ashgate, Aldershot; Burlington VT, 2003
- *Church and Religious 'Other'*, T&T Clark, London, 2008

HOOSE Bernard, 'Should the Church Change?,' in Gerard MANNION (ed), *Church and Religious 'Other,'* [pp 221-231]

MANNION Gerard

- *Ecclesiology and Postmodernity: Questions for the Church in Our Time*, Liturgical Press, Collegeville MN, 2007
- *Comparative Ecclesiology: Critical Investigations (Ecclesiological Investigations)*, Bloomsbury / T&T Clark, London, 2008

MANNION Gerard and Lewis S. MUDGE (eds), *The Routledge Companion to the Christian Church*, Routledge, Abingdon, 2008

- BEST Thomas F., 'Ecclesiology and Ecumenism', in Gerard MANNION and Lewis S. MUDGE, (eds), *The Routledge Companion to the Christian Church* [pp 402-420]

- CHAPMAN Mark, 'Authority,' in Gerard MANNION and Lewis S. MUDGE Mudge (eds), *The Routledge Companion to the Christian Church* [pp 497-510]

MARMION Declan and Mary E. HINES (eds), *The Cambridge Companion to Karl Rahner*, Cambridge University Press, Cambridge, 2013

MARTI Gerardo and Gladys GANIEL, *The Deconstructed Church – Understanding Emerging Christianity*, Oxford University Press, Oxford, 2014

MARTIN David

– *Tongues of Fire: The Explosion of Protestantism in Latin America*, Blackwell, Oxford, 1991

– *Forbidden Revolutions*, SPCK, London, 1996

MEYER Harding—see PUGLISI James F.

MIRANDA Beatriz V. DIAS and Mabel SALGADO PEREIRA (eds), *Memorias Eclesiasticas: Documentos Comentados [Ecclesiastical Memoirs: Commentated Documents]*, Editora UFJF / Centro da Memoria da Igreja de Juiz de Fora, Cehila / Juiz de Fora, Brasil, 2000

MÖHLER Johann Adam, *Unity in the Church, or, the Principle of Catholicism* Catholic University of America Press, Washington DC, 1996

NEWMAN John Henry, 'IX. Catholicity of the Anglican Church,' [pp 1-73], in *Essays Critical and Historical, 3rd Edition, Volume II*, Basil Montagu Pickering, London, 1873

O'CALLAGHAN Joseph F., *Electing Our Bishops – How the Catholic Church should choose its leaders*, Rowman & Littlefield – a Sheed & Ward Book – Lanham MD, 2007

OLIVEIRA Dom Raimundo Augusto DE, *Dom Salomão Ferraz e o Ecumenismo [Dom Salomão Ferraz and Ecumenism]*, Feira de Santana, Bahia, undated document

ORSY Ladislas SJ—see POPE Stephen J.

PAPROCKI Thomas J.—see BEAL, John P.

PARTRIDGE Christopher, (ed) *Encyclopedia of New Religions: New Religious Movements, Sects and Alternative Spiritualities*, Lion Hudson, Oxford, 2006

PELYPENKO (Obispo) [Bishop] Alejo, *Infiltración Comunista en las Iglesias de América [Communist Infiltration in the Churches of America]*, Pia Sociedad de San Pablo, Buenos Aires, 1961

PHAYER Michael, *Pius XII, the Holocaust, and the Cold War*, Indiana University Press, Bloomington IN, 2008

PILETTI Nelson and Walter PRAXEDES, *Dom Hélder Câmara: entre o poder e a profecia [Dom Hélder Câmara: between power and prophecy]* Editora Atica, São Paulo SP, 1997

PLUMMER John P. and John R. MABRY, *Who Are The Independent Catholics?* Apocryphile Press, Berkeley CA, 2006

PLUMMER John P., *The Many Paths of the Independent Sacramental Movement*, Apocryphile Press, Berkeley CA, 2006

POPE Stephen J. (ed), *Common Calling – The Laity and Governance of the Catholic Church*, Georgetown University Press, Washington DC, 2004

• BUCKLEY Michael J. SJ, 'Resources for Reform from the First Millennium' in Stephen J. POPE (ed), *Common Calling – The Laity and Governance of The Catholic Church*, [pp 71-86]

• ORSY Ladislas SJ, 'The Church of the Third Millennium: In Praise of *Communio*,' in Stephen J. POPE (ed), *Common Calling – The Laity and Governance of The Catholic Church*, [pp 229-251]

POTTMEYER Hermann J., *Towards a Papacy in Communion – Perspectives from Vatican Councils I and II*, Crossroad, Herder and Herder, New York, 1998

PRÜTER Karl

– *Bishops Extraordinary*, Saint Willibrord's Press, Highlandville MO, 1985

– *The Directory of Autocephalous Bishops of the Churches of the Apostolic Succession* (8th Edition, Revised and Expanded), St. Willibrord's Press, San Bernardino CA, 1996

PUGLISI James F. (Ed), *Petrine Ministry and the Unity of the Church: Toward a Patient and Fraternal Dialogue*, Liturgical Press, Collegeville MN, 1999

• HIND John, 'Primacy and Unity: An Anglican Contribution to a Patient and Fraternal Dialogue,' in PUGLISI James F. (ed), *Petrine Ministry and the Unity of the Church* [pp 35-57]

• MEYER Harding, '"Suprema auctoritas ideo ab omne errore immunis": The Lutheran Approach to Primacy,' in PUGLISI James F. (ed), *Petrine Ministry and the Unity of the Church* [pp 15-34]

• SCHATZ Klaus SJ, 'Historical Considerations Concerning the Problem of the Papacy,' in PUGLISI James F. (ed), *Petrine Ministry and the Unity of the Church* [pp. 1-13]

QUINN John R., *The Reform of The Papacy – The Costly Call to Christian Unity* Crossroad, a Herder and Herder Book, New York, 1999

RADFORD RUETHER, Rosemary—see WEAVER Mary-Jo and R. Scott APPLEBY

RAHNER Karl SJ
– *The Shape of the Church to Come*, SPCK, London, 1974
– *Theological Investigations XVII*, Darton, Longman and Todd, London, 1981

RAMSEY Arthur Michael, *The Gospel and the Catholic Church*, Longmans, Green and Co., London, 1936

RATZINGER Joseph
– *Salt of the Earth – The Church at the End of the Millennium, an interview with Peter Seewald*, Ignatius Press, San Francisco, 1997
– *Faith and the Future*, Ignatius Press, San Francisco, 2009

REDMILE Robert D., *The Apostolic Succession and the Catholic Episcopate in the Christian Episcopal Church of Canada*, Xulon Press, Maitland FL, 2006

RICHARDS Michael, *A People of Priests – the Ministry of the Catholic Church* Dartman, Longman and Todd, London, 1995

RUSH Ormond, *Still Interpreting Vatican II, Some Hermeneutical Principles*, Paulist Press, New York / Mahwah NJ, 2004

RYCHLAK Ronald J., *Hitler, The War, and The Pope*, Our Sunday Visitor, Huntington IN 2000

SCHATZ Klaus SJ—see PUGLISI James F.

SCHREITER Robert J., *The New Catholicity – Theology between the Global and the Local*, Orbis Books, Maryknoll NY, 2004

SCOTT Peter and William T. CAVANAUGH (eds), *The Blackwell Companion to Political Theology*, Blackwell, Oxford, 2004
• BELL Daniel M. Jr., 'State and Civil Society', in SCOTT Peter and William T. CAVANAUGH (eds), *The Blackwell Companion to Political Theology* [pp 423-438]

- CAVANAUGH William T., 'Church,' in SCOTT Peter and William T. CAVANAUGH (eds), *The Blackwell Companion to Political Theology*, Blackwell, Oxford, 2004, [pp 393-406]

SEISDEDOS Gabriel, *Hasta Los Oidos De Dios*, Ediciones San Pablo, Buenos Aires, 1999

SELIN Gary, *Priestly Celibacy, Theological Foundations*, Catholic University of America Press, Washington DC, 2006

SHIRILAU Mark S., *History and Overview of the Ecumenical Catholic Church*, Healing Spirit Press, Villa Grande CA, 1995

SMIT Peter-Ben, *Old Catholic and Philippine Independent Ecclesiologies in History: The Catholic Church in Every Place*, Brill, Leiden / Boston, 2011

SPITZECK Heiko, M. PIRSON, W. AMANN, S. KHAN, E. VON KIMAKOWITZ (eds) *Humanism in Business*, Cambridge University Press, Cambridge, 2009

SULLIVAN Francis A. SJ, *From Apostles to Bishops: The Development of the Episcopacy in the Early Church*, The Newman Press, New York / Mahwah NJ, 2001

TILLEY Terrence W., *Inventing Catholic Tradition*, Orbis Books, Maryknoll NY, 2000

THAVIS John, *The Vatican Diaries*, Penguin, London, 2013

THIEL John E., *Senses of Tradition – Continuity and Development in Catholic Faith*, Oxford University Press, Oxford, 2000

THORNTON Sister Mary Crescentia, *The Church and Freemasonry in Brazil, 1872-1875*, Catholic University of America Press, Washington DC, 1948

VIGNOT Bernard, *Les Églises Parallèles [The Parallel Churches]*, Cerf–fides, Paris, 1991

VORGRIMLER Herbert (ed) *Commentary on the Documents of Vatican II, 6 Volumes*, Crossroad, New York, 1989

VORGRIMLER Herbert, *Sacramental Theology*, Liturgical Press, Collegeville MN, 1992

WARD Gary L., Bertil PERSSON, Alan BAIN, *Independent Bishops: an International Directory*, Apogee Books, Detroit MI, 1990

WEAVER Mary-Jo Weaver and R. Scott APPLEBY (eds):
– *Being Right: Conservative Catholics in America*, Indiana University Press, Bloomington IN, 1995
– *What's Left? Liberal American Catholics*, Indiana University Press, Bloomington IN, 1999
• COOKE Bernard J. 'Progressive Approaches to Ministry,' in WEAVER Mary-Jo and R.Scott APPLEBY (eds), *What's Left? Liberal American Catholics*, [pp 135-146]
• RADFORD RUETHER Rosemary, 'Women-Church,' in WEAVER Mary-Jo and R.Scott APPLEBY (eds), *What's Left? Liberal American Catholics*, [pp 46-64]
WIJNGAARDS John, *Ordination of Women in the Catholic Church: Unmasking a Cuckoo's Egg Tradition*, Bloomsbury Academic, London, 2001
WILSON George B. SJ, *Clericalism – The Death of Priesthood*, Liturgical Press, Collegeville MN, 2008
YÉPEZ CASTILLO Aureo, *La Universidad Católica Andrés Bello: en el marco histórico–educativo de los Jesuitas en Venezuela [Andrés Bello Catholic University: in the historical-educational framework of the Jesuits in Venezuela]*, Universidad Católica Andrés Bello, Caracas, 1994
ZAGANO Phyllis, *Women & Catholicism – Gender, Communion, and Authority*, Palgrave Macmillan, New York, 2011

Articles

BETTENCOURT Dom Estêvão OSB, 'Igreja Católica Brasileira,' in *Pergunte e Responderemos, [Ask and We Will Answer]*, Number 55, July 1962 online archive at http://www.pr.gonet.biz/revista.php
BREYER Carol Ann, 'Common Collars: A Study of Collaboration between Roman Catholic Married Priests and Roman Catholic Women Priests,' in *CORPUS Reports*, Vol. 37, No. 5, Sept./Oct. 2011, pp 23ff

BYRNE Julie, 'Catholic But Not Roman Catholic,' *American Catholic Studies*, Vol. 125, No. 3, Fall 2014, pp 16-19

CHIRICO Peter, 'Dominus Iesus as an Event,' in *America: The Jesuit Review*, 26th March 2001, https://www.americamagazine.org/issue/332/article/dominus-iesus-event

CONDE TUDANCA Rodrigo, 'Un Incidente Olvidado del Trienio Adeco: La Creacion de la Iglesia Católica, Apostólica, Venezolana' [A Forgotten Incident of the Adeco Period: The Creation of the Venezuelan Catholic Apostolic Church], in *Boletin de la Academia Nacional de la Historia*, Caracas, No. 302, Apr.-June 1993, pp 87-117 [also in Boletín CIHEV No. 8, Yr. 5, Jan.-June 1993, pp 41-81]

CUCCHETTI Humberto, 'Algunas lecturas sobre la relación iglesia/ peronismo (1943–1955): entre el mito de la "nación católica" y la "iglesia nacional",' [Readings of church-peronism relations (1943-1955): between the myth of the 'catholic nation' and the 'national church'] in *Revista Confluencia*, No. 1, 2003, Mendoza, Argentina, pp 1-18

HIBBERT Giles OP, 'Apostolic Succession – Magic, Power and Priesthood' (a paper first given to the Newman Association, Wilmslow, Cheshire, 4th Nov. 2002), [booklet] Belfriars Publications, London, 2002

HORTAL Jesús SJ, 'O valor dos sacramentos administrados nas "Igrejas Brasileiras"' [The validity of the sacraments administered in the *'igrejas brasileiras'*], in *Direito e Pastoral* [Brazilian Canon Law Review, Pontifical Higher Institute of Canon Law, Brazil], No. 14, Oct. 1989, pp 58 (124)-62 (128)

IBGE – Brazilian Institute of Geography and Statistics, *Censo Demografico 2010 [Demographic Census 2010]* IBGE, Rio de Janeiro, 2010

KÜNG Hans, 'Towards an Ecumenical Theology of Religions: Some Theses for Clarification,' in KÜNG, Hans and Jürgen MOLTMANN (eds), *Concilium: Religion in the Eighties; Christianity Among World Religions*, T&T Clark, Edinburgh, 1986, pp 119-125

LESLIE Kenneth, *Protestant Digest*, Volume 6, Issue 7, Protestant Digest Incorporated, New York, 1945

LORSCHEIDER Aloísio, '"Igreja Brasileira," Esclarecimento e Procedimento' ['Igreja Brasileira,' Clarifications and Procedures], in *Convergência* [Journal of the CRB – Conference of Religious of Brazil], Yr. 25, No. 231, Apr. 1990, pp 137-142

McDONNELL Kilian, 'The Ratzinger / Kasper Debate: The Universal Church and Local Churches,' in *Theological Studies*, No. 63, 2002, pp 227-250

OVIEDO CAVADA Carlos 'Obispos Irregulares' [Bishops Irregular] the Repository of the Pontifical Catholic University of Chile, 1986

SILVA Wagner PIRES DA, 'Another Catholicism: The Bishop of Maura and the Brazilian Catholic Apostolic Church,' in *Revista de História Bilros* (Fortaleza), Vol. 5, No. 8, Jan.-Apr. 2017, pp 106-125

SPIAZZI Raimondo OP, 'Annotazioni' [Annotations], *Monitor Ecclesiasticus*, No. 84, Desclée, Rome, 1959, pp 369-409

Roman Catholic Church Documents

CONFERÊNCIA NACIONAL DOS BISPOS DO BRASIL – CNBB
[National Conference of Bishops of Brazil]
- 'Letter from the Congregation for the Doctrine of the Faith, 4th March 1972,' in *Comunicado Mensal [Monthly Communique]* No. 234, Mar. 1972, p 12
- 'Pastoral Letter of the Bishops of the Ecclesiastical Province of São Paulo on the *"Igreja Brasileira,"*' in *Comunicado Mensal*, No. 243, Dec. 1972, pp 90-97
- 'The *Igreja Brasileira*,' in Report of the Meeting of the Presidency of CNBB, in *Comunicado Mensal*, No. 252, Sept. 1973, pp 1129-1130

- 'Responses from the Congregation for the Doctrine of the Faith about the *"Igreja Brasileira",*' in *Comunicado Mensal,* No. 406, Nov. 1986, pp 1471-1473
- 'Explicatory Note on Marriages carried out in the Igreja Brasileira,' in *Comunicado Mensal,* No. 406, Nov. 1986, p 1646
- HORTAL Jesús SJ, 'Guia Ecumênico' [Ecumenical Guide], in *Estudos da CNBB [CNBB Studies]* Number 21 (three editions: 1979, 1983, 1993

REVISTA ECLESIÁSTICA BRASILEIRA (REB) [Brazilian Ecclesiastical Review]

- 'Circular letter of the Ecclesiastical Chamber of Rio de Janeiro, 6th July 1945,' *REB,* Sept. 1945
- 'Bishops of the Province of Belo Horizonte,' *REB,* No. 18, Vozes Limitada, Petrópolis, 1958

ARCHDIOCESE OF CARACAS

- 'Letter to the Papal Nuncio, 13th December 1946' in the file 'Castillo Mendez'
- *Adsum,* the journal of the Archdiocese of Caracas, No. 107, Nov. 1946
- *Adsum,* the journal of the Archdiocese of Caracas, No. 128, Aug. 1948

POPE JOHN XXIII, 'Virtutes Dignitati Sacerdotum Necessariae: Caput, Cor et Lingua' in *Acta Apostolicae Sedis,* Number 52, Vatican City, 1960

CONGREGATION FOR THE DOCTRINE OF THE FAITH

- *'Dominus Iesus',* 6th August 2000 http://www.vatican.va/roman_curia/congregations/cfaith/documents/rc_con_cfaith_doc_20000806_dominus-iesus_en.html
- *Decree of Excommunication,* 5th August 2002 http://www.vatican.va/roman_curia/congregations/cfaith/documents/rc_con_cfaith_doc_20020805_decreto-scomunica_en.html

Other Documents in Chronological Order

COMMISSIONE PER LA PUBBLICAZIONE DEI DOCU-
MENTI DIPLOMATICI, '28th April 1936' in *Documenti
Diplomatici Italiani*, Ministero degli Affari Esteri, Libreria dello
Stato, Rome, 1992

ANDRADA Ministro Lafayette DE, 'Liberdade Religiosa –
Igreja Católica Apostólica Romana, 17th Nov. 1949,' *Revista
Archivo Judiciário [Judicial Archives Review]*, Vol. CI /6-15, Rio
de Janeiro, Jan.-Mar. 1952

CÂMARA MUNICIPAL DE SÃO PAULO, SEÇÃO DE
PROTOCÓLO [City Hall, Protocol Section]
- Case number 3779 of 1963, "Naming after Dom Jorge Alves de
Sousa [sic] of the current planned street between [...]."
- Case number 5192 of 1968, "Granting of freedom of the city to
Dom Luigi Mascolo"

IGREJA CATÓLICA APOSTÓLICA BRASILEIRA
- *Luta!* issue 1: January 1947, issue 2: November 1947, issue 4:
January-February 1948, issue 5: June 1948, issue 6: July 1948,
issue 7: August 1948, issue 8: July 1949, issue 9: October 1949,
issue 10: January 1950, issue 11: April 1950, issue 12: September
1950, issue 13: January 1951, issue 14: May 1951, issue 15:
August 1951, issue 16: March 1952, issue 17: October 1952,
issue 18: April 1953, issue 19: December 1953, issue 20: August
1954, issue 21: April 1955, issue 22: July 1955, issue 23: March
1956, issue 24: February 1957, issue 25: January 1958
http://diocesedecabofrio.blogspot.com.br/p/revista-luta.html
- 'Preâmbulo Comemorativo dos 65 anos de Organização
Jurídico-Eclesial da Igreja Católica Apostólica Brasileira'
[Commemorative Preamble for the 65th Anniversary of the
Juridical-Ecclesial Foundation of the Brazilian Catholic
Apostolic Church], 2010
http://docplayer.com.br/21642059-Preambulo-comemorativo-
65-anos-icab-preambulo-comemorativo-dos-65-anos-de-

organizacao-juridico-eclesial-da-igreja-catolica-apostolica-
-brasileira.html

- 'Declaração Acerca do Arcebispo David Bell' [Declaration
  Regarding Archbishop David Bell], 12th July 2013
  http://noticiasicab.blogspot.com.br/2013/07/declaracao-acerca-
  do-arcebispo-david.html?m=1